Bulldog:
A Compiler for VLIW Architectures

ACM Doctoral Dissertation Awards

1982
Area-Efficient VLSI Computation
by Charles Eric Leiserson

1983
Generating Language-Based Environments
by Thomas W. Reps

1984
Reduced Instruction Set Computer Architectures for VLSI
by Manolis G. H. Katevenis

1985
Bulldog: A Compiler for VLIW Architectures
by John R. Ellis

Bulldog:
A Compiler for VLIW Architectures

John R. Ellis

The MIT Press
Cambridge, Massachusetts
London, England

VLIW(TM) and Trace Scheduling(TM) are trademarks of Multiflow Computers, Inc.

This dissertation was submitted in May 1984 to the Department of Computer Science, Yale University, in partial fulfillment of the requirements for the degree of Doctor of Philosophy. The thesis research was sponsored in part by National Science Foundation grants #MCS81-06181 and #MCS83-08988 and Office of Naval Research grant #N000014-82-K-0184.

This book was typeset by the author in TeX and printed on an Imagen 8/300 printer. Printed and bound in the United States of America.

Library of Congress Cataloging-in-Publication Data

Ellis, John R. (John Rolfe), 1956–
 Bulldog: a compiler for VLIW architectures.

 (ACM doctoral dissertation awards; 1985)
 Originally presented as the author's thesis (doctoral)—Yale, 1985.
 Bibliography: p.
 1. Compiling (Electronic computers) 2. Bulldog (Computer program) 3. Computer architecture.
 I. Title. II. Series: ACM doctoral dissertation award; 1985.
 QA76.76.C65E45 1986   005.4′53   85-24092
 ISBN 0-262-05034-X

Contents

Appendices

Series Foreword

Each year the Association for Computing Machinery (ACM) conducts a world-wide competition to select the best doctoral dissertation. The only restriction is that the dissertation be written in English. A cash award of $1000 is given to the author by ACM, and the winning dissertation is published by The MIT Press with appropriate royalties. The award is presented annually at ACM's Computer Science Conference.

The ACM has appointed a selection committee with members from academia and industry. This year the committee reviewed thirty-four dissertations and chose the thesis "Bulldog: A Compiler for VLIW Architectures" by John R. Ellis as the winner. The thesis work was supervised by Professor Joseph Fisher of Yale University and Multiflow Computer, Inc. The selection committee was composed of Larry Dowdy, Nicholas Findler, David Johnson, Michael Marcotty, and Fred Maryanski, with John White of the Xerox Palo Alto Research Center serving as chairman.

John Ellis was judged to have made an outstanding contribution to the problem of exploiting the parallelism available in emerging multiprocessor architectures. Ellis's thesis is that high-quality compilers can be written for VLIW (Very Long Instruction Word) computers. These machines drive multiple parallel RISCs (Reduced Instruction Set Computers) with a single instruction stream. Each instruction, however, is long enough to command all of the RISCs at once.

Exploiting the parallelism available in VLIW machines can be very difficult if done by hand. Thus, Ellis developed a compiler that incorporates a number of optimizations based on *trace scheduling* and *memory reference* and *memory bank disambiguation*. Trace scheduling increases parallelism by scheduling several basic blocks at once. The compiler increases parallelism further by unrolling loops and by using disambiguation algorithms to tell at least some of the time when vector and bank references cannot collide.

In addition to the results Ellis obtained, the selection committee was extremely impressed with the quality of the dissertation. Ellis shows an understanding of the scientific method rarely seen in systems work. The dissertation clearly describes sound experimental analysis of a first-rate implementation of a new and interesting kind of compiler. The work represents a truly outstanding example of doctoral research in computer science.

John R. White, Chairman
ACM Doctoral Dissertation Award Subcommittee

Preface

Very Long Instruction Word architectures are reduced-instruction-set machines with a large number of parallel, pipelined functional units but only a single thread of control. These machines offer the promise of an immediate order-of-magnitude speed-up for general-purpose scientific computing. But unlike previous machines such as the Cray and the FPS-164, it is impossible to program VLIW machines in machine language—only a compiler for a high-level language (Fortran?) makes these machines feasible. My thesis demonstrates, via a working compiler, that this symbiosis of new architecture and new compiling technology is practicable.

A traditional compiler couldn't find enough parallelism in scientific programs to utilize a VLIW effectively. The Bulldog compiler uses several new compilation techniques: **trace scheduling** to find more parallelism, **memory-reference** and **memory-bank disambiguation** to increase memory bandwidth, and new code-generation algorithms.

My dissertation includes the results of preliminary experiments testing both the Bulldog compiler and various aspects of VLIW architectures. I've successfully compiled and simulated a respectable set of numerical subroutines, including simple matrix operations, FFT, LU decomposition, singular value decomposition, tridiagonal solvers, routines from SIMPLE, and adaptive quadrature. The results show that, at least for many scientific applications, VLIW architectures buildable today can achieve order-of-magnitude speed-ups over current machines.

Though originally developed for VLIWs, many of the ideas in Bulldog could be applied to pipelined reduced-instruction-set architectures such as the MIPS. My experiments indicate that speed improvements of perhaps 30–80% are possible for scientific code on such machines.

Acknowledgements

Josh Fisher, my advisor, rescued me from the thesis tarpit and suggested I work on the Bulldog compiler. I finished only because of his leadership of the ELI project.

John Ruttenberg, Charles Marshall, Alex Nicolau, John O'Donnell, Abhiram Ranade, Mark Sidell, Joe Rodrigue, and Richard Kelsey all contributed to the ELI project; their efforts were indispensable.

Bill Gropp, Jack Dongarra, and Alan Perlis diligently read and corrected my lengthy manuscripts. Bill answered innumerable questions about scientific computing and provided several of the benchmarks; he was also the local Tex wizard, and he kept our printers working.

Tom Karzes read two difficult chapters very closely, and his suggestions resulted in clearer prose and better notation.

Faisal Saied provided the TRID benchmarks. Dennis Gannon sent me the SIMPLE benchmark. Paul Dubois helped me make SIMPLE more realistic.

Stan Eisenstat and Martin Schultz answered many questions about scientific computing.

Charles Hedrick supplied us with ELISP, the DEC-20 Lisp we used for most of our programming, and he quickly fixed several of its bugs as we found them.

Steve Wood, Nat Mishkin, Bob Nix, Mary-Claire van Leunen and I worked together as the Tools group for several years. From our systems hacking I learned more about computer science than by any other means, and our long-term friendship made Yale bearable. Mary-Claire showed me that writing prose is harder than writing programs. Nat shamed me into finishing my thesis by finishing before me (Bob shamed Nat into finishing (Udi Shapiro shamed Bob into finishing)).

Mary-Claire helped make the index. The Systems Research Center, Digital Equipment Corporation, provided the computer and typesetting facilities used in the final preparation of the camera-ready copy.

Alan Perlis taught me there is more to life than Algol. He encouraged me to learn about APL, Lisp, and Smalltalk at a time when most systems researchers were embedded in C-Pascal-Mesa-Clu-Ada.

Janet Cowan proofread the final draft. Most graduate students have dark, depressed moments at some point in the game, and Janet helped me persevere through mine.

Bulldog:

A Compiler for VLIW Architectures

Chapter 1
My Thesis

Ordinary scientific programs can be compiled for a new parallel architecture called VLIW (Very Long Instruction Word), yielding order-of-magnitude speed-ups over scalar architectures.

Introduction

Compilers have traditionally played second fiddle to hardware projects in parallel processing. Parallel architectures have been built to be hand coded, and attempts at compiler writing were mere afterthoughts. These attempts have been unsurprisingly unsuccessful.

The two most common types of parallel architectures built to date have been vector machines and multiprocessors. Compiling (or simply hand coding) for either requires matching an overview of the coarse structure of the application to that of the hardware. It's conceivable that hand coders and compilers might someday be good at this; but so far they haven't been, and there's no reason for optimism. There has been a general failure at culling large amounts of parallelism from existing programs automatically.

So instead of building an architecture first and a compiler second, the ELI project at Yale has simultaneously developed a compiler and an architecture intended for scientific computing [Fisher 82, Fisher 83, Fisher 84, Fisher 84b]. Using a technique called **trace scheduling**, the Bulldog compiler finds large amounts of parallelism in ordinary scientific code. Taking advantage of this parallelism requires a new hardware architecture, which we call VLIW (Very Long Instruction Word). The compiler and the hardware form an integrated pair—neither is very useful without the other.

Unlike other proposed parallel architectures, we think VLIWs are practical in the very near future. In fact, a new company, Multiflow Inc. of Branford, CT, has been formed specifically to produce a commercial attached processor for scientific computing using VLIW and trace-scheduling technology.

The Bulldog compiler is finished, and it compiles ordinary scientific programs into highly parallel machine code for a large class of VLIWs, achieving order-of-magnitude speed-ups over traditional scalar architectures. This dissertation describes the compiler and the experiments investigating its capabilities.

Previous Architectures

What's wrong with previous parallel architectures?

Currently, architectures supporting the so-called functional languages are quite fashionable in academy. But over a decade of research into data-flow, reduction, and logic-based architectures has produced not one believable prototype, much less a commercial machine. There are many unsolved problems (by unsolved, I mean lacking a working demonstration of a solution). One of the most serious is efficiently handling large aggregate data structures such as vectors without the side-effects of traditional architectures: The naive approach requires huge amounts of garbage collection, while more sophisticated approaches involve significant access overhead. Another serious problem is keeping the communications overhead within practical limits. Yet another problem is providing sufficient memory bandwidth for the large number of processors envisioned. Functional architectures might yet prove workable in the long term, but what about the next ten years?

Highly parallel machines that actually have been built fall into two broad classes: multiprocessors and vector machines. Both classes provide coarse-grained parallelism, which is hard for a compiler to use.

With multiprocessors, a compiler must minimize communication and synchronization while trying to keep all the processors busy, avoiding the delays when one processor must wait for another. This forces a compiler to look for large sections of relatively independent control and data; compilers have only been able to do this for programs consisting of simple data-independent inner loops.

With vector machines, a compiler must find large data aggregates in the program that can be fetched and operated upon simultaneously using relatively simple operators. This requires finding a high degree of regularity in the data and control, and compilers haven't been too successful at that either (though vectorizing compilers are getting better all the time).

LIW Machines

Recently, several numerical attached processors offering low cost/performance ratios have appeared on the market. These processors, typified by the MARS-432 [Numerix 83] and the FPS-164 [FPS 82], provide fine-grained parallelism as opposed to the coarse-grained parallelism of vector machines and multiprocessors. Several pipelined functional units, a large memory, and register banks are connected by partial crossbars and buses. All these elements are controlled by a single, wide instruction stream capable of independently initiating an operation on every functional unit in each cycle (hence the name LIW, Long Instruction Word).

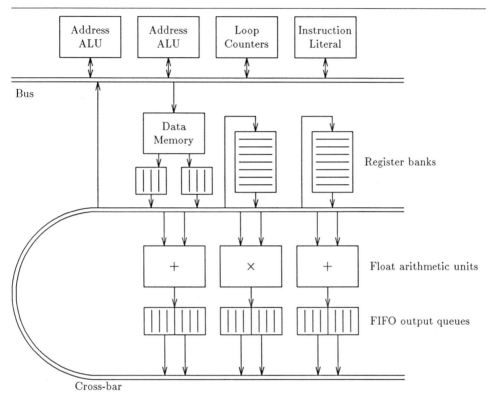

Figure 1.1. The MARS-432 architecture.

LIWs are essentially reduced-instruction-set processors like the MIPS [Hennessy 82] but with a few more functional units. The functional units and register banks handle scalars only, and all aggregate operations must be explicitly programmed. All scalar data movements between memory, the register banks, and the functional units are also explicitly programmed. Unlike machines such as the CDC 6600 and the Cray, there are no hardware interlocks for the pipelines—the compiler (or the hand coder) must track when and where pipeline results are available.

Figure 1.1 shows a block diagram of the MARS-432. The 432's instruction word has a separate field controlling each of the elements. So two memory reads, two address calculations, two floating adds, a floating multiply, two register-bank writes and two reads, and the necessary crossbar connections can all be initiated by a single instruction. As a consequence, the instruction word is quite wide: 128 bits.

The manufacturers call these machines "horizontally microcoded," but the term is deceptive. Unlike the microarchitecture of traditional machines, these LIWs have comparatively clean architectures without most of the detailed dirt and asymmetry usually associated with microcode. LIWs have much more in common with reduced-instruction-set processors.

But despite this comparative cleanliness and the little parallelism actually offered, LIWs are still incredibly difficult to program by hand. To get maximum utilization for even the simplest programs, the operations of inner loops must be severely reordered and overlapped with other operations, and the programmer must keep track of the state of each pipeline and register bank [FPS 82]. A much improved Fortran compiler has recently been released for the FPS-164, but it handles only a simple class of inner loops [Touzeau 84].

VLIW Architectures

Given the commercial success of LIW machines, the natural question is: How wide can we profitably make an LIW? Such a VLIW (Very Long Instruction Word) machine would have many more functional units, register banks, memories, buses, and crossbars, all controlled in lockstep by a single instruction stream. Given the difficulty of programming the MARS-432 or FPS-164 in assembly language, hand coding a VLIW would be impossible. Would a compiler be able to take advantage of the potential parallelism offered by a VLIW machine?

Instead of the coarse-grained parallelism of vector machines and multiprocessors, VLIWs provide a fine-grained parallelism that a trace-scheduling compiler can easily use. In a VLIW, every resource is completely and independently controlled, by which I mean:

> *Timing control.* Every single action takes an amount of time predictable by the compiler. The time may vary according to the operation.
>
> *Flow control.* There is a single thread of control, a single instruction stream, that initiates each fine-grained operation; many such operations can be initiated each cycle.
>
> *Communications control.* All communications are completely choreographed by the compiler and are under explicit control of the compiled program. The source, destination, resources, and time of a data transfer are all known by the compiler. There is no sense of packets containing destination addresses or of hardware scheduling of transfers.

Such fine-grained control of a highly parallel machine requires very large instructions, hence the name Very Long Instruction Word architecture.

Figure 1.2 shows a hypothetical VLIW machine. It has 8 **clusters** connected by simple data buses. Each cluster is similar to a MARS-432, containing a memory, a floating adder, a floating multiplier, two integer ALUs, and interconnections to the other clusters. As in an LIW, all the elements run in lockstep and are controlled by a single instruction stream, and each instruction specifies the action of every element independently. Consequently, instructions will be very large (at least several hundred bits).

VLIW machines are far too large to have a single crossbar connecting all their elements. Instead the clusters are connected by buses for transferring scalar values. It may well take several hops to move a value between distant clusters, and those hops must be explicitly programmed by the compiler.

VLIWs need not have the regularity implied by the example. The interconnections between the clusters, the type and number of elements within the clusters, and the connections between cluster elements can (and probably will) be asymmetric.

Before the advent of trace scheduling, it wasn't practical to build VLIW machines because no mere mortal could program them by hand. It is just barely possible to program machines like the FPS-164 and the MARS-432 in assembly language, but the amount of effort involved is tremendous. Hand-coding a VLIW with 8 or 16 or 32 times the number of functional units is out of the question. Without a compiler for a high-level language, VLIWs are useless.

Compilers for VLIWs

At first blush compiling high level languages for VLIWs might appear to be an impossible task, given that they are programmed at such a fine-grained level. But in fact the Bulldog compiler isn't that much different from a traditional optimizing compiler.

A traditional compiler parses the source program into an intermediate code, optimizes that intermediate code, and then translates the intermediate code into machine code. Usually, the translation to machine code is done one basic block at a time, perhaps after registers have been globally allocated.

It wouldn't be hard to construct a basic-block code generator for VLIWs. Several such code generators were written for machines with limited fine-grain parallelism such as the FPS-164, the CDC 6600 and 7600, and the scalar portion of the Cray [Sites 78]. Part of the problem is equivalent to that of statically scheduling a set of interdependent jobs with different resource requirements on a fixed set of processors; this problem has been studied for years and there are many practical solutions [Fisher 79].

But basic blocks have severely limited parallelism; experiments showed early on that one could expect at most a two- or three-times speed-up by executing basic blocks in parallel [Foster 72, Tjaden 70]. A basic-block-based code generator couldn't hope to keep a VLIW with 8 or 16 processors busy.

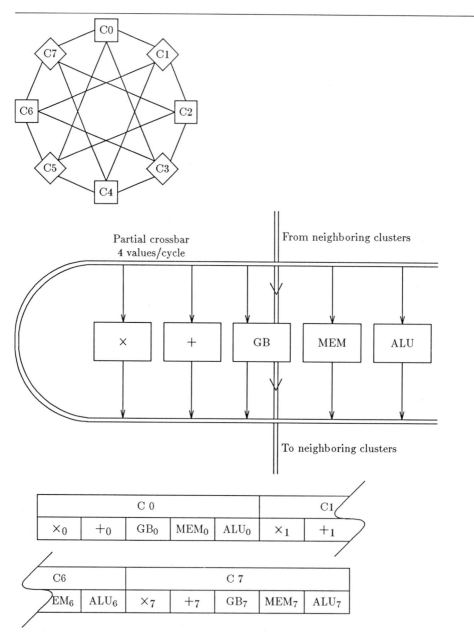

Figure 1.2. A Hypothetical ELI. Each of the 8 clusters is connected to 4 neighbors. A close-up of a cluster is shown in the middle. A separate field in the instruction word controls each element in every cluster, as shown at bottom.

Later experiments showed, however, that if one ignored the artificial constraints imposed by basic blocks, ordinary scientific programs contained large amounts of parallelism—factors of 90 on average [Riseman 72, Nicolau 81]. If only a compiler could find it, such parallelism is more than enough to keep a VLIW busy.

Trace Scheduling

Trace scheduling finds much of that factor-of-90 parallelism by giving more than one basic block at a time to the code generator. To generate machine code for a routine, the compiler repeatedly traces out a path of many basic blocks in the intermediate-code flow graph of the routine and hands that entire path to the code generator. These paths, or **traces**, contain much more parallelism than basic blocks. The code generator treats a trace of blocks almost as if it were a single very large basic block.

The compiler picks a trace, generates machine code for it, and replaces the trace by the machine code. Then it picks another trace and does the same thing. It repeats this until the entire flow graph has been translated to machine code. Estimates of execution frequency guide the compiler in picking traces; the blocks most likely to be executed comprise the first trace, those next likely to be executed comprise the second trace, and so on. Figure 1.3 shows the flow graph of a simple program and the traces selected from it.

The current compiler uses loop nesting and programmer-supplied hints to make reasonable guesses about block execution frequency; this method appears to work fairly well without too much help from the programmer.

For various reasons, a trace never extends past a loop boundary. That is, a trace can include only blocks from the same loop, but no blocks from containing or contained loops.

The underlying premise of trace scheduling is that the most likely execution paths through a program can be predicted at compile time, and that most of the execution time is spent in those likely paths. Is this a valid assumption? For most scientific programs, yes. The time-critical control structures of scientific code tend to be quite simple and highly predictable, consisting mainly of nested loops with a few conditionals that usually branch one way most of the time. Clearly, this premise is less likely to be true for other domains such as systems programs—that's why we restricted the ELI project to scientific programs.

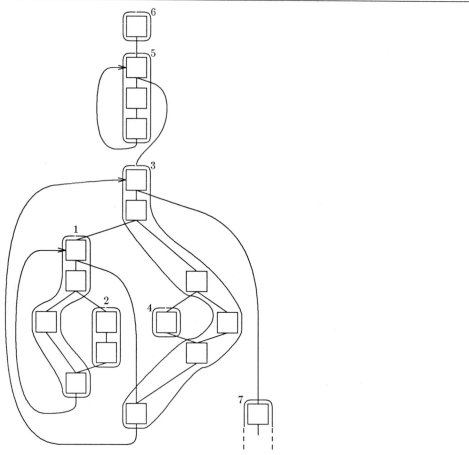

Figure 1.3. A flow graph of basic blocks and the traces selected from it.

To further increase the parallelism of traces, the compiler unrolls the bodies of inner loops as many as 32 times immediately after parsing the source program into intermediate code. For example, a loop such as:

```
i:=1
LOOP
    IF i>n THEN EXIT
    ...body...
    i:=i+1
```

unrolled three times would look like:

```
i:=1
LOOP
    IF i>n THEN EXIT
    ...body...
    i:=i+1
    IF i>n THEN EXIT
    ...body...
    i:=i+1
    IF i>n THEN EXIT
    ...body...
    i:=i+1
```

This unrolling produces much longer traces, increasing the potential parallelism available to the code generator. (Later we'll see other uses for unrolling.)

To get parallel machine code, the code generator must substantially reorder the trace's intermediate-code operations, filling machine instructions with operations that come from widely separated places in the trace; time-critical operations are usually scheduled early, while non-critical operations are often delayed.

In a basic-block code generator of a traditional compiler, this reordering is simple [Aho 77, Sites 78]. By doing one basic block at a time, the traditional code generator is assured that all jumps into the block from the outside are to the block's first instruction, and that there is at most one conditional jump in the block, which must be at the end. But looking at figure 1.3, one immediately notices that traces consisting of many blocks might have more than one conditional jump and that there might be jumps from outside the trace into the middle of the trace. This complicates the task of reordering considerably; in addition to the normal data-precedence rules for basic block operations, the compiler must also worry about jumps off the trace and jumps into the trace.

For example, suppose that in the following flow-graph fragment, the current trace consists of operations 1, 2, and 3:

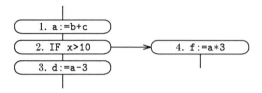

If when reordering the trace the code generator decides to move `a:=b+c` below the conditional jump, then to preserve correctness it must place a copy of `a:=b+c` on the other edge of the jump:

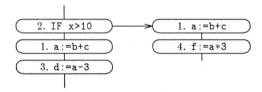

An analogous transformation is required when the code generator moves a trace operation above a jump into the trace; the operation must be copied onto the edge jumping into the trace. For example, suppose a trace consists of operations 1, 2, 3, and 4 below:

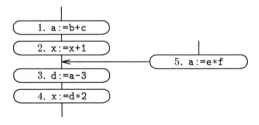

If the code generator decides to move `d:=a-3` above `x:=x+1` and the incoming edge, it must place a copy of `d:=a-3` on the incoming edge:

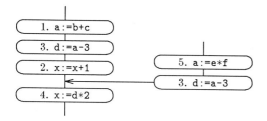

When the compiler replaces a trace by machine code, the copies of operations produced by the code motions are inserted at the trace boundaries; this process is called **bookkeeping**. Figure 1.4 shows a trace before and after it is replaced by its machine code and the correctness-preserving copies. The copies are treated just like original intermediate-code operations and will be included as part of later traces.

Memory-reference Disambiguation

Indirect memory references arising from pointer dereferencing and array indexing pose special problems for a trace-scheduling compiler. Long traces contain many such indirect references, and in order to take advantage of the potential parallelism in the trace, the code generator must be able to reorder the references as it does other operations in the trace. To see why, consider this fragment of a trace:

```
1. x1:=v[i]
2. v[i]:=y1
3. x2:=v[j]
4. v[j]:=y2
```

Without knowing anything about the indices `i` and `j`, a compiler must assume that `i` could equal `j`, and thus that operation 3 must be executed after 2; under this assumption, there is no available parallelism in the fragment. But if the compiler knew somehow that `i` and `j` were never equal, then 1 and 3 could be performed in parallel and 2 and 4 in parallel, a doubling in speed. Analogous situations arise from dereferencing pointers.

To achieve the most parallelism, the compiler must **disambiguate** as many memory references as possible, determining whether they could possibly be to the same memory location. Disambiguating pointer dereferences is tough; there are few obvious clues in the program to help the compiler determine whether two pointers might point at the same object. But in our target domain of scientific code, the inner loops consist almost entirely of array references, and it usually isn't hard to disambiguate such references.

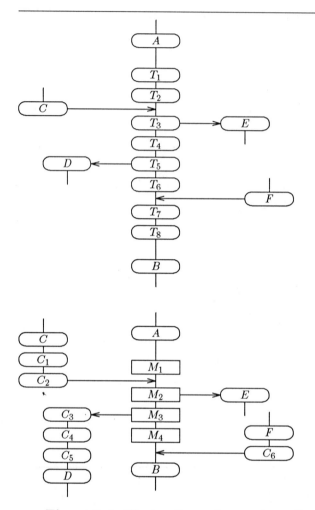

Figure 1.4. The top figure shows a trace through a flow graph consisting of operations T_1–T_8. The bottom figure shows the flow graph with the trace replaced by the machine instructions M_1–M_4 generated by the code generator. After inserting the machine instructions, the compiler inserted the copies C_1–C_6 of operations to preserve correctness of the program.

The disambiguator is a separate module of the Bulldog compiler. The code generator asks the disambiguator questions of the form, "Can these two vector references possibly refer to the same memory location?" The disambiguator answers yes, no, or I-don't-know. The yes and I-don't-know answers are the ones that restrict parallelism.

Sometimes the compiler isn't able to disambiguate automatically two vector references. There is an assertion facility that lets the programmer tell the compiler key facts about the program; if the compiler can't automatically distinguish two memory references, it consults the programmer-supplied assertions. This avoids the catastrophic all-or-nothing behavior of many sophisticated compilation techniques.

The Global-memory Bottleneck

Many designs of parallel architectures fail because of lack of memory bandwidth. They have small, fast, local memories clustered around the computing elements, with large aggregate data stored in a larger, slower, shared global memory. For programs that manipulate large aggregates, especially for scientific programs, the global memory is a severe bottleneck; it can't fetch and store elements of the aggregate data fast enough to keep the computing elements busy. Put another way, it is easy to build a dual-ported memory, but very hard (and expensive) to build an 8- or 16-ported memory. Even if the global memory does supply enough bandwidth, the compiler or operating system is hard-pressed to move data transparently through the memory hierarchy.

Most fast machines use a cache combined with interleaved memory banks to provide higher bandwidth. For example, by putting even addresses into one bank and odd addresses into another, the bandwidth doubles, since the two banks operate in parallel. But this design doesn't scale up easily, because there is still a single central controller that accepts memory requests and distributes them to the individual banks. Servicing two requests at a time is easy; servicing 8 or 16 at a time becomes a nightmare.

We solved the memory bottleneck problem as we solved other problems, using a combination of new architecture and smart software. We noticed that in scientific programs most of the memory references result from small inner loops enumerating through the elements of large arrays. Further, the central memory controller isn't really needed for those accesses, since the particular bank of each access could be predicted at compile time. If computing elements could access individual banks without going through the central controller, the memory bottleneck would be alleviated.

Unfortunately, even in scientific code it is not always possible to compute the banks of memory references at compile time. Even if the architecture supports direct reference to banks, it must still support general references for which the bank is not known statically.

In the ELI architecture, each cluster has its own bank. Logical memory addresses are interleaved among the b banks, with logical address a in bank $a \bmod b$. Each bank has a **front door** that provides direct access for memory references known at compile time to be in the bank. There is also a central memory controller connecting all the banks and accessed through one or more **back doors**. A memory reference whose bank is unknown at compile time must be made through the controller's back door. If the compiler can statically determine the bank of a memory reference, it will generate code to reference the bank directly through the front door; otherwise, it will generate a slower back-door reference.

Determining the banks of memory references at compile time is called **bank disambiguation** because the compiler uses techniques similar to memory-reference disambiguation. If these automatic techniques fail, the programmer can help by adding assertions. But the compiler also has to apply some source transformations. For example, consider the following implementation of vector addition:

```
i:=1
LOOP
    IF i>n THEN EXITLOOP
    a[i]:=b[i]+c[i]
    i:=i+1
```

Suppose the machine has 8-way interleaving. The bank of each of the vector references will be different on successive iterations through the loop. But by unrolling the loop 8 times:

```
i:=1
LOOP
    IF i>n THEN EXITLOOP
    a[i]:=b[i]+c[i]              /* bank 0 */
    i:=i+1
    IF i>n THEN EXITLOOP
    a[i]:=b[i]+c[i]              /* bank 1 */
    i:=i+1
    ...
    IF i>n THEN EXITLOOP
    a[i]:=b[i]+c[i]              /* bank 7 */
    i:=i+1
```

the vector references are now to the same banks on successive iterations, and the compiler can easily determine the banks using the symbolic analysis.

Unfortunately, more sophisticated transformations are needed for loops that aren't as well-behaved. For example, unrolling doesn't help with loops having variable initial-index values:

```
FOR i:=m TO n DO
    a[i]:=b[i]+c[i]
```

Even after unrolling, the bank of a[i] will be different for different executions of the loop, depending on the value of m mod 8 (assuming 8 banks). I'll present several source transformations that solve these problems. Currently, the compiler only implements loop unrolling automatically; the more sophisticated transformations must be done by hand.

The Conditional-jump Bottleneck

In order to achieve order-of-magnitude speed-ups, the compiler must compact every time-critical trace into a schedule 1/10 (say) the length of the trace. But it's well-known that, even in scientific code, conditional jumps comprise a large fraction of executed instructions; such jumps could well become a bottleneck if only one can be executed per instruction. To achieve large speed-ups, a VLIW will probably have to execute several jump operations each cycle.

Several existing microarchitectures execute multiple conditional jumps per instruction. Typically, two or more test conditions are evaluated in parallel and a boolean bit-vector of the results is appended to the address field stored in the instruction, yielding the actual target address of the branch.

Our approach is slightly different [Fisher 80, Fisher 83], yet another example of the symbiosis of hardware and compiler development. The ELI architecture allows up to n conditional jumps within an instruction:

$$branch_0 \ label_0; \ branch_1 \ label_1; \ldots branch_{n-1} \ label_{n-1}$$

These jumps are executed like a Lisp cond statement. Semantically, the branch conditions $branch_i$ are tested sequentially, and the first one that is true causes a jump to the corresponding $label_i$; if none are true, control "falls through" to the next instruction. Of course, the hardware can evaluate all n conditions in parallel and use a priority encoder to select the first one that is true. (The actual value of n will be decided by experimentation and the constraints of hardware design.)

When generating code for a trace, the compiler doesn't have to do anything special to take advantage of this hardware. It treats conditional jumps within a trace just like any other operations, fitting as many as possible into each instruction. If several jumps are placed in an instruction, they are ordered according to their position within the trace. The transformations needed for code motions past jumps still apply. As explained later, the rest falls out naturally.

Because the fetch-execute cycle of machines is often pipelined, especially in reduced-instruction-set processors, jump operations can take several cycles to execute [Hennessy 82]. Many machines simply freeze instruction execution until the jump completes; but in high-performance architectures the typical hardware trick is to allow other non-jump instructions to be executed while waiting for the jump to complete. It's the responsibility of the compiler or assembly-language programmer to fill the empty cycles following a jump with operations that can be safely executed no matter which way the jump eventually goes.

Gross and Hennessy [Gross 82] describe a system for optimizing such "delayed branches." Their method has several drawbacks. It is a separate pass in the compiler that runs after code generation. It only looks at neighboring basic blocks and can't do more global code motion. It doesn't have reliable information for making static predictions of branch directions. It doesn't allow jumps to overlap—that is, only one jump can be in the execution pipeline at a time. And their experiments show that for longer jump delays (3 cycles or more), the performance of the method deteriorates.

The Bulldog compiler, via trace scheduling, handles multicycle jumps more effectively. It treats multicycle jumps like any other multicycle operation, during code generation. The choice of traces implicitly directs the compiler to optimize those jumps and jump directions which are most time-critical. Jumps within a trace are overlapped with other operations taken from anywhere on the trace, increasing the likelihood that a time-critical jump will be overlapped with other operations. And with a very small amount of extra hardware support, jumps can overlap other jumps freely, allowing full pipelining of jump execution.

Code Generation

Generating machine code from intermediate-code basic blocks for a traditional architecture is well understood. The two main problems are register allocation and instruction selection. A compiler must decide whether to keep particular values in memory or in registers. It must also map intermediate operations onto one or more machine instructions, which may be difficult if the machine has a rich instruction set.

The problems faced by a VLIW compiler generating code for a large trace are somewhat different and more complex.

Foremost, a VLIW compiler must worry about packing many machine operations into a single, large, parallel machine instruction. A traditional code generator merely outputs a stream of machine instructions, one or more per intermediate operation, that are appended together to form the object code. But a VLIW code generator must juggle the machine operations to get as many as possible to fit into each parallel machine instruction.

Because VLIWs are essentially reduced-instruction-set processors, there is no problem with instruction selection; there is a direct mapping from intermediate-code operations onto the machine operations of the machine model. But unlike a traditional machine, a VLIW offers many hardware functional units implementing the same operator, and the compiler must choose which one to use for a particular intermediate operation. Because of the long data paths between distant elements, the code generator must try to cluster operations to minimize data movements between elements, while at the same time trying to utilize fully all of the functional units. This problem is called **operation placement**.

For example, a VLIW machine may have 16 memory banks and 32 different functional units implementing the integer-add operation. To minimize data movement, the compiler must try to perform the vector-indexing calculations on integer ALUs near the memory bank containing the vector elements.

Data routing is the problem of choosing data paths (buses and registers) to move data between elements of the machine. Between a source and destination there might be several paths, and the compiler must pick one that will least conflict with other activities. The move might take several hops between the source and destination, and the compiler must allocate a register after each hop to hold the value temporarily.

Finally, register allocation is tougher with a VLIW, since it could have at least as many register banks as functional units. The compiler must not only decide when to move a value into a register from memory but also which banks will hold the value. Sometimes it's advantageous to copy a value into several banks so that it can be used by many functional units simultaneously.

Obviously, operation placement, data routing, and register allocation are all interdependent. Compilers for existing horizontally microcoded machines such as the FPS-164 haven't had to deal with these problems because the target architectures offer little choice: An operation can be done in only one or two functional units, there are only one or two paths between any two points in the machine, and a functional unit is serviced by only one or two register banks.

Ruttenberg and I have each written a code generator for the Bulldog compiler. Ruttenberg's code generator [Ruttenberg 85] uses a complex branch-and-bound strategy and a simple, somewhat unrealistic machine model. My code generator uses a simpler strategy more similar to traditional code generators but generates code for a more realistic machine model. The two code generators differ primarily in their approach to operator placement and register allocation. I will refer to Ruttenberg's as "Ruttenberg's code generator" and to mine as "the code generator."

The code generators get a trace of basic blocks as input and produce parallel machine code as output, treating the trace as if it were one very large basic block. Like many traditional code generators, our code generators convert the intermediate-code operations into a directed acyclic graph. The nodes of the DAG represent operations, and there is an edge between two nodes if one node uses the value produced by another. The code generators then form a **schedule** of machine instructions by traversing the nodes in some topological order, choosing machine operations for intermediate-code operators and filling the instructions of the schedule with the machine operations chosen. To prevent illegal code motions past jumps and to force undisambiguated memory references to be evaluated in the correct order, new edges are introduced to prevent one node from being evaluated before another.

The Bulldog Compiler

Figure 1.5 shows the overall structure of Bulldog. The source language is parsed into a traditional intermediate code and optimized using the standard Fortran-compiler optimizations, producing highly optimized intermediate code. Then the memory-bank disambiguator tries to determine the bank of every vector reference.

The resulting program is then handed to both the trace scheduler and the disambiguator. The trace scheduler repeatedly picks traces from the program's flow graph, gives them to the code generator, and replaces the trace by the machine code generated. While generating code, the code generator asks the disambiguator whether pairs of vector references in the trace could possibly refer to the same memory location.

Unlike a traditional compiler, the interfaces between the components are quite simple and purely procedural. The only shared data structure is the optimized intermediate code, which is represented as a simple list; individual components build their own flow graph if they need one. The only data structures passed through the interfaces are simple lists of numbers, symbols, and other lists.

Keeping the interfaces simple enabled the four people working on the compiler at various times to work independently. If you've ever worked on a large project, you know that shared data structures and data types can be a big headache in a program undergoing rapid change, even (or especially) in a strongly typed language like Mesa or Modula-2. The mild inefficiencies created by our procedural interfaces were far outweighed by the savings in programmer effort. The procedural interfaces also allowed us to identify precisely which information is needed where in the compiler.

The compiler is implemented in ELISP, a dialect of Lisp for the DEC-20. Compared to the Algol family (C, Pascal, Mesa, Ada, Modula-2), Lisp is a better tool for compiler research . The ELI project probably saved several man-years by using Lisp in preference to C or Pascal. No other programming environment provides: automatic storage reclamation, an interpreter, a single-stepper, a debugger, formatted input/output of data structures, pretty printers that print *all*

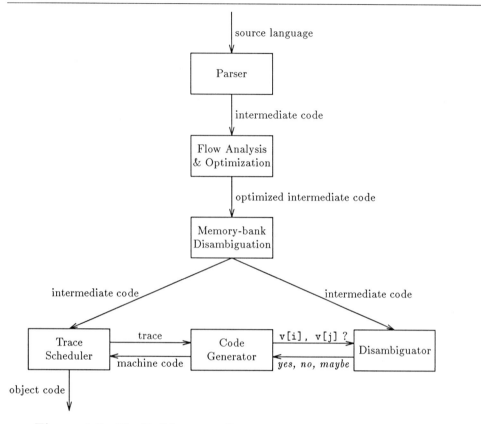

Figure 1.5. The Bulldog compiler.

data structures, a rich set of control and data structures, a large library of utilities for manipulating aggregate structures such as vectors and lists, space and time efficiency when you need it, a compiler as good as typical C and Pascal compilers, mixed interpreted and compiled code. A good Lisp provides all of this in a unified environment with a read-eval-print loop accessible at all times. If you haven't used Lisp in the last five years or you think it is a toy language, stop reading this thesis and read "Programming in the interactive environment: The Lisp experience" [Sandewall 78], a recent collection of papers on Lisp [Lisp-84 84], and the Common Lisp manual [Steele 84].

Experiments

The Bulldog compiler, like any compiler, is a collection of many algorithms and heuristics whose interactions are complex and sometimes unpredictable. It is over 30,000 lines long and not susceptible to abstract analysis of performance. The only convincing measure of such a large program is to run realistic experiments on a large set of test data.

I've assembled a library of numerical scientific routines and run them through the compiler. The library consists of:

> matrix multiply
> FFT
> LU decomposition
> singular value decomposition
> routines from the SIMPLE benchmark from Lawrence Livermore
> tridiagonal solvers
> integration using adaptive quadrature
> one-dimensional optimization
> zero-finding

These represent a broad spectrum of the likely data and control structures in scientific programming.

I've run the routines through the compiler and measured their performance on several machine models via simulations. The **ideal machine**, an abstract, unrealistic model, helps measure the maximum amount of parallelism that trace scheduling and disambiguation can find. The **realistic ELI** is as close to a practical, 8-cluster VLIW as I could make it, based on the evolving design of the ELI architecture [Fisher 80, Fisher 84]. The **pipelined-sequential machine** is "built with the same technology" as the realistic ELI, but it has only one cluster and resembles the MIPS [Hennessy 82] or the scalar portion of the Cray; operations are pipelined but only one may be initiated per cycle. Comparing the realistic ELI with the pipelined-sequential machine shows how much faster the combination of VLIWs and trace scheduling are compared to traditional architectures.

The results of these benchmarks strongly support my thesis that ordinary scientific programs can be successfully compiled for VLIWs, yielding order-of-magnitude speed-ups.

Who Did What

The ELI project, now disbanded, was started by Josh Fisher around 1980 to investigate trace scheduling and VLIW architectures. The Bulldog compiler is one result of that project.

As in many group projects, the ideas in Bulldog were often the result of group synthesis. Trying to ascertain exact authorship is difficult, if not pointless. This dissertation presents the Bulldog compiler in its entirety, and it must necessarily include ideas that are not solely, or even partially, mine. But I am obligated to try to identify the major contributions made by others.

Originally, I was charged with assembling and interfacing the various components of Bulldog. But I ended up writing nearly all of the code in the working compiler. A number of the ideas and algorithms were strictly mine, but many were not.

The basic idea of trace scheduling and its application to VLIWs is due to Josh Fisher. Trace scheduling was originally intended for compacting vertical microcode into the horizontal microcode of traditional architectures [Fisher 79, Fisher 81]. But Fisher realized that trace scheduling could find much more parallelism than available in current machines, so he started thinking about VLIWs.

Fisher implemented a trace scheduler, not much different from the one described in his thesis, for a simplistic machine model. I substantially reimplemented the same algorithm, refining the trace-picking heuristics, interfacing it to the rest of the compiler, and designing the numerous hairy modifications necessary for realistic VLIWs.

Alex Nicolau proved that trace scheduling is correct and terminates, and in the process corrected an important but obscure bug in Fisher's original algorithm [Nicolau 84]. He also designed and implemented the first version of the disambiguator. After some initial experience with that version, I reimplemented the disambiguator using a different, more efficient algorithm. I also added in the assertion facility.

Fisher and I developed the basic idea of memory-bank disambiguation. I designed the symbolic analysis algorithm and worked out the various source transformations needed to bank-disambiguate the programs in our library.

John Ruttenberg wrote the first VLIW code generator in the compiler, using the technique he calls operation scheduling [Ruttenberg 85]. After seeing the early results of his efforts, I wrote another code generator, the one described in detail later on. My code generator is quite different from his, but I definitely profited from his efforts. My functional-unit assignment algorithm (Bottom-up Greedy) was partly inspired by operation scheduling.

Charles Marshall worked on a code generator for the FPS-164 that was never finished but did generate code for individual traces. He may have had the hardest task, trying to force a compiler intended for VLIWs onto an existing, not-so-clean commercial machine. My discussions with him about the FPS-164 and other hardware helped me nail down my ideas about parameterized machine models.

Fisher and Ruttenberg worked out the early seminal ideas of VLIWs [Fisher 83, Ruttenberg 83]. Later the rest of us joined in and added our two cents. Mark Sidell and then John O'Donnell worked on making a real VLIW prototype, the ELI (Enormously Long Instructions). My machine modeling, and the actual model used in the experiments, is based on their work.

Others made smaller contributions: Richard Kelsey wrote a nifty algorithm for drawing directed acyclic graphs, an invaluable debugging tool. Abhiram Ranade talked with us about memory architectures, parallel algorithms, and instruction execution. Joe Rodrigue hacked the Unix program "struct" to convert Fortran into Tinylisp, and he helped exercise the compiler. Doug Baldwin participated in many of the early hardware discussions.

Finally, I did most of the experiments, collecting the programs in our library, converting them to our Fortran-like language Tinylisp, adding in assertions, discovering the needed source transformations, and coaxing them through the compiler and the machine simulator.

Previous Work

Early parallelism experiments [Foster 72, Tjaden 70] indicated that there was very little parallelism in ordinary programs. The pessimism of those experiments combined with the difficulty of hand-coding VLIWs focused research on multiprocessors, vector machines, and data-flow and reduction machines, and away from VLIWs.

Data-flow and reduction machines are still a gleam in the researcher's eye. Maybe they'll eventually provide thousand-fold parallelism, but there are still too many unsolved problems. Meanwhile, the ELI project has demonstrated a practical hardware and software architecture that offers mere 8-fold speed-ups right now.

There has been little success in compiling programs for multiprocessors. For example, the Cm* project [Jones 80] was hamstrung by the difficulty in distributing programs among the multiple processors.

The major effort in automated compilation for vector machines and multiprocessors was undertaken at the University of Illinois. Kuck and his group developed a system, Parafrase, whose main goal is to generate code for fast, highly parallel machines [Padua 80]. Parafrase relies on extensive global data-dependence analysis and no global flow information. A memory-reference disambiguation system eliminates superfluous dependency edges in the data-dependency graph due to ambiguous array references [Banerjee 79]. Using a large library of source transformations, Parafrase attempts to fit the available parallelism to the target architecture. Because the architectures cannot use fine-grained, operation-level parallelism, the disambiguator and the transformations operate at a coarse, all-or-nothing level, ignoring anything that cannot fit the mold. As a result, Parafrase ignores large amounts of parallelism existing in ordinary programs.

Many of the ideas of the ELI project were originally motivated by the research on the compilation of high-level languages into horizontal microcode. Fisher's thesis introduced the concept of trace scheduling and discussed heuristics for using list scheduling to generate horizontal microcode from vertical microcode [Fisher 79]. Since then there have been many papers about variants on trace scheduling and other techniques attempting translation into horizontal microcode [Landskov 80, Micro-12 79, Micro-16 83].

Our research differs significantly from this microcode research. First, the VLIW architectures we've been studying are not horizontally-microcoded machines—they are reduced-instruction-set processors that hide the complexity and asymmetry of microcode, while offering many times the architectural parallelism of current microcoded machines. Second, most of the microcode compilation techniques generate vertical microcode with registers, functional units, and data paths already assigned; then they try to compact the vertical microcode into horizontal microcode, perhaps reassigning registers in the process. The problem with this approach is that the register and functional unit assignments made for the vertical microcode can significantly affect the compaction into horizontal microcode, and for parallel machines it isn't clear how best to make the assignments. Finally, most of the microcode research is paper research with very few people actually building real compilers.

A number of existing machines offer pipelined execution of operations; a program can initiate one or two multicycle operations every instruction cycle. On the MIPS [Hennessy 83], the compiler is responsible for ensuring the correct synchronization of data-dependent operations; whereas the scalar part of the Cray provides that synchronization in hardware, if necessary temporarily suspending instruction execution until an operation's operands become available. For both machines, researchers have written peephole optimizers that reorder basic blocks of machine instructions in an attempt to get the most overlapped pipelined execution of operations. On the Cray, Sites [Sites 78] used list scheduling and reported 5–20% speed-ups for scalar code compared with no reordering (the hardware always pipelines execution—Site's system only reduced the number of times the hardware needed to suspend instruction execution). On the MIPS, Hennessy and Gross used a generalization of list scheduling and reported 2–10% speed-ups compared with no pipelining at all (that is, no operation was started until the previous one completed). The main drawback of both systems is that there is little parallelism inherent in basic blocks; Gross told me that the MIPS could be changed to allow only one operation initiated per cycle (instead of two) without significantly affecting performance, since the MIPS compiler can't find enough parallelism in basic blocks to keep the second operation field of the instruction busy. And like the microcode compaction systems, the Cray and MIPS optimizers suffer from trying to reorder instructions with the registers already bound to operations.

The Fortran compiler for the FPS-164 [Touzeau 84] is perhaps the only compiler to date that generates good code for LIWs. It uses list scheduling on basic blocks of intermediate code to generate the wide, parallel instructions for the FPS-164. For simple loops, however, it uses a clever "software pipelining" technique to generate near-optimal code. It combines binary search with list scheduling to find the shortest pipelined sequence of instructions for the loop body. "Simple loops" are those that iterate the induction variables through linear sequences and that have no conditionals in the body. For much scientific code this restriction on loops isn't serious, and the compiler is quite adequate. But the main problem is that the technique doesn't scale up to larger VLIWs; the compiler assumes there is one of each type of functional unit and that there is a single crossbar connecting all the units.

The Polycyclic Architecture [Rau 81, Rau 82] is an ingenious combination of hardware and software. The core of the architecture is a full crossbar connecting the outputs and inputs of all the computing elements; at each crosspoint in the bar is a small FIFO-like register file. This guarantees that an operation on a functional unit will never be delayed because of contention for register bandwidth when either reading the operands or writing the result. Provably optimal code can be produced for simple loops using a fast algorithm; near-optimal code can be produced for some other simple classes of loops. A VLSI chip implementing the Polycyclic crossbar has been designed and supposedly fabricated, though I'm not sure any fully working chips actually have been produced.

There are several problems with the Polycyclic architecture. Though it could be used to build a powerful LIW, scaling it up to a VLIW with 8 or 16 times the number of functional units would be out of the question. However, it could be used as the local interconnect for individual clusters of a VLIW, but then the nice algorithmic compilation properties would no longer hold; all the problems of compiling for VLIWs that I've described previously would apply here as well. The Polycyclic Architecture would make a nice crossbar for a VLIW cluster; with only minor modifications to accommodate the FIFO register files, the Bulldog compiler wouldn't have problems modeling the crossbar. Unfortunately, the Polycyclic suffers from the "not invented here" syndrome; because it is so different from traditional architectures and because it is not in commercial production, there is a natural resistance to considering it as part of a realistic machine design.

Chapter 2
The Front End

The front end of the Bulldog compiler is like any other Fortran compiler: A parser translates the source language into an intermediate code, and an optimizer optimizes the intermediate code in preparation for code generation.

Tinylisp

The source language of the current compiler is Tinylisp, a Fortran-like expression language with Lisp syntax. (Tinylisp is a misnomer, since the only thing it has in common with Lisp is its syntax.) Tinylisp includes all the basic Fortran constructs used to write portable scientific routines.

We made a separate language instead of implementing a Fortran parser because we wanted a clean, malleable research vehicle that we could fiddle with. For example, we've added syntax that allows the programmer to specify the jump probabilities of conditional branches, how many times loops are expected to be executed, and how many times loops should be unrolled. We've also added syntax for specifying assertions to help the disambiguators.

Tinylisp's data types are integer, float, complex, and multidimensional arrays of those types. Tinylisp provides all the basic operators on expressions of the types, including variable assignment. Tinylisp's control primitives are blocks, conditionals, loops, and exits from blocks and loops. The Bulldog compiler is designed primarily to compile the time-critical kernels of scientific code, so the Tinylisp parser expands all procedure calls inline (this prohibits recursive procedures, of course). Like Lisp, every control construct is an expression and returns a value.

It's straightforward to convert most clean scientific code written in portable Fortran into Tinylisp. In fact, we hacked the Unix utility Struct to convert Fortran into Tinylisp (Struct translates vanilla Fortran into structured Ratfor). Appendix B contains examples of Tinylisp and the original Fortran. Some were converted by hand, others automatically.

Because Tinylisp uses Lisp syntax, we didn't have to write a real parser; instead, the compiler merely invokes Lisp **read**. The Lisp syntax also makes source transformations simple. For example, the high-level looping constructs are actually Lisp-like macros that expand into the low-level primitives. (This is all well-known Lisp craft, I'm just proselytizing.)

Bulldog currently lacks the more exotic features that make Fortran useful as a production language: double precision, common blocks, equivalence statements, and so on. These are irrelevant to the task at hand, demonstrating that trace scheduling and VLIWs work. After reading the rest of this dissertation it should become obvious that there is nothing in any of the techniques used in Bulldog that couldn't be applied straightforwardly to a production Fortran compiler.

Intermediate Code

The compiler translates the source language into a traditional intermediate code. For example, this source statement:

```
x := (v[i+1] * y) + a
```

would be translated as:

```
IADD   t1,i,1
FVLOAD t2,v,t1
FMUL   t3,t2,y
FADD   x,t3,a
```

where t1, t2, and t3 are newly introduced temporaries.

The general form of an intermediate-code operation is:

$$\text{operator } [\text{dest,}] \text{ operand}_1, \ldots, \text{operand}_n$$

Each operator takes a fixed number of operands of fixed types and optionally produces a result of a fixed type. The operands are either variables or constants. For example,

```
FADD x,y,z
```

takes two floating operands y and z and produces a floating result, assigning it to x.

Because VLIWs are reduced-instruction-set processors, there is generally a direct mapping from the intermediate-code operators to the available machine-code operators of the machine model. Thus, the code generator doesn't need to worry about the complexities of instruction selection.

The operators fall into several broad classes:

Arithmetic operators. These include all the standard unary and binary integer and floating operators available on most scientific processors: multiplication, subtraction, addition, logical operations, logical and arithmetic shifts, type conversions, minimum and maximum. Simple assignment is considered to be a unary operator.

Comparison operators. These operators compare two operands and produce a boolean result. There is a fully symmetric set of comparisons for both integers and floats: $<, \leq, =, \neq, \geq, >$. For example:

```
FGT b,x,y
```

compares x and y and sets b to be true or false, depending on whether x is greater than y.

Jump operators. These include unconditional and conditional branches. The conditional branches have the form:

```
IF comparison-operator, operand1, operand2, label, probability
```

The `comparison-operator` is one of the comparison operators above; `label` specifies the target of the branch, and `probability` specifies the estimated probability that the branch condition will be true and the jump taken. There are also two boolean-comparison jumps:

```
IF-TRUE  operand, label, probability
IF-FALSE operand, label, probability
```

that branch depending on whether the operand is true or false. Some of the machine models we've studied don't implement conditional branches for floating comparisons as a single machine operation. (A possible motivation for such machine models is given in chapter 4 in the discussion on multicycle jumps.) For those models, a Tinylisp statement of the form:

```
IF x>y THEN ...
```

would be translated into a sequence of a comparison followed by a boolean test:

```
FGT     t2,x,y
IF-TRUE t2, label, probability
```

Assertions. The ASSERT operator has the form:

```
ASSERT comparison-operator, operand1, operand2
```

At runtime, `ASSERT` verifies that the asserted relation between the operands is true. Assertions are used by the disambiguators at compile time and are normally deleted by the code generators; but a debugging option retains the assertions in the machine code, helping the programmer identify errors.

Vector operations. These load and store elements from vectors. Vectors are one-dimensional arrays stored contiguously in memory and use 0-based indexing; the Tinylisp parser translates a multidimensional array reference into an index calculation and a vector reference. Unlike Fortran (but in conformance with most other languages), Tinylisp arrays are laid out in row-major order. (The choice between row-major and column-major isn't crucial, since the programmer can use inline procedures to produce alternate layouts. As we'll see in chapter 6, this ability to control array layout is needed for memory-bank disambiguation.)

The only intermediate-code operations on vectors are load and store. For example:

    FVLOAD x,v,i

assigns the float x to be the ith element of vector v, and

    IVSTORE v,i,a

assigns the ith element of v to be the integer a.

An intermediate pseudo-operation declares the size and type of every vector. The address of the vector needn't be known at compile time (it could well be a procedure parameter).

Some machine models don't implement the indexed-addressing mode implied by VLOAD and VSTORE. For those machines, VLOAD and VSTORE are translated to lower-level pointer operations. For example,

    FVLOAD x,v,i

would be converted to:

    VBASE   t1,v
    IADD   t2,t1,i
    FPLOAD x,t2,v

The VBASE operator assigns t1 to be the address of the first element of vector v. The IADD adds i to that address, yielding the address t2 of the ith element. The FPLOAD loads the float stored at the address t2. (The name of the vector, v, isn't used by the FPLOAD operator; it is retained as an operand merely to tell the disambiguator which vector is being referenced.) Almost all of the excess address arithmetic resulting from this conversion will be eliminated by induction variable simplification, described later.

Pseudo-operators. These provide various declarative pieces of information about the program. The DECLARE pseudo-op declares the types, sizes, and initial values of variables. The LABEL pseudo-op defines a label (the target of a branch). There are several other pseudo-ops, none worth mentioning here.

Unlike most compilers, Bulldog has an interpreter for the intermediate code. This was quite useful for debugging both the compiler, especially the intermediate-code optimizations, and the programs being compiled. It also makes optimizations like constant folding easier, since the interpreter is invoked directly to evaluate an operation at compile time.

From now on, I'll usually use a more readable infix notation for intermediate code. For example, instead of:

```
IADD    t1,m,n
FVSTORE v,t1,x
```

I'll write:

```
t1:=m +i n
v[t1]:=x
```

The suffixes i and f indicate the datatype of operations, but I'll drop them when they're not necessary for the discussion at hand. And for conditional jumps:

```
IF IGT, x, y, label
```

I'll usually write:

```
IF x>y THEN label
```

Intermediate-code Optimizations and Transformations

The Bulldog compiler implements most of the intermediate-code optimizations of the better traditional Fortran compilers. Of course, these optimizations would be essential in a commercial trace-scheduling compiler. But they are also essential to prove my thesis: Without highly optimized intermediate code, the speed-up results from trace scheduling would be highly suspect, since the speed-up (parallelism) found by trace scheduling might be strongly biased by the code that otherwise would have been optimized away.

A great deal of my time was spent implementing the optimizations. Unfortunately, I couldn't simply rip out the guts from an existing Fortran compiler. There are very few excellent compilers on the market, and they are all proprietary. But even if I had access to an optimizing Fortran compiler, it wouldn't have been worth my time to hack it, since all such compilers are extremely complicated. They are highly tuned for efficiency and for their target machines. Re-tuning such a complicated program for Bulldog would have taken longer than simply reimplementing the algorithms from scratch.

I relied on *Principles of Compiler Design* (the Dragon Book) [Aho 77] for almost all of the optimizations. They all operate on the intermediate-code flow graph, which is sectioned into basic blocks. I won't describe them in detail here, except to note particular modifications made for VLIW trace scheduling.

Constant folding. Constant expressions are evaluated at compile time:

```
x:=3+5         ⇒      x:=8
. . .                 . . .
y:=x*2                y:=16
```

Copy propagation. This helps eliminate useless assignments:

```
x:=y                    ⇒        x:=y
...                              ...
IF x>n THEN ...                  IF y>n THEN ...
```

The assignment `x:=y` will be deleted later by dead-code removal if that value of `x` is no longer used.

Common-subexpression elimination. Common subexpressions are removed within basic blocks only:

```
x:=a+b        ⇒         x:=a+b
...                     y:=x
y:=a+b
```

Global CSE is more difficult and results in little improvement, since most of the global common subexpressions in scientific code occur in inner loops and are eliminated via loop-invariant motion and induction-variable simplification followed by basic-block CSE.

Dead-code removal. An operation is dead and useless if:

It is unreachable by any path from the start of the program, or

It produces a value that is not used, or

It is an **IF** whose true and false edges lead to the same successor in the flow graph.

A simple iterative algorithm repeatedly removes all such dead operations from the flow graph.

Variable renaming. New names are introduced for disjoint uses of the same variable. For example:

```
x:=a+b        ⇒         x:=a+b
y:=x*2                  y:=x*2
...                     ...
x:=d-e                  x1:=d-e
z:=x+1                  z:=x1+1
```

Variable renaming increases the parallelism available to trace scheduling. In the original fragment, the operations must be done sequentially to prevent the second value of `x` from overwriting the first. But in the transformed fragment, the last two operations can be done in parallel with the first two because the second use of `x` has been renamed to `x1`.

Not all opportunities for variable renaming are due to the programmer. When a loop is unrolled, the variables in the body can often be renamed. For example, when the following loop is unrolled three times:

```
LOOP                    ⇒      LOOP
    x:=a+b                         x:=a+b
    v[i]:=x                        v[i]:=x
    . . .                          . . .
                                   x:=a+b
                                   v[i]:=x
                                   . . .
                                   x:=a+b
                                   v[i]:=x
                                   . . .
```

the uses of x in each copy of the original loop body are disjoint and can be renamed.

Bulldog uses a renaming algorithm similar to the simple one used by Parafrase [Padua 80]. The definitions and uses of a variable x are represented as nodes in a bipartite graph, and there is an edge between a definition node and a use node if the definition reaches the use. Each maximal connected component of the graph can then be assigned a different variable name.

Loop unrolling. Inner loops are unrolled by some amount currently specified by the programmer for each loop individually. Here is a loop unrolled 8 times:

```
i:=1                       ⇒      i:=1
LOOP                              LOOP
    IF i>n THEN EXITLOOP              IF i>n THEN EXITLOOP
    body                             body₀
                                     IF i>n THEN EXITLOOP
                                     body₁
                                     . . .
                                     IF i>n THEN EXITLOOP
                                     body₇
```

Loop unrolling is currently implemented by the Tinylisp parser. The amount of unrolling is specified in the source language:

```
FOR i:=1 TO n UNROLL 8
    body
```

There is some trickiness with loop variables and induction-variable simplification that is discussed below.

Loop-invariant motion. Operations producing values that are invariant across iterations of a containing loop are moved out of the loop. For example:

```
i:=1                                    i:=1
LOOP                       ⇒            x:=a+b
    IF i>n THEN EXITLOOP                LOOP
    x:=a+b                                  IF i>n THEN EXITLOOP
    v[i]:=x                                 v[i]:=x
    i:=i+1                                  i:=i+1
```

The compiler also detects many invariant vector references. A vector reference is invariant within a loop if the vector isn't stored into anywhere in the loop.

Loop invariants aren't always the result of programmer laziness. For example, the index calculations for accessing multidimensional arrays give rise to many loop invariants, and the programmer has no control over that.

Induction-variable simplification. IVS removes integer multiplications, additions, and subtractions from a loop by introducing new induction variables and eliminating old ones. For example, suppose that the following Tinylisp loop was accessing a vector v with declared bounds 1:n:

```
Tinylisp:          Before IVS:          After IVS:
FOR i:=1 TO n      i:=1                  t1:=0
    x:=v[i]        LOOP                  t2:=n-1
    ...                IF i>n THEN       LOOP
                           EXITLOOP          IF t1>t2 THEN
                   t1:=i-1                        EXITLOOP
                   x:=v[i]                   x:=v[t1]
                   ...                       ...
                   i:=i+1                    t1:=t1+1
```

One subtraction has been removed from the loop body by replacing the induction variable i by a new induction variable t1.

IVS really pays off in scientific code that accesses multidimensional arrays. For example, suppose the following code references an array a with bounds 1:m

$\times$ 1:n:

Tinylisp:	Before IVS:	After IVS:

```
Tinylisp:            Before IVS:              After IVS:
FOR i:=1 TO m        i:=1                     t4:=j-1
    x:=a[i,j]        LOOP                     t6:=(m-1)*n
    ...                  IF i>m THEN          t7:=t4+t6
                             EXITLOOP         LOOP
                         t1:=i-1                  IF t4>t7 THEN
                         t2:=t1*n                     EXITLOOP
                         t3:=j-1                  x:=a[t4]
                         t4:=t2+t3                ...
                         x:=a[t4]                 t4:=t4+n
                         ...
                         i:=i+1
```

IVS has removed a multiplication, an addition, and two subtractions from the loop at the expense of a new multiplication, an addition, and a subtraction outside the loop.

The Bulldog compiler uses a slightly more general algorithm than the one presented in *Principles of Compiler Design*. And there is some tricky interaction between loop unrolling, variable renaming, and IVS that requires special handling for VLIWs. Suppose a simple loop is unrolled 8 times merely by repeating the body. After unrolling and variable renaming, the code looks like:

```
i:=1                               i0:=1
LOOP                   ⇒           LOOP
    IF i>n THEN EXITLOOP               IF i0>n THEN EXITLOOP
    body                              body₀
    i:=i+1                            i1:=i0+1
                                      IF i1>n THEN EXITLOOP
                                      body₁
                                      i2:=i1+1
                                      ...
                                      IF i7>n THEN EXITLOOP
                                      body₇
                                      i0:=i7+1
```

There are two problems with the transformed code. The first is that the Dragon Book's IVS algorithm won't recognize the variables i0, i1, ..., i7 as induction variables. The second problem is that the transformed code is less parallel than it could be. If the copies of the loop body are data-independent (often the case in scientific code), they can be overlapped completely. But because the induction variables must be incremented sequentially, that is, i2:=i1+1 must be executed after i1:=i0+1, copies of the later bodies can't be fully overlapped with the earlier ones; $body_7$ can't be started until at least 7 cycles after the start of $body_0$.

To get around these problems, increment/decrement loop variables are treated specially by loop unrolling:

```
FOR i:=1 TO n          ⇒          i0:=1
      body                        i1:=2
                                  . . .
                                  i7:=7
                                  LOOP
                                        IF i0>n THEN EXITLOOP
                                        i:=i0
                                        body₀
                                        i0:=i0+8
                                        IF i1>n THEN EXITLOOP
                                        i:=i1
                                        body₁
                                        i1:=i1+8

                                        . . .

                                        IF i7>n THEN EXITLOOP
                                        i:=i7
                                        body₇
                                        i7:=i7+8
```

Now all of the induction variables are independent from each other, the increments and the copies of the body can be fully overlapped, and IVS will also recognize $i0, \ldots, i7$ as induction variables.

There is another minor hassle with IVS. It tries to rewrite all comparisons in the loop that refer to the original induction variables in terms of the newly introduced variables. The original IVS algorithm tended to rewrite the above code into:

```
t0:=...
t1:=...
. . .
t7:=...
LOOP
      IF t0>c0 THEN EXITLOOP
      body₀
      t0:=t0+8
      IF t0>c1 THEN EXITLOOP
      body₁
      t1:=t1+8
      . . .
      IF t0>c7 THEN EXITLOOP
      body₇
      t7:=t7+8
```

That is, all the exit tests have been rewritten in terms of one induction variable t0. This is unsatisfactory for VLIWs, since it is likely that the different comparison functional units will be widely scattered throughout the machine (one per cluster). The code generator will produce code that either copies t0 to all the comparison functional units or performs the exit tests sequentially, both of which are time-consuming and less parallel than necessary. So the modified IVS algorithm tries to use all the new induction variables evenly, making sure no one induction variable is used more than another when rewriting comparisons:

```
t0:=...
t1:=...
...
t7:=...
LOOP
     IF t0>c0 THEN EXITLOOP
     body₀
     t0:=t0+8
     IF t1>c1 THEN EXITLOOP
     body₁
     t1:=t1+8

     ...
     IF t7>c7 THEN EXITLOOP
     body₇
     t7:=t7+8
```

Thus, all the exit tests can be executed in parallel, without any long-distance data movements of an induction variable.

There is still one more minor hassle with IVS involving the assertions supplied by the programmer to help the disambiguator. For example, consider this loop:

```
FOR i:=1 TO n
     ASSERT i<=k
     x:=v[i]
     ...
```

If this loop is unrolled 8 times and optimized by IVS, a family of 8 new induction variables will replace the original uses of i in the vector references v[i+0], v[i+1], ..., v[i+7]. But the assertion is in terms of i. Somehow the disambiguator's assertion mechanism, described in chapter 5, must be able to relate i to the newly introduced induction variables. IVS could either add a new rewritten version of the assertion for each new induction variable, or it could record the linear function that relates i to each new variable. I chose the latter method (though the former should work just as well).

When IVS introduces a new induction variable j, it will necessarily be some linear function of the original induction variable i: $j = ai + c$. At the top of the loop, IVS records this linear function using the EQUIV pseudo-op:

```
i:=...
j:=...
LOOP
    t1:=a*i
    t2:=t1+c
    EQUIV j,t2
    ASSERT i<=k
    ...
    i:=i+d
    j:=j+d1
```

Normally, the compiler ignores the EQUIV. But the disambiguator treats the EQUIV as if it were a normal assignment. Thus it is able to express j in terms of i and relate uses of j to the programmer-supplied assertion. After the disambiguator is finished, all ASSERT and EQUIV operations are deleted, and a later pass of dead-code removal will eliminate the old induction variables (in this example, i).

Replacing VLOADs and VSTOREs. As discussed previously, this transformation replaces the VLOAD and VSTORE operators by PLOAD and PSTORE:

```
FVSTORE v,i,x        ⇒        VBASE    t1,v
                              IADD     t2,t1,i
                              FPSTORE  t2,x,v
```

The transformation is invoked only for machine models that don't have an indexed-addressing mode.

Replacing comparison branches. As discussed previously, this transformation replaces branches with integer or floating comparisons (or both) by a comparison followed by a boolean branch:

```
IF FGT,x,y, label        ⇒        FGT t1,x,y
                                  IF-TRUE t1, label
```

The transformation is invoked only for comparison branches not directly implemented by the machine model.

Loading constants. This transformation replaces uses of non-immediate constants by variables initialized to contain the constants. A non-immediate constant is one that can't be generated by the immediate field of an instruction—it must be loaded from memory. Each machine model defines precisely which constants are immediate. A use of a non-immediate is transformed as follows:

```
x:=y*3.9        ⇒        FCONSTANT t1,3.9
                         x:=y*t1
```

The `FCONSTANT` operator merely assigns `t1` the value of 3.9. Several `FCONSTANT`s of the same value in a loop will all get moved out of the loop by loop-invariant motion, and common-subexpression elimination and copy propagation will then replace them by a single `FCONSTANT`. In this way, the memory loads needed for non-immediate constants are moved out of the loops. (The section on constants in chapter 7 discusses the motivation for this transformation.)

The optimizations and transformations are applied in this order:

> replacing `VLOAD`s and `VSTORE`s
> variable renaming
> constant folding
> loading constants
> loop-invariant motion
> common-subexpression elimination
> copy propagation
> dead-code removal
> induction-variable simplification
> constant folding
> common-subexpression elimination
> copy propagation
> replacing comparison branches
> memory-reference disambiguation
> memory-bank disambiguation
> deletion of assertions
> dead-code removal

Several of the optimizations are repeated twice to clean up after previous optimizations. Currently, the optimizations are reinvoked on the whole flow graph; but that is often unnecessary. For example, the optimizations invoked after induction-variable simplification need be invoked only on the blocks that were changed by IVS.

The Costs of Optimization

The data-flow analyses needed to support these optimizations are live variables, reaching definitions, reaching uses, reaching copies, and dominators. To compute them, the Bulldog compiler uses the simple iterative set algorithms, implemented with bit vectors representing the sets [Aho 77]. In practice, the algorithms perform $O(n)$ set operations (union and intersection), where n is the number of nodes in the flow graph. When implemented with bit vectors, each set operation takes $O(n/w)$ time, where w is the word size of the machine on which compiler runs. Thus, the algorithms take $O(n^2)$ time.

For a typical flow graph encountered by a traditional compiler, the n/w factor is small enough so that the running time is quite acceptable and appears to be linear. Unfortunately, the running time is still asymptotically n^2. Unrolling the inner loops of scientific programs 16 or 32 times or more effectively increases the size of the flow graph by almost the same amount. On such large flow graphs, the running time of the flow-analysis algorithms becomes significant; the results in chapter 8 show that the compiler spends roughly 1/3 to 2/3 of its time in flow analysis (up to 40 minutes of CPU time on a DEC-2060).

As I'll discuss at the end, these large running times don't make trace scheduling impractical. Currently people spend weeks hand-coding a small algorithm such as a tridiagonal solver for a machine like the FPS-164. Replacing those expensive man-weeks by an hour or two of time on a large computer is quite economical.

Nevertheless, let's consider three ways the flow analysis might be improved.

The first possible improvement is to implement sets more efficiently than bit vectors. In the current algorithm, the bit vectors tend to be sparse, consisting of either mostly one bits or mostly zero bits. Perhaps some type of sparse vector representation would reduce the time needed for an average set operation. I'm not sure that this would work, however. Even though the sparse representation might be asymptotically faster, the comparatively large overhead required for manipulating the representation could well make it slower than simple bit vectors for the sizes of flow graphs actually encountered. (The current bit-vector operations are hand-coded in assembly language and are very simple and fast.)

The second possible improvement is to implement incremental reanalysis. Currently, the compiler assumes that an entire analysis is destroyed by an optimization; for example, the live-variable analysis is invalidated by loop-invariant motion. Thus, the analyses are recomputed several times as needed by the various optimizations. But instead the optimizations could incrementally update the analyses each time it makes a change to the flow graph. Unfortunately, incremental reanalysis is very complicated in general; easy and efficient methods are still open research topics.

The third possible improvement is to adopt different algorithms. The interval-based algorithms could well be more efficient than the iterative ones for the large flow graphs of trace scheduling [Aho 77]. The recursive-descent analyses can be even more efficient, but they require a structured, tree-like flow graph; if the source language includes GOTOs (Fortran), the compiler would have to convert the flow graph (luckily, almost all Fortran programs have reducible flow graphs). If you can afford to exclude gotos from the source language, the recursive-descent analyses are probably the way to go.

Chapter 3
The Machine Model

The Bulldog compiler uses a parameterized machine model capable of describing a large class of realistic VLIW architectures. A parameterized machine model was essential, since we were developing the compiler and hardware simultaneously. Using the model, arbitrary topologies of register banks and functional units can be constructed and simulated. By compiling programs under various models, we can explore the interactions between the compiler and the hardware design.

The model presented here is not intended as a general hardware description language. Rather, it is tailored for the specific needs of the Bulldog compiler and is parameterized just enough to characterize the class of VLIW architectures in which we were interested.

Some basic terminology:

A **machine element** is either a register bank, a functional unit, or a constant generator (such as the immediate-constant field of an instruction).

A **machine operator** is an operator of a hardware functional unit, such as floating-point add.

A **machine operation** is the specification of machine operator, functional unit, operands, and destination; for example

    r1:=r2 +₅ r3

(Register **r1** gets the result of adding **r2** and **r3** on the fifth integer adder.)

An **instruction** is a collection of many machine operations that will all be executed in the same cycle. Instructions are stored in the wide instruction words in instruction memory.

Building a model involves specifying the number and parameters of each machine element and the connections between the elements. In the Lisp tradition, an embedded, imperative, object-oriented language is used to concisely specify a model. Appendix A contains some example model specifications.

Data Types

The only data types currently recognized by the model are integer and float, both one word. All the data paths in the model are one word wide. Since memory is word-addressed, the actual width of the word doesn't matter to the compiler.

These two primitive data types are quite sufficient for our purposes. The time-critical routines of most scientific programs use only integers and floats, with either single precision or double precision predominating. Because most memory references are for full-word integers and floats, word-based addressing isn't a limitation. (The scientific processors with which I'm familiar are all word addressed.)

Extending the model to handle different sized data types is a matter of detail: Registers and data paths would be flagged with the data types they could hold or transmit. A production compiler certainly has to deal with more data types, but their absence in the Bulldog compiler has no bearing on my thesis.

Register Banks

Specified for each register bank are:

> The number of registers.
>
> The number of input ports.
>
> The number of output ports.
>
> The machine elements connected to the input ports.
>
> The machine elements connected to the output ports.
>
> The resources needed to read a register.
>
> The resources needed to write a register.

(Resources are described below.)

The registers are all identically sized, holding either a float or a real.

All the input ports are identical in that they are all connected to the same set of input machine elements. Similarly, the output ports are all connected to the same set of output machine elements.

The operations on a register bank are "read register i to output port j" and "write register i from input port j." A transfer between registers in the same bank is specified by the combination of a read and a write operation in the same cycle; one of the output elements of the bank must be itself to allow such a transfer.

More than one of the output elements can read a register being read out on a port during a cycle. For example, if an adder and a multiplier were output elements of a bank, then if "read register 3 to output port 2" were executed in some cycle, both the adder and the multiplier could read the value of register 3 via port 2.

The registers are write-after-read; that is, a register's old value can be read at the beginning of the cycle and overwritten at the end of the cycle.

Functional Units

A functional unit is a machine element that computes some output value based on its inputs. Examples are adders, multipliers, integer ALUs, and memory units. Specified for each functional unit are:

The machine elements connected to the functional unit's inputs.

The machine elements connected to its outputs.

The intermediate-code operators implemented by the unit.

The pipeline delay of the unit (the number of cycles required for an operation to complete).

The resources needed to execute an operation on the unit.

A constraint function that operations must satisfy.

Because VLIWs are simple reduced instruction set processors, there is a one-to-one mapping between intermediate-code operators and machine operators; for simplicity, they have the same names. So to find a functional unit that could implement the intermediate-code operation IADD (integer add), the code generator merely looks for a functional unit that has IADD listed as one of its operators.

A memory unit is simply a functional unit that implements the memory-reference intermediate-code operators.

The inputs of a functional unit are all identical with respect to their connections to other machine elements and are not distinguished "left" or "right." For example, suppose an integer ALU was connected to two register banks A and B. Then for any registers l in A and r in B, the ALU could compute $l - r$ or $r - l$ with the same ISUB operator; if bank B had two output ports, then the ALU could also use B for both of its inputs, computing $l - m$ and $m - l$ for any two registers l and m in B.

The advantage of this symmetry for a code generator should be obvious. Asymmetric operands for machine operations make code generators much more complex, and should be avoided whenever possible. Providing the symmetry costs a bit extra in hardware, true, but not that much when considering the benefit of simpler code generators: A compiler writer has only so much time, and every minute he devotes to handling asymmetric hardware is a minute not devoted to improving the quality of generated code, and generating quality code is much harder in the presence of asymmetry. I think the current code generator could be extended to handle asymmetric machine operations, but only by making it even more complex; the extra hardware is probably worth it. (Decide for yourself after reading the chapter on code generation.)

All the operations of a functional unit have identical pipeline delay. A unit with different delays for different operators could be modeled by having two functional units with the same inputs and outputs but different delays and operators; the resources required by each would ensure that only one of the units could be used in any cycle (resources are described below).

Some actual hardware pipelined functional units can have operations initiated only every n cycles. This too can be modeled using resources and is described below.

The constraint function is a boolean predicate that takes an intermediate-code operation as its argument and returns true if the operation can be implemented on the functional unit. Currently the only use of this is to implement memory banking. Before code generation starts, the bank disambiguator records in each memory-reference operation the bank number of the reference (if the number is known at compile time). Each memory-bank functional unit has a constraint function that tests the bank number of intermediate-code operations being considered for execution on the unit; only memory references marked with the required bank number are allowed to be executed on the unit.

Constant Generators

A constant generator is a machine element that produces constant values on demand. A constant generator is used to model the immediate fields of instructions and the special 0, 1, and -1 inputs of some functional units.

Specified for each constant generator are:

The machine elements connected to the output of the generator.

The resources needed to generate a constant.

A constraint function.

The constraint function is a boolean predicate that takes a constant as its argument and returns true if the constant can be generated by this generator. For example, to model the immediate field of an instruction, the constraint function would allow, say, only integers that could be represented with 11 bits.

Many integer ALUs have special increment and decrement operations that don't require a second input. Such ALUs can be modeled by making one of the inputs of the ALU a constant generator that generates only 1 and -1; this simplifies code generation considerably, since the code generator need deal only with the general add and subtract and not worry about special-casing increment and decrement.

Resources

Each of the different types of machine elements has a **resources** field specifying which ephemeral hardware resources are needed for element operations. One example of a resource is the field within an instruction needed to initiate an operation; another example is a bus which can transmit at most one value per cycle. In this model, resources need not correspond with actual hardware and can be used to model many sorts of hardware constraints.

A **resource class** is a set of n identical resources, any one of which can be substituted for any other. In any cycle, no more than n of the resources can be used.

A **resource request** is a requirement for resources needed to execute a machine-element operation. Abstractly, it is a two-dimensional matrix A; assuming the operation is initiated in cycle c, $a_{i,j}$ specifies the number of resources needed in cycle $c + i$ from resource class j.

The simplest use for resource requests is to constrain the compiler from initiating more than one operation on a functional unit per cycle. By convention, each functional unit requires 1 resource from a corresponding resource class of size 1. (Of course, a model could be constructed that would allow a functional unit to start two operations every cycle, as in the MIPS [Hennessy 83]; the size of the corresponding resource class would be 2 instead of 1.)

Similarly, a register bank having 4 output ports would request for its read operation 1 resource from a corresponding class of size 4.

Some real hardware functional units such as memories can initiate an operation only once every other cycle. This constraint can be modeled using a resource request that requires 1 unit of the functional unit's resource class for the first cycle and 1 for the second cycle.

Connecting Machine Elements

There is one restriction on connecting machine elements: Only register banks may be connected to the outputs of functional units. That is, a functional unit always delivers its results to some register bank. The rationale for this is discussed in a later section on "hot spots" (page 46). Other than this restriction, arbitrary topologies can be constructed.

Every connection between machine elements has an associated resource request that must be satisfied to move data across the connection. This models the hardware constraints on data paths. For example, to model a one-value-per-cycle bus, all the elements writing the bus would be connected to all the elements reading the bus. Associated with the bus is a resource class, *bus*, of size 1. Every point-to-point connection between a writer and a reader would request the resource class *bus*. Thus, only one value per cycle could be put on the bus.

You might think that under this scheme only one reader could read the value on the bus in any one cycle, since another point-to-point connection from the same writer to another reader would not be able to satisfy its resource request for class *bus*. But the model assumes that once a value appears at the output port of a register bank or constant generator, it may be read by any of the machine elements connected to the port; only one of the point-to-point resource requests (chosen nondeterministically) is required to be satisfied, and the others are ignored.

A full crossbar is modeled simply by connecting all the readers with all the writers, with no associated point-to-point resource requests. A partial crossbar that connects all the readers with all the writers but allows only n values to be transmitted per cycle is modeled just like a bus, except that the associated resource class has size n instead of 1.

The point-to-point resource requests can be arbitrary, except for one restriction: For any two elements A and B that are inputs to a functional unit F, the resource request for the A–F connection must be **non-conflicting** with the request for the B–F connection. Two resource requests R and S conflict if, taken as a pair, they can never be satisfied; that is, if R and S jointly request more than the maximum amount available from some resource class. (Formally, R and S conflict if there exists some i and j such that $r_{i,j} + s_{i,j} > \text{size}(j)$, where $\text{size}(j)$ is the size of the jth resource class.)

This conflict constraint makes life considerably easier for the code generator without seriously affecting the class of architectures that can be modeled. Without the constraint, the code generator would have to go to a bit of trouble to make sure that all the operands of a machine operation were suitably placed so that they could all be moved to the functional unit in the same cycle. For example, suppose that the inputs of functional unit F were connected to register banks A, B, and C, each with one output port, and that the A–F and B–F connections have conflicting resource requests (each, say, requests the same class of size 1). The code generator would have to guarantee that for two-operand operations, at least one of the operands was in C, since it couldn't move the operands from A to F and from B to F in the same cycle. While one could imagine a code generator smart enough to handle such conflicts, I didn't see any real need for it. (In fact, the current code generator handles very similar constraints imposed by the number of output ports on a register bank.)

Shortest-path Table

The code generator needs to know how to move a value from any machine element to any other machine element in the machine. Instead of trying to compute such information on the fly during compilation, the compiler constructs a shortest-path table that gives the shortest path between any pair of machine elements.

Only paths consisting solely of register banks are considered. (Though it might be possible to move values through functional units using the identity operator, it wouldn't be necessary on any sane architecture.) The cost of a path from machine element i to machine element j is the number of cycles needed to move a value along the path. A move between directly connected register banks takes one cycle, so the cost of a path is the number of register banks along the path.

A standard transitive closure algorithm computes the path table, yielding the cost matrix C and the path matrix P. The cost of the shortest path from machine element i to machine element j is given by $c_{i,j}$. The list of register banks immediately adjacent to element i that are on the shortest paths from i to j is given by $p_{i,j}$.

Hot Spots

Many microprogrammed architectures have so-called "hot spots," latches, that will hold a value for only one cycle or until another value displaces it. For example, the outputs of the multiplier and adder pipelines in the FPS-164 [FPS 82] are latched and can be fed back to the register banks or directly to the inputs of the pipelines. There isn't enough bandwidth into the register banks, so to keep the pipelines full the programmer is often forced to use the latched pipeline outputs directly as pipeline inputs. But the programmer must be very careful to synchronize the pipelines' inputs and outputs, since the next value coming out of the pipeline will overwrite the previously latched value.

With a lot of work a code generator could do a fair job of handling the FPS-164's hot spots in the limited situations of optimizing simple pipelined loops [Touzeau 84]. But handling hot spots in general is very difficult, since potentially many operations in many cycles all have to be synchronized exactly. For example, when the code generator schedules some operation that leaves its value in a latch, it must ensure that latched value is not overwritten by successive operations until it is safely moved out of the way. Unfortunately, on machines like the 164 it often isn't feasible to move the value into a register bank; instead, the compiler must try to use the latched value directly as an input to another operation on the same or nearby functional unit. But scheduling that reading operation of the value might itself entail the use of latches, possibly even the original latch in question; the code generator must recursively synchronize the use of those latches as well. This suggests a recursive backtracking algorithm for code generation; such algorithms tend to be expensive and very complicated in practice.

Instead we decided to adopt the approach of the MARS-432 [Numerix 83], the Polycyclic Architecture [Rau 82], and most traditional high-level architectures: We outlawed hot spots. Every value-producing operation and every data transfer reads its operands from a register bank and delivers its result to a register bank. The advantage of this is that operations don't have to be tightly synchronized—a value can be left for an extra cycle or two in a register without worrying about it getting overwritten. The disadvantage is that more register banks, more register-bank ports, larger crossbars, or some combination of these are needed. But given the practicality of the MARS-432 hardware (it works and is cost-effective) and the threat of a backtracking code generator if we allowed hot spots, outlawing hot spots seemed the best approach.

The issue of hot spots illustrates the interaction of hardware design and compiler design. Architectures with hot spots are easy to build, but building compilers for them is hard. (It took years to build the FPS-164 compiler.) Better that the compiler and hardware are designed in parallel, avoiding hardware features that can't be used easily by the compiler.

Multicycle Machine Operations

In real hardware, many operations, such as floating arithmetic and memory references, take multiple cycles to execute and are pipelined. The code generator views these multicycle operations as atomic, and specifies the operator, the input registers, and the result register all on the first cycle of the operation. There are two ways of implementing these operations in the hardware instructions, typified by the MARS-432 and the FPS-164.

In the MARS-432, the operator, the operands, and the destination of an operation are specified on the first cycle, and the hardware buffers them in internal registers until the operation completes. But in the FPS-164, a multicycle template of micro-operations is used: The operator and operands are specified on the first cycle, the pipeline is "pushed" with a special opcode over the succeeding cycles, and the result is stored with a register-write operation on the last cycle:

```
FMUL r1,r2
PUSH
PUSH
WRITE r3
```

These implementations differ with respect to their behavior across jumps. In the MARS-432, if a jump occurs during execution of a multicycle operation, the operation will complete anyway, since the hardware has buffered the specification of the operation, including the destination register. But in the FPS-164, if a jump occurs in the middle of a multicycle operation, the operation won't complete (and won't store its results in a register) unless the instruction template is explicitly continued at the destination of the jump. For example, a 4-cycle multiply would be written as:

```
     FMUL r1,r2
     PUSH          ; BRANCH-IF-TRUE L1
     PUSH
     WRITE r3
     ...
L1:  ...
```

If the branch to L1 was taken in the second instruction, then the floating multiply wouldn't complete and nothing would be stored in the destination r3, unless the tail end of the multiply template was continued at L1:

```
L1:  PUSH
     WRITE r3
```

The two machines also differ in their behavior at joins. For example, in the MARS-432 a 4-cycle multiply can execute across a join:

```
     BRANCH-IF-TRUE L1

     ...
     r3:=FMUL r1,r2
     NOOP
L1:  NOOP
     NOOP
```

If the branch isn't taken, then the multiply is started and completes 4 cycles later. If the branch to L1 is taken, then the multiply is ignored completely. But in the FPS-164, the behavior is different:

```
     BRANCH-IF-TRUE L1

     ...
     FMUL r1,r2
     PUSH
L1:  PUSH
     WRITE R3
```

If the branch to L1 is taken, garbage from the multiplier's pipeline will be stored in r3 because the multiply template wasn't started before the branch was taken.

Bulldog's machine model and code generator are compatible with either implementation. As we'll see, the compiler guarantees that a multicycle operation will be continued on either branch of a conditional jump:

```
      r3:=FMUL r1,r2
      FMUL2 ; BRANCH-IF-TRUE L1
      FMUL3
      FMUL4
        . . .
  L1: FMUL3
      FMUL4
```

And if a multicycle operation spans a join, it will be initiated on both incoming branches with identical operands and destination:

```
      r3:=FMUL r1,r2
      FMUL2 ; BRANCH-IF-TRUE L1
      FMUL3
      FMUL4
        . . .
      r3:=FMUL r1,r2
      FMUL2
  L1: FMUL3
      FMUL4
```

(The $FMUL_i$ merely indicate the successive cycles of an FMUL.) In both cases, whether the hardware uses buffering or micro-operation templates, the effect is the same.

Multiple Conditional Jumps

The machine model allows up to n conditional jumps within an instruction:

$$branch_0\ label_0;\ branch_1\ label_1;\ \ldots\ branch_{n-1}\ label_{n-1}$$

These jumps are executed like a Lisp **cond** statement. Semantically, the branch conditions $branch_i$ are tested sequentially, and the first one that is true cause a jump to the corresponding $label_i$; if none are true, control "falls through" to the next instruction. The number n of conditional jumps allowed per instruction can be controlled by defining a resource class.

The actual hardware needn't necessarily store n target addresses in the instruction word. For example, Fisher discusses an encoding scheme that requires only one address per instruction [Fisher 80, Fisher 83]. In this scheme, every instruction has a *nextPC* field that specifies the address of the next instruction to be executed. The target address of an $n+1$-way conditional jump is computed as $nextPC + i$, where $branch_i$ is the first test in the instruction that evaluates to true ($i = n$ if no test is true). Fisher shows how to layout a compiled program in memory to accommodate this encoding scheme without wasting too much space. The layout is done in an independent post-pass, making the encoding transparent to the rest of the compiler.

Pipelined Memory Operations

The model allows for several memory operations to be initiated simultaneously and for them to be overlapped in the pipelines. It assumes that a memory write actually stores its result into memory at the end of the last cycle of the write and that a memory read gets its value from memory at the beginning of the last cycle of the read. Thus, in the following example, assuming memory references take 3 cycles, the memory read returns the value y, not x:

cycle 1   write x to address 1093
cycle 2   noop
cycle 3   noop
cycle 4   write y to address 1093
cycle 5   read from address 1093
cycle 6   noop
cycle 7   noop

The meaning of two writes or a write and read to the same location at the same time is undefined.

Simulation

The Bulldog compiler includes a machine-model simulator that lets us debug our compiler and experiment with proposed architectures. The flexibilities provided by a simulator are well known: easy debugging, detailed instrumentation, quick changes to the "hardware." The disadvantage (slow simulation) isn't so bad; any of our benchmarks running small inputs for debugging can be simulated in less than a minute on our DEC-2060, and most of the largest inputs (which we rarely need to run) in less than an hour.

There is nothing unusual in the implementation of the simulator. It is driven by the same model (data structures) that the compiler uses, with simple event queues to simulate pipelined operations. The simulator is instrumented to gather many sorts of statistics (presented in chapter 8). And it has some debugging checks that find compiler bugs early. For example, the compiler tags the register operands and results of operations with the source-variable names of the operands; during execution, the simulator stores the tags next to the values in the registers, and it will flag any operations that reference a register with a variable-name tag that doesn't match the one stored in the register. This quickly identifies value-location bugs in the compiler, which are typically very hard to find when using real hardware.

Usefulness

How useful is the machine model? I described three potential unrealities, and downplayed each:

Data types. The model supports only two primitive data types, float and integer, but that is sufficient for most time-critical scientific routines. It's quite feasible to extend the model and the code generator to include more data types (though it would be a lot of work).

Symmetry. The model requires that the outputs of a register bank be identical, all connected to the same set of elements. Similarly, the inputs of functional units must be identical and are not distinguished "left" or "right." I argued that processors, especially reduced-instruction-set processors, should always have such symmetry—the small extra cost in hardware is offset by a much simpler code generator. It would be possible to build a code generator that could handle asymmetric register banks and functional units in a VLIW, but only at great cost.

Hot spots. The model requires that value-producing machine operations always store their results in a register bank; at the level seen by the code generator, there can be no latched outputs that get overwritten the next cycle. Handling hot spots in general would require an expensive, complicated backtracking code generator. Many machines, including the wide MARS-432, are built without hot spots.

The model used for most of our experiments is described in detail in chapter 8 and accurately mirrors the designs of the ELI project [Fisher 83].

Chapter 4
Trace Scheduling

Picking Traces

When picking the next trace from the flow graph, the trace picker tries to identify
a path of untranslated intermediate-code operations that are most likely to be
executed. (I first described trace picking in terms of basic blocks, but the actual
implementation is in terms of operations.) The code generator will optimize the
early traces at the expense of later ones, on the assumption that the early traces
are more time critical.

To understand the importance of picking good traces, consider this example:

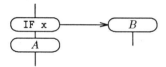

Suppose the trace picker decides that x is usually false and picks a trace including
IF x and A. Given the trace, the code generator might well decide that A is
a time-consuming operation and that to generate a shorter schedule of machine
code, it will move A up above IF x:

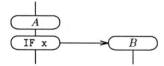

Notice that A is now executed regardless of which way the jump goes. If in fact x
is usually false, the extra execution cost of evaluating A needlessly when the jump
goes right is outweighed by the faster execution that results when the jump goes
left. But if the trace picker was wrong and x is usually true, A will be executed
needlessly most of the time; worse, it will be consuming machine resources that
could be used for other, more time-critical operations (such as B).

The trace picker uses estimates of execution frequency to guide its selection
of traces. Each operation O has an associated count(O), the number of times
it is expected to be executed during an entire run of the program (I'll say more
about where these estimates come from in a later section). Each edge e out of
a conditional branch operation has an associated prob(e), the probability that e

---

seed := the untranslated intermediate-code operation with the largest execution count

/* Grow the trace forward from the seed */
current-end := *seed*
loop
 s := the good successor of *current-end*
 if there is no such *s* **or** *s* is already translated to machine code **or** the
   edge from *current-end* to *s* is a loop back edge
 then
  exitloop
 Add *s* to the end of the trace
 current-end := *s*

/* Grow the trace backward from the seed */
current-beginning := *seed*
loop
 p := the good predecessor of *current-beginning*
 if there is no such *p* **or** *p* is already translated to machine code **or** the
   edge from *p* to *current-beginning* is a loop back edge
 then
  exitloop
 Add *p* to the beginning of the trace
 current-beginning := *p*

Figure 4.1. The trace-picking algorithm.

---

will be taken once control reaches the branch. The expected number of times an edge e from a conditional branch operation C is executed is thus:

$$\mathrm{count}(e) = \mathrm{count}(C)\,\mathrm{prob}(e)$$

To pick a trace, the trace picker first finds the untranslated intermediate-code operation with the highest estimated execution count. This operation becomes the "seed"; the trace picker then grows the trace forward and backward from the seed. To grow forward, the picker looks at the operation currently at the end of the trace and considers all its successors, picking a good one based on the execution estimates. The successor is added to the end of the trace, and the process is repeated. The trace stops growing forward when there is no good successor, when the chosen successor has already been translated to machine code by an earlier trace, or when the edge to the successor is a loop back edge (an edge from an operation in a loop body that jumps to the top of the loop). I'll discuss later why traces aren't allowed to cross loop back edges. Then the trace is grown backward using a similar method. Figure 4.1 shows the algorithm in detail.

When growing the trace both backward and forward, the same criteria are used for picking the next "good" operation to add to the trace. In either case, the best flow-graph edge is chosen from a set of candidate edges: Going forward, the candidate edges are those leaving the current end of the trace; going backward, the candidate edges are those entering the current beginning. An edge is best among all the candidates if the trace picker considers flow most likely to proceed along that edge.

Specifically, suppose there is an edge e from predecessor P to successor S:

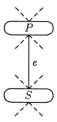

When the trace is growing forward, P is the current end of the trace, and when it is growing backward, S is the current beginning of the trace. Whether growing backward or forward, the edge e is selected for the trace as the best candidate edge if it meets the following conditions:

Of all the edges leaving P, e has the highest execution count. (This is equivalent to saying e has the highest probability.)

Of all the edges entering S, e has the highest execution count.

Intuitively, these criteria specify that if the program reaches P, then it most likely will proceed down e to S, and that if the program is already at S, it most likely got there via e from P. Thus it makes sense to include e as part of the trace.

Note that under these criteria sometimes no best edge will be selected, and the trace will stop growing in that particular direction. For example:

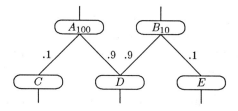

Suppose count(A) = 100 and count(B) = 10, and the branch edges have the probabilities shown. Further suppose that B was the current end of the trace. The edge with maximum count leaving B is B–D, but the edge with maximum count coming into to D is A–D. So the trace will stop at B, on the assumption that the most likely path of execution that reaches D comes down from A, not from B.

In this example, it probably doesn't matter that a trace would stop at B, since it is likely that A and D, being more time-critical, would have been included on an earlier trace anyway. Unfortunately, there are other situations in real programs where the trace-picking algorithm does stop growing a trace prematurely. Consider this example from an inner loop of one of the benchmarks:

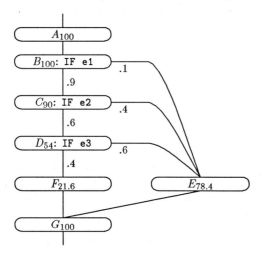

The cascaded conditional structure results from optimizing a single IF whose test is a disjunction:

```
A
IF e1 OR e2 OR e3 THEN
     E
ELSE
     F
G
```

Intuitively, the most likely path of execution is A, B, C, D, E, and G. But the trace picker stops prematurely when it gets to D, because the edge D–E is the highest-count edge leaving D, but edge C–E is the highest-count edge entering E. As a result, the trace is half as long as it should be.

One fix is to modify the heuristic to ignore edges to or from operations previously selected for the current trace. Here are the modified criteria for deciding whether edge e from P to S is the best candidate edge:

> Consider all edges P–X such that either X is the current beginning of the trace or X isn't already selected for the trace. Then e must have the highest execution count of all those edges.

Consider all edges X–S such that either X is the current end of the trace or X isn't already selected for the trace. Then e must have the highest execution count of all those edges.

But now the heuristic almost has the aura of magic—it's not quite as intuitive as before. (I haven't actually implemented this fix.)

As is the case with many other compiler heuristics, it might be that a much simpler heuristic will do as well or better. For example:

When growing the trace forward, pick the edge with maximum execution count.

When growing the trace backward, pick the predecessor (not the edge) with maximum execution count.

This simpler heuristic is guaranteed not to stop growing the trace prematurely.

As with most heuristics, the only sure way to distinguish them is by measuring their performance on realistic benchmarks. I've implemented this last heuristic, but I've only had time to run a very few comparisons with the original; one benchmark did slightly better, one did slightly worse, but the differences were only a few percent.

Loop Back Edges

The trace-picking algorithm ensures that a trace never crosses the back edge of a loop. This restriction makes the disambiguator much simpler, since it is assured that all the operations in a trace will be from the same iteration of a loop body.

For outer loops, this restriction on picking traces is a little too severe. Nested loops have the form:

```
LOOP
      outer loop code
      initialization for inner loop
      LOOP
            inner loop body
      finalization for inner loop
      outer loop code
```

Under the normal rules, the first trace will be:

inner loop body

The second trace will be:

outer loop code
initialization for inner loop

and the third trace will be:

finalization for inner loop
outer loop code

For many programs in the benchmark library, the second and third traces are individually not very parallel. Experiments showed that a significant fraction of execution time was spent in these traces. The front-end loop optimizations attempt to create a family of induction variables for each copy of the unwound inner loop body, and the initialization code for each of those variables can consist of many integer operations.

However, but for the loop back edge restriction, the third and second traces could easily form one larger trace:

finalization for inner loop
outer loop code
outer loop code
initialization for inner loop

This larger trace potentially has more parallelism in it. In fact, some experiments with the benchmarks showed that if traces were allowed to cross outer-loop back edges in this way, the execution time of several of the programs improved roughly 5 to 10%.

Unfortunately, the current disambiguator relies on the fact that traces don't include loop back edges. Chapter 5 discusses possible modifications to the disambiguator that will lift this restriction.

Execution Estimates

Where does the trace picker get its execution estimates? The programmer can supply them, or he can use an automatic profiler. By default the compiler assumes each branch of an IF will be taken with equal probability and that the body of a loop is executed 100 times each time the loop is entered. The programmer can override these defaults for an individual IF or loop by giving an explicit probability (for IFs) or iteration-count estimate (for loops). Alternatively, the programmer can use the automatic profiler to measure and record these same quantities over one or more program runs.

Given the probabilities and iteration-count estimates, the compiler propagates execution count estimates to all the operations and edges in the flow graph, using these rules:

$$\mathrm{count}(S) = 1$$
$$\mathrm{count}(O) = \sum_{e \in \mathrm{in}(O)} \mathrm{count}(e)$$

where S is the entry into the flow graph, O is any operation, and $\text{in}(O)$ is the set of edges entering O. A loop header H (the unique entry to a loop to which all the loop back edges lead) is treated as a special case:

$$\text{count}(H) = \text{iteration-count}(H) \sum_{e \in \text{in}(H)} \text{count}(e)$$

where iteration-count(H) is the iteration-count estimate of the loop. That is, the execution count of a loop header (and thus all the operations within the loop) is multiplied by the estimated iteration count of the loop. As defined previously, the execution count of an edge e leaving operation O is defined as:

$$\text{count}(e) = \text{count}(O)\,\text{prob}(e)$$

Performance of the Trace Picker

How good is the trace picker? For our scientific benchmarks, at least, it is quite adequate. The control structures of these programs are very simple, consisting mainly of nested loops. The time-critical sections contain few explicit conditionals, and the trace picker has no problems picking maximal traces for the inner loops first, then the next outer loops, and so on.

Often, the default execution estimates for loops are sufficient to completely identify the time-critical traces. And for most of the few time-critical conditionals, it's been obvious to the programmer which way they usually go. A typical conditional looks like:

```
IF x~=0 THEN
    y:=z/x
```

and it's usually clear from the algorithm whether x is almost always non-zero or almost always zero. Because most of the control structures in scientific code are so simple, it's not necessary to have accurate estimates; grossly exaggerated estimates will guide the trace picker just as well. In the example above, it wouldn't matter whether the branch probability supplied by the programmer was .6 or .9—the trace picker would still pick the same trace.

Three of the benchmarks, ZEROIN, FMIN, and EOS, had a large number of nested conditionals, and it wasn't clear to me which way the conditionals went on average (but I wasn't familiar with the algorithms). For these, I used the automatic profiler and obtained significant improvements in execution time of the compiled code (roughly 25 to 75%). But as discussed in chapter 8, even with the automatic profiler these programs had little available parallelism. They had many branches with probabilities close to half (branches that went each way about the same number of times). Trace scheduling will never do very well on such programs, because the core assumption of trace scheduling is that branches mostly go one way or the other. So having a profiler is nice, but it probably isn't crucial.

Bookkeeping

After the code generator generates a schedule of machine instructions for a trace of intermediate-code operations, the trace scheduler must remove the trace from the flow graph and replace it by the machine instructions. This isn't as simple as it sounds. The code generator has substantially reordered the trace, filling each machine instruction with operations from widely separated points on the trace; time-critical operations are usually scheduled early, while non-critical operations are often delayed. Because of the movement of operations with respect to conditional jumps off the trace and jumps into the trace, simply replacing the trace by the schedule would result in an incorrect program. To preserve correctness, the code generator must insert new intermediate code around the boundaries of the flow graph. For no really good reason, this process of replacing the trace with the schedule and inserting new, correctness-preserving operations is called **bookkeeping**.

Some definitions: A **split** is a conditional jump on the trace. A **join** is a jump into the trace. The **on-trace edge** of a conditional jump on the trace is the edge leading from the jump to the next trace operation; the **off-trace edge** is the other edge of the jump. If a conditional jump is the last operation in the trace, one edge is arbitrarily identified as the on-trace edge. Similarly, the on-trace edge of a join is the edge coming from the previous trace operation; one of the edges joining the first trace operation is arbitrarily identified as the on-trace edge.

First, let's consider splits. Suppose the trace consisted of the operations between A and B:

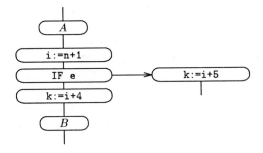

and suppose the code generator produced the following schedule of machine operations for it:

1	IF e1
2	i:=n+1
3	k:=i+4

(In this example and succeeding ones, the actual registers and functional units of the machine operations are suppressed for simplicity. For now, we'll assume all machine operations take one cycle.) Replacing the trace by the schedule in the flow graph yields:

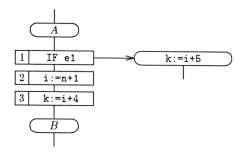

But this is incorrect—k:=i+5 gets the wrong value of i because i:=n+1 has moved below the split in the schedule. The solution is to place a copy of the intermediate-code operation i:=n+1 on the off-trace edge of the split:

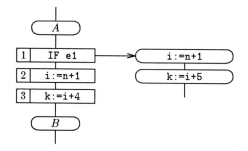

If more than one operation moves below a split in the schedule, then they are all copied out onto the split in original trace order. Figure 4.2 shows an example of this.

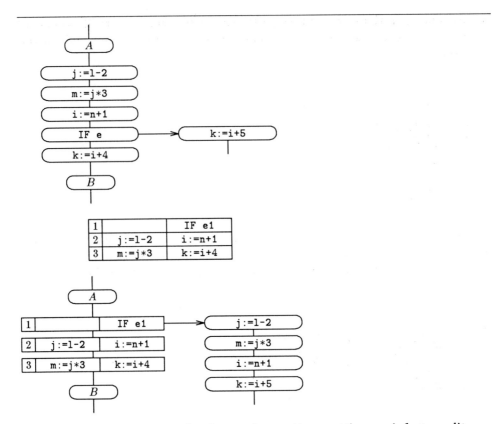

Figure 4.2. An example of several operations getting copied at a split. The top shows the trace, the operations between A and B. The middle shows a schedule for the trace. The bottom shows the schedule replacing the trace and the necessary split copies.

Now consider joins. Suppose that for this trace:

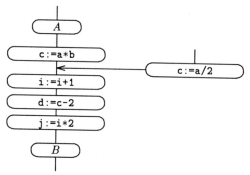

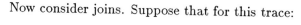

the code generator produced the following schedule:

1	c:=a*b	i:=i+1
2	d:=c-2	j:=i*2

Unlike the split example, it's not clear here how to replace the trace by the schedule. Where should the join from c:=a/2 be placed? If it is placed before cycle 1, then unlike the original program, c:=a*b is now below the join. Whenever execution proceeds from c:=a/2 through the join into the schedule, d:=c-2 will get the wrong value of c. If the join is placed before cycle 2, i:=i+1 is now above the join instead of below; if the program enters the schedule through the join, j:=i*2 will get the wrong value of i. Similarly, if the join is placed after cycle 2, j:=i*2 will also now be above the join, and the succeeding operations will get the wrong value of j.

The solution is to place the join as early in the schedule as possible such that no trace operations originally above the join are now below it. In the example, the join would thus be placed between cycles 1 and 2:

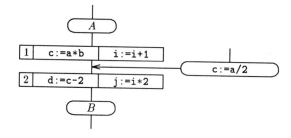

Then, if an operation was originally below the join but is now above it, it must be copied onto the joining edge to preserve program correctness:

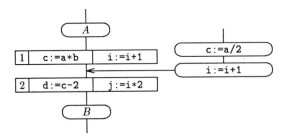

If more than one operation has moved above the join, then they all must be copied into the join in trace order.

The joins are made as early as possible in the schedule to minimize the number of operations that need to be copied into it. Note that sometimes a join must be placed after the last cycle of the schedule; this happens when some operation originally above the join in the trace is scheduled in the last cycle.

The copies of operations created at splits and joins as a result of code motions are treated just like other intermediate-code operations. They will be selected and compiled as part of later traces.

We've seen what happens when an operation moves below a split in the schedule. But what about an operation moving above a split? For example, consider this trace:

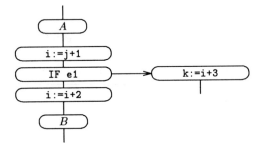

Suppose the code generator produced the following schedule:

1	i:=j+1
2	i:=i+2
3	IF e1

That is, `i:=i+2` has moved above the jump. The flow graph would look like:

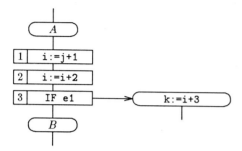

This would be incorrect, since now `k:=i+3` gets the wrong value of `i`. But if `i` were dead on the off-trace edge of the jump (that is, no operation read its value) it would have been ok to move `i:=i+2` above the jump, since no operation on the off-trace edge reads `i`'s value. In general, an operation writing some variable `x` can be moved above a split in the schedule only if `x` is dead on the off-trace edge of the jump. But the trace scheduler doesn't have to worry about this—as described in chapter 7, the code generator won't generate such illegal code motions.

Jumps

In the examples so far we've only considered simple value-producing operations moving past splits and joins in the schedule. But jumps can move past other splits and joins as well, getting copied just like other operations. To copy a jump into a split or join, the edges of a jump must be distinguished as "off-trace" and "on-trace," where the on-trace edge leads to the next operation in the trace and the off-trace edge leads to some off-trace operation:

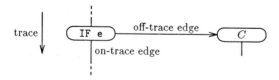

Depending on the sense of the jump's test, the on-trace edge can be either the true or false edge of the jump.

When the jump is copied, the copy's off-trace edge is left pointing at the same spot as the original (C), while the on-trace edge points to the next operation in the split or join. For example, consider this trace and schedule:

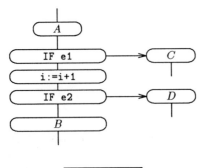

1	IF e2
2	IF e1
3	i:=i+1

Note that the off-trace edge of IF e1 leads to C, and that IF e1 and i:=i+1 have moved below IF e2 in the schedule and thus need to be copied onto its off-trace edge:

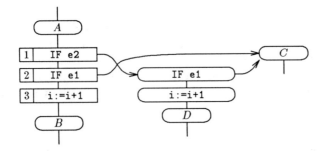

The off-trace edge of the new copy of IF e1 points at C (where the original's off-trace edge points), while its on-trace edge leads to the next operation in the split, the copy of i:=i+1.

You can convince yourself that the new flow graph is equivalent to the original by trying out all four combinations of truth values e1 and e2. For example, when e1 and e2 are both true, the operations executed in the original are

A, IF e1, C

while the operations executed in the new flow graph are

A, IF e2, IF e1, C

The fact that IF e2 is executed in the new flow graph but not in the original doesn't affect program correctness. It probably doesn't affect the speed of the compiled code, either, since the assumption that **e1** and **e2** are false most of the time is implicit in the way the trace was picked. The idea of trace scheduling is to optimize the most likely paths of execution (early traces) at the expense of less likely paths (later traces).

Jumps are copied into joins just as with splits:

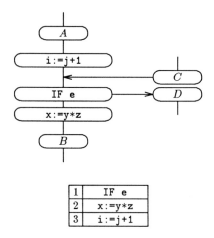

1	IF e
2	x:=y*z
3	i:=j+1

The earliest the join can be made is after cycle 3:

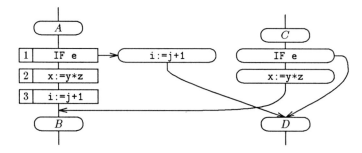

Operation `i:=j+1` moved below `IF e` and so is copied onto its off-trace edge; `IF e` and `x:=y*z` moved above the join and so are copied into it.

Again, you can convince yourself that the new flow graph is equivalent to the original by trying all combinations of truth values for **e** and entry points *A* and *C*.

There is some extra hair when jumps get copied up into joins. Consider this trace and schedule:

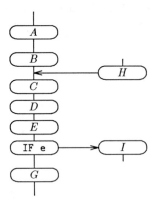

1	*D*	IF e
2	*B*	
3	*C*	*E*

The join is made between cycles 2 and 3:

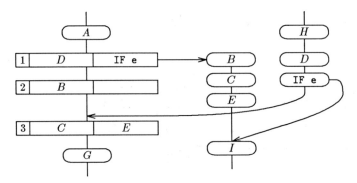

Operations *B*, *C*, and *E* moved below IF e1 in the schedule, so they get copied into the split. Operations D and IF e1 moved above the join in the schedule, so they get copied into the join.

But as it stands, this new flow graph is incorrect. Suppose e was true. Then in the original flow graph, if control entered at *H* the operations executed would be:

H, C, D, E, IF e, I

But in the new flow graph, the operations executed would be:

H, D, IF e, I

Operations C and E don't get executed as they should. They must be placed on the off-trace edge of the new copy of IF e:

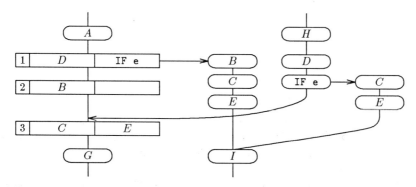

Now, no matter which entry point is taken and what the value of **e**, the new flow graph is equivalent to the original.

The general rule for a jump copied into a join is: All operations on the trace below the join and above the jump that weren't copied into the join (because they were scheduled below it) must be copied onto the off-trace edge of the jump's new copy. If any of those copied operations are jumps, they are copied like any other jump, but this rule is *not* recursively applied to them.

Buffering the Trace

In the examples so far, I've assumed that a conditional jump on the trace always jumps to some operation not on the trace. But that's not always the case:

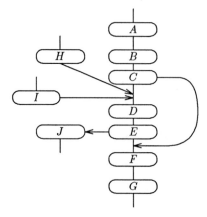

Assume the trace consists of operations B–F. The off-trace edge from C immediately joins the trace below *E*. Handling such an edge during bookkeeping could be quite tricky, since neither end is anchored to a fixed, off-trace operation, and both ends could move after scheduling.

To make the bookkeeping simpler, temporary buffering nodes are inserted between the trace and the rest of the flow graph, insuring that all split and join edges are anchored:

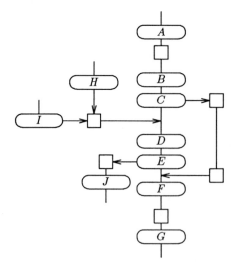

At splits, a buffering node is spliced into the off-trace edge. At joins, a single buffering node is spliced between the trace operation and all the incoming off-trace edges joining to that operation.

After the buffering nodes are inserted, every split edge now leads to an off-trace node, and every join edge comes from an off-trace node. Each buffering node represents one split or join point, and there is now at most one off-trace join edge and one off-trace split edge for every operation on the trace.

To replace the trace by the schedule, the buffering nodes are detached from the trace and reattached to the schedule. Then the copies of operations produced at the splits and joins are spliced between the schedule and the buffering nodes. Lastly, the buffering nodes are removed from the flow graph.

Multiple Conditional Jumps

The machine model used by the compiler allows multiple conditional jumps in a machine instruction:

IF e_1 THEN l_1; IF e_2 THEN l_2; ...; IF e_n THEN l_n

The conditions e_i are tested sequentially, and the first e_i that is true causes a jump to the corresponding label l_i.

When generating code for a trace, the code generator doesn't do anything special to handle multiple jumps—it simply places as many jumps into the current instruction as the hardware resources allow, subject to the same data-precedence rules as all other operations (for example, a jump IF x>y must follow the operations producing the values of x and y).

After a schedule is generated, the jumps within an instruction are ordered by their original trace order. Then the normal bookkeeping rules are applied to each jump individually. To see why this works, consider the following trace and the schedule produced for it:

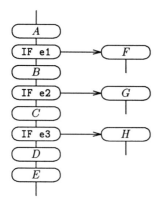

1	A			
2	E	IF e1	IF e2	IF e3
3	B	C	D	

The code generator decided to place all three jumps into the same instruction. Applying the normal bookkeeping rules yields the following flow graph:

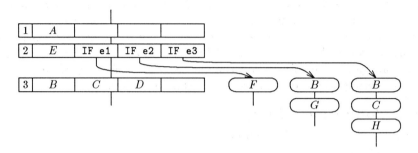

If none of the jump conditions are true, the second instruction will fall through into the third. Because B moved below IF e2 in the schedule, it was copied onto its off-trace edge. Similary, B and C were copied onto the off-trace edge of IF e3. Trying out all combinations of values for e1, e2, and e3 shows that this is equivalent to the original program.

There is a slight complication if the on-trace edge of one of the jumps placed in an instruction is the true edge instead of the false, or fall-through, edge. For example, consider this trace and schedule:

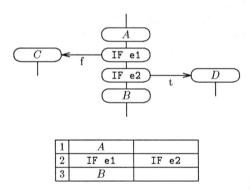

1	A	
2	IF e1	IF e2
3	B	

The on-trace edge of IF e1 is its true edge. Putting the schedule into the flow graph yields:

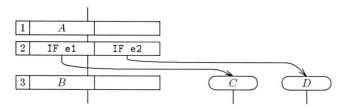

But this is incorrect, since now if **e1** is true, control passes to C instead of **IF e2** as it should. So the bookkeeper must replace the condition **e1** by its complement **~e1**:

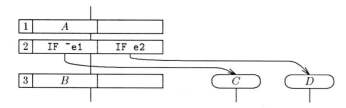

For example, if the condition **e1** was $x > y$, its complement would be $x \le y$.

In general, when one or more jumps are placed into an instruction, the bookkeeper complements the jump condition of each jump whose on-trace edge is its true edge. The destinations of the off-trace edges of the jumps remain the same, and the fall-through of the instruction is the next instruction in the schedule. While it's not necessary to do this for instructions containing only one jump, the bookkeeper does it anyway for simplicity.

Multicycle Operations

Operations taking more than one cycle to complete add further complexity to trace scheduling. Once an n-cycle machine operation is initiated, it finishes execution n cycles later, whether or not any branches were taken during those n

cycles. Consider this trace and schedule:

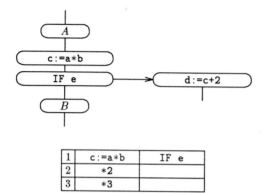

1	c:=a*b	IF e
2	*2	
3	*3	

The multiply machine operation takes three cycles (*2 and *3 in the schedule indicate the successive cycles of the multiply). If the branch in the first cycle is taken, it can't simply jump directly to the machine instruction for d:=c+2, because the multiply producing c won't be finished until two cycles later.

So the bookkeeper inserts a two-cycle stub of machine instructions on the off-trace edge of the jump:

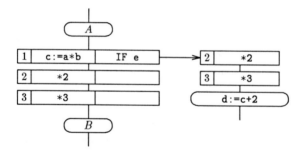

This stub, or **partial schedule**, allows the multiply to finish before the machine instruction containing d:=c+2 can start.

If several multicycle operations are bisected by a jump, their tail ends are all placed in a partial schedule. Consider this trace and schedule:

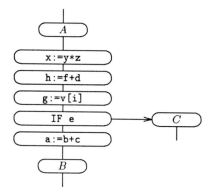

1	x:=y*z				
2	*2	h:=f+d	g:=v[i]		
3	*3	+2	[]2	a:=b+c	IF e
4	*4	+3	[]3	+2	
5			[]4	+3	
6			[]5		

(Here, multiplies take 4 cycles, adds 3 cycles, and memory references 5 cycles.) The jump IF **e** bisects 4 multicycle operations; after inserting the partial schedule the flow graph would look like:

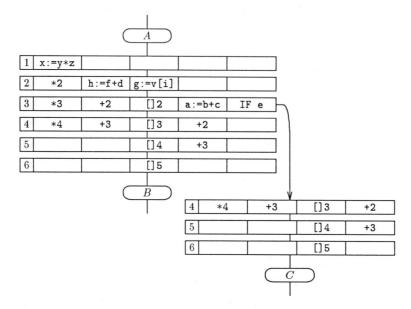

If **e** is true and the jump is taken in cycle 3, the partial schedule will allow all the multicycle operations in progress to finish before starting the instructions at C (which may depend on the values produced by those multicycle operations).

An operation originally above a split but scheduled completely below it will be copied (as an intermediate-code operation) onto the split edge as usual. All split copies are placed after the partial schedule.

Multicycle operations bisected by joins require similar handling. For example:

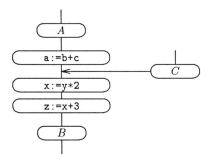

1	a:=b+2	
2	+2	x:=y*2
3	+3	*2
4		*3
5		*4
6	z:=x+3	
7	+2	
8	+3	

The bookkeeper will place the join as high as possible such that no operation originally above the join in the trace is now below it; in this case, between cycles 3 and 4. But C can't jump directly into the schedule between 3 and 4, because the multiply is in progress. So the bookkeeper inserts a partial schedule between C and the schedule that starts up the multiply and then joins the schedule two cycles later:

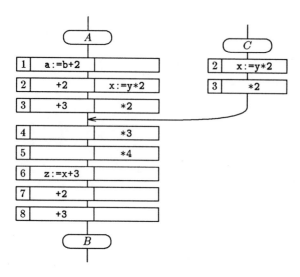

Thus, no matter which way control enters the schedule, the multiply will be started and produce the value of x for z:=x+3 in cycle 6.

If several machine operations are bisected by a join, then the initial parts of the operations above the join are all placed in a partial schedule. For example, if the bookkeeper decided to place a join between cycles 2 and 3 in this schedule:

1	a:=b+c	g:=v[i]	
2	+2	[]2	x:=y*z
3	+3	[]3	*2
4		[]4	*3
5		[]5	*4

the following flow graph and partial schedule would result:

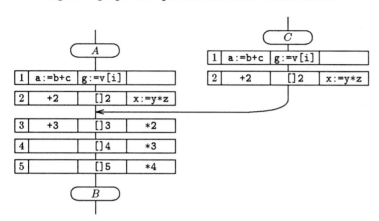

Whether control enters from *A* or from *C*, the pipelines will be in the same state of completion when control reaches cycle 3 of the schedule.

A machine operation originally below the join but scheduled completely above it (that is, the last cycle of the operation is above the join) will be copied onto the join edge as usual. All the join copies are placed between the off-trace predecessor of the join and the partial schedule.

Recording Variable Locations

When the code generator is handed a trace, it needs to know the initial and final register and memory locations of variables referenced on the trace. The locations of variables at a trace's boundaries must be recorded so that the code generator will know where to find the variables or store them when it produces code for later adjoining traces.

The simplest traditional code generators store variables back into known memory locations (such as a stack frame) at the end of each basic block or even each statement. This strategy is unacceptable for a VLIW compiler intended for scientific code, since memory bandwidth is often the limiting resource in the inner loops. More sophisticated code generators have a prepass that globally allocates registers for the entire flow graph. But this strategy won't work either. Unlike a traditional machine, a VLIW has many register banks and functional units separated by long, slow data paths. As explained in chapter 7, the decision of which register should hold a variable is secondary to which functional units should compute the operations that use the variable, and assigning functional units to intermediate-code operations is best delayed until code-generation time for each trace.

Thus, in the Bulldog compiler registers are allocated to variables by the code generator as it is producing code for a trace. When the bookkeeper replaces a trace by the generated schedule of machine instructions, it records at every entrance and exit from the schedule the locations of live variables. Later traces adjoining the exits and entrances are constrained to use those locations as initial or final variable locations.

Consider a schedule that has just replaced a trace in the flow graph:

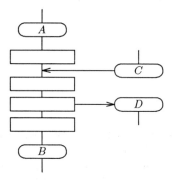

At every exit from the schedule, the bookkeeper inserts a DEF pseudo-operation (supplied by the code generator) that specifies the final machine locations of every variable live at that exit:

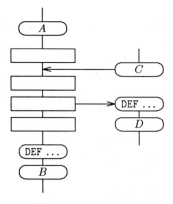

A DEF pseudo-operation has the form:

DEF $v_1\, l_1,\ v_2\, l_2,\ \dots,\ v_n\, l_n$

where v_i is a live variable and l_i is one of its memory or register locations at the exit. Since a variable can occupy many locations in the machine at a given point in the program, there will be a separate v_i/l_i pair for each location of the variable.

Similarly, at every entrance to the schedule, the bookkeeper inserts a USE pseudo-operation (also supplied by the code generator) specifying the initial live-variable locations assumed by the schedule at that entrance:

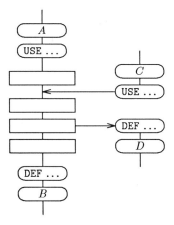

A USE has the form:

USE $v_1\ l_1,\ v_2\ l_2,\ \ldots,\ v_n\ l_n$

where v_i is a variable live at the entrance and l_i is one of its locations.

The DEFs and USEs will be picked up as part of the later adjoining traces. When a DEF is the first operation of a trace (DEFs will always be first), it tells the code generator the initial register and memory locations of the variables live on entrance to the trace. Similarly, when a USE occurs at the end of a trace (USEs will always be last), it tells the code generator the final locations of variables live on exit from the trace; the code generator must ensure that the variables end up in at least those locations by the end of the schedule, if necessary generating code to move the variables into position.

If there is no DEF at the beginning of a trace, the code generator is free to make up any convenient initial locations for live-on-entry variables. When the schedule is inserted into the flow graph, a USE at the entrance to the schedule records the initial locations chosen. A later trace will include that USE as its last operation and will guarantee that the variables do indeed end up in the chosen locations.

Similarly, if there is no USE at the end of a trace, the code generator leaves the variables in whatever locations are convenient. When the schedule is inserted into the flow graph, a DEF at the exit of the schedule records the final locations chosen, and a later trace adjoining the exit will pick up the DEF and be informed of the locations.

A trace could consist of just a DEF and USE, in which case the code generator may need to generate code to move variables from the initial locations specified by the DEF into the final locations specified by the USE. No code is needed for a variable if its final locations are a subset of its initial locations.

DEFs and USEs actually record the variable locations at the boundary between the partial schedule of the split or join and the operations outside the trace (including any split or join copies inserted by the bookkeeper). Schematically, an exit looks like:

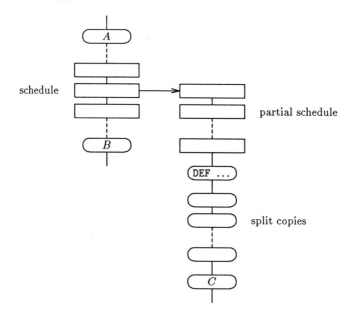

where C is the original off-trace successor of the split. Similarly, a join looks like:

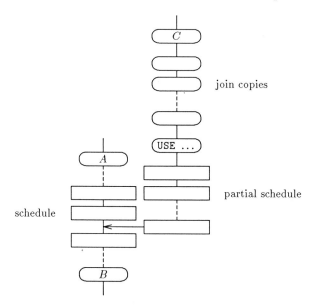

A DEF at a schedule exit records for all its uncompiled successors the locations of live variables for use by later traces. But if all the successors of a schedule exit (including split copies) are machine instructions, that is, if all the successors have already been translated into machine operations by previous traces, then a DEF would serve no purpose, and the bookkeeper doesn't insert one. Similarly, if all the predecessors of a schedule entrance are machine instructions, no USE is inserted.

At this point, an extended example hopefully will make the DEF/USE mechanism clearer. Suppose the compiler is given a simple program that computes the average of i^2 over all integers i between 1 and n:

```
s:=0
FOR i:=1 TO n DO
    s:=s+i*i
s:=s/n
```

The intermediate-code flow graph initially looks like:

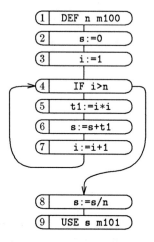

The DEF at the beginning specifies memory location 100 as the initial location of the input parameter n, and the USE at the end specifies memory location 101 as the final location of the output parameter s.

The first trace picked and compiled is the inner loop (the most time-critical operations), operations 4–7. Because there is no DEF or USE on the trace, the code generator is free to choose initial and final locations for variables. Inserting the schedule for the trace into the flow graph yields:

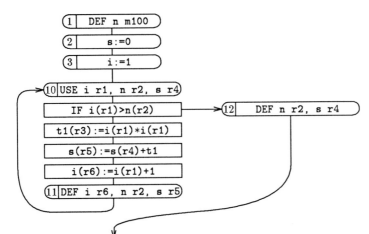

(Instances of variables in machine operations are annotated with the registers used to hold their values.) The new DEFs and USEs inserted in the flow graph record the locations of the variables live at the entrances and exits. Notice that the code generator was dumb and picked new registers for the new values of i and s instead of updating them in place. (The real code generator would keep an induction variable in one register.)

The next trace consists of operations 11 and 10 (in that order), the DEF and USE on the back edge of the inner loop. Because the locations of i and s in the USE aren't the same as those in the DEF, the code generator will generate code to move them from the DEF's locations to the USE's locations:

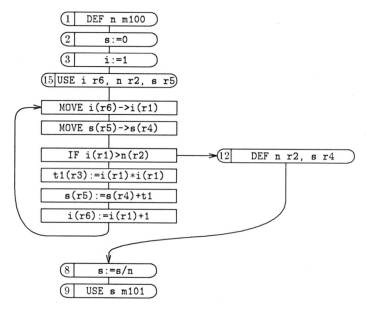

The operation i:=1 originally joined the USE at the end of the trace; that join was placed on the schedule using the normal rule—as high as possible such that no operation originally above the join on the trace is now below it. In this example, "as high as possible" is the beginning of the schedule. Consequently, the new USE inserted at that join reflects the variable locations at the beginning of the schedule, not the end. (Remember this is just an example and that the code generator would really have kept the induction variables i and s in the same register throughout the loop.)

The next trace includes the exit from the loop, operations 12, 8, and 9. This trace also has a DEF and a USE giving the required initial and final locations of the live variables. The resulting flow graph is:

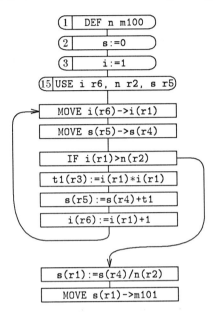

Because the final location specified by the USE for **s** was memory location 101, the code generator generated a memory store to move **s** from its register to **m101**.

The final trace consists of operations 1–3 and 15. The finished object code is:

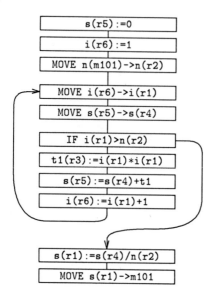

```
        s(r5):=0
        i(r6):=1
   MOVE n(m101)->n(r2)

   MOVE i(r6)->i(r1)
   MOVE s(r5)->s(r4)

     IF i(r1)>n(r2)
   t1(r3):=i(r1)*i(r1)
    s(r5):=s(r4)+t1
    i(r6):=i(r1)+1


   s(r1):=s(r4)/n(r2)
   MOVE s(r1)->m101
```

Because the initial location of **n** was **m101**, a memory fetch was necessary to put **n** into register **r2** as required by the USE at the end of the trace. The code generator was pretty smart here, noticing that since the USE required **s** in **r5**, it makes sense to use **r5** for previous references to **s** on the trace.

This example suggests that traces are always maximal and either include a DEF and a USE or else stop at loop boundaries. While this is usually the case, there is nothing in trace scheduling or the DEF/USE mechanism that requires traces to be maximal.

Incremental Live Analysis

Just as a basic-block code generator needs to know the variables live on entrance and exit from the block, the Bulldog code generator needs to know the variables live on every entrance and exit from the trace. This live information is used to allocate and free registers and to prevent illegal code motions. Before trace scheduling begins, a standard live analysis [Aho 77] calculates the sets of live variables at every point in the flow graph. Unfortunately, this pre-trace-scheduling analysis isn't sufficient, because the flow graph is changed during trace scheduling by the bookkeeper adding in split and join copies of operations. Thus, the bookkeeper must perform an incremental reanalysis after each trace.

When a trace is replaced by a schedule and split and join copies added to the flow graph, the live-in and live-out variable sets of all the other operations in the flow graph remain unchanged. Intuitively, this is precisely because the code

generator and the bookkeeper are designed to replace the trace by a semantically equivalent combination of machine instructions and bookkeeper operations.
Therefore, the bookkeeper need only compute the live-in and live-out sets of
the new split and join copies. (Nicolau [Nicolau 84] provides a more rigorous
justification for this observation.)

Consider a typical split after the partial schedule, DEF, and split copies have
been inserted:

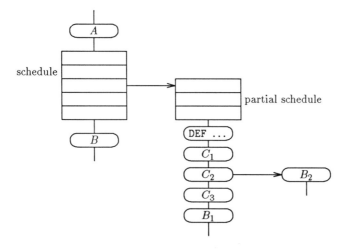

The C_i operations are split copies of operations from the trace, and the B_i are
the buffering nodes inserted at the beginning of bookkeeping. The sets of live
variables at the buffering nodes remain unchanged when the schedule and copies
replace the trace. Since the variables live at the buffering nodes are already
known, it is easy to calculate the live-in and live-out sets for each of the copies
C_i by simple backward propagation from B_1 and B_2. That is, the variables live
at C_3 are calculated in terms of the variables live at B_1, C_2 in terms of B_2 and
C_3, and C_1 in terms of C_2.

Now consider a typical join after bookkeeping:

Notice that C_2 is a copied jump and that operations C_4 and C_5 were copied onto its off-trace edge. As at a split, the variables live at the buffering nodes remain unchanged when the schedule and copies replace the trace. Also, the USE specifies the locations for exactly those variables live on entry to the partial schedule. (The code generator computes the USE from the schedule using the variables live on exit from the trace supplied to it by the trace scheduler. This computation is described in chapter 7.) Since the variables live at the USE and at the buffering nodes B_2 and B_3 are known, the variables live at the copies can be calculated just as at a split by backward propagation from the known points.

A simple backward-propagation algorithm suffices for both splits and joins. It uses the standard data-flow equations:

$$\text{live-out}(O) = \bigcup_{S \in \text{succ}(O)} \text{live-in}(S)$$
$$\text{live-in}(O) = (\text{live-out}(O) - \text{def}(O)) \cup \text{use}(O)$$

That is, the set of variables live on exit from an operation O is the union of the sets of variables live on entry to all of O's successors. And the set of variables live on entry to O is the set of variables live on exit from O minus the variables written by O, plus the variables read by O.

The algorithm keeps a set *to-do* to remember all the operations O whose live-in and live-out sets are ready to be computed (all of O's successors have known live-in sets). The algorithm repeatedly picks an operation O from *to-do*, calculates O's live sets using the live-in sets of its successors, and then adds to *to-do* all the predecessors of O that are now ready to have their live sets computed:

> *to-do* := ∅
> **for** each node O such that O is either a USE for the schedule or a buffering
>   node at a split from the schedule
> **do**
>   *to-do* := *to-do* ∪ *ReadyPredecessors*(O)
>
> **while** *to-do* ≠ ∅ **do**
> O := any operation in *to-do*
>   Remove O from *to-do*
>   *live-out*(O) := $\bigcup_{S \in \text{succ}(O)}$ *live-in*(S)
>   *live-in*(O) := (live-out(O) − def(O)) ∪ use(O)
>   *to-do* := *to-do* ∪ *ReadyPredecessors*(O)

The procedure *ReadyPredecessors(O)* returns the set of all predecessors of operation O that can now have their live sets computed. Each of the returned predecessors P satisfy the following:

The live-in and live-out sets of P aren't yet known.

The live-in and live-out sets of all the successors of P are known.

This algorithm is fast. Each operation examined is examined exactly once, and the total number examined is the sum of the number of split and join copies, the number of splits, and the number of joins.

A Detailed Summary of Bookkeeping

By now, it might seem that bookkeeping is incredibly complicated—split and join copies, jumps, multicycle operations, partial schedules, USEs and DEFs, etc. It is complex, but manageably so; its implementation in the current compiler consists of only 20 pages of code. This section presents a concise summary of bookkeeping.

In what follows, the entrance to the beginning of the trace is considered a join, and the exit from the end of the trace is considered a split even if the last operation of the trace isn't a conditional jump.

The schedule returned by the code generator is opaque to the trace scheduler and can only be examined using interface procedures exported by the code generator. The bookkeeper decides where splits and joins should be placed and then invokes the interface procedures to construct the partial schedules, DEFs, and USEs for the splits and joins. The implementation of the interface procedures is described in chapter 7. The procedures are:

Schedule:length(schedule) returns the length of the schedule.

Schedule:[](schedule,cycle) returns the machine instruction for the given cycle from the schedule. A machine instruction is simply an ordered list of machine operations. Supplied with each machine operation is the corresponding intermediate-code operation from the trace.

Schedule:split(schedule,cycle) returns the partial schedule and DEF for a split from the schedule at the end of the given cycle. The DEF contains the locations of all the variables live on exit from the partial schedule.

Schedule:join(schedule,cycle) returns the partial schedule and USE for a join that the bookkeeper has decided to make to the beginning of the given cycle. The USE contains the locations of all the variables live on entry to the partial schedule.

The following functions on machine and intermediate-code operations are derived from the original trace and the information supplied by the interface functions:

Cycle(M) is the first cycle of a machine operation M in the schedule, that is, the cycle the operation is scheduled.

LastCycle(M) is the last cycle of a machine operation M in the schedule, that is, $Cycle(M) + Time(M) - 1$, where $Time(M)$ is number of cycles needed to execute the operation.

ICO(M) is the original intermediate-code operation from the trace that gave rise to machine operation M. In the machine model used by the compiler, an intermediate-code operation causes at most one machine operation to be generated; machine operations that simply move data from one part of the machine to another don't have associated intermediate-code operations.

TracePos(O) is the position of intermediate-code operation O within the trace.

OffTraceSucc(O) is the off-trace successor of an intermediate-code jump on the trace; after the buffering nodes are inserted, this successor is always a buffering node.

The steps in bookkeeping are:

1. Buffering the trace. Dummy buffering nodes are inserted at every entrance and exit from the trace, so that every split edge exiting the trace leads to a buffering node, and every joining edge to the trace comes from a buffering node. The set of variables live at each buffering node is recorded in the node.

2. Setting flow-graph successors. The successor of every machine instruction in the schedule not containing a conditional jump is set to be the next instruction in the schedule; the successor of the last instruction is set to be the buffering node at the end of the trace. If a machine instruction does contain one or more jumps, its fall-through successor is set to be the next instruction in the schedule, and the target of each jump J in the instruction is set to be *OffTraceSucc(ICO(J))*. If the on-trace edge of *ICO(J)* is its true edge, then the branch condition of J is complemented (for example, $<$ becomes $\geq$).

3. Setting the flow-graph predecessors. The predecessor of every machine instruction in the schedule is set initially to be the previous machine instruction in the schedule; the predecessor of the first machine instruction is set to be the buffering node at the beginning of the trace. Then the joins to the trace are moved over to the appropriate points in the schedule. Each join to the trace at position t has an associated buffering node B. The joining edge from B is moved to the earliest machine instruction in the schedule such that no operations originally above the join in the trace are now below it in the schedule. That is, a join originally to trace position t is placed at the beginning of the earliest cycle c in the schedule such that for every machine operation M with $Cycle(M) \geq c$, then $TracePos(ICO(M)) \geq t$.

4. Split partial schedules and DEFs. At every conditional jump J in an instruction at a given cycle in the schedule, *Schedule:split(schedule,cycle)* is invoked and returns a partial schedule and a DEF for the split. The partial schedule and the DEF are spliced between J and its associated buffering node B on the split:

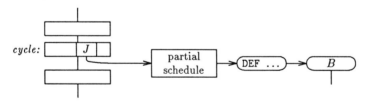

An operation M is in the partial schedule if it spans the split, that is if $Cycle(M) \leq cycle$ and $LastCycle(M) > cycle$. Only those cycles of M above the split (from $Cycle(M)$ to $cycle$) are included in the partial schedule.

5. Join partial schedules and USEs. At every join to a cycle in the schedule (there may be several), *Schedule:join(schedule,cycle)* is invoked and returns a partial schedule and a USE for the join. The partial schedule and the USE are spliced between the buffering node B for the join and the instruction at *cycle*:

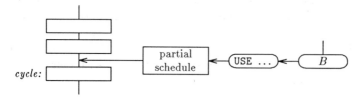

An operation M is in the partial schedule if it spans the join, that is if $Cycle(M) < cycle$ and $LastCycle(M) \geq cycle$. Only those cycles of M below the join (from *cycle* to *LastCycle(M)*) are included in the partial schedule.

6. Split copies. At every conditional jump J in the schedule, the bookkeeper finds all the machine operations M originally above J in the trace but now scheduled completely below it, that is, $TracePos(ICO(M)) < TracePos(ICO(J))$ and $Cycle(M) > LastCycle(J)$. For each such M, the intermediate-code operation *ICO(M)* is copied onto the off-trace edge of the split between the DEF and the buffering node B. If there are several such operations $O_1, O_2, \ldots, O_n$ that are copied, they are arranged in increasing trace order starting at the DEF, so that $TracePos(O_i) < TracePos(O_{i+1})$:

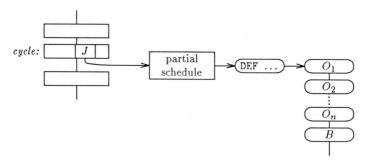

If some machine-operation jump J is copied into the split as O_i, then its on-trace edge points to O_{i+1} (or B if $i = n$), and its off-trace edge points to *OffTraceSucc(ICO(J))*.

7. Join copies. At every join originally to trace position t but now to cycle *cycle* in the schedule, the bookkeeper finds all the machine operations M originally below the join but now completely above it, that is, $TracePos(ICO(M)) \geq t$ and $LastCycle(M) < cycle$. For each such M, the intermediate-code operation *ICO(M)* is copied into the join between the USE and the buffering node B. If there are several operations $O_1, O_2, \ldots, O_n$ that are copied, they are arranged in increasing trace order starting at B, so that $TracePos(O_i) < TracePos(O_{i+1})$:

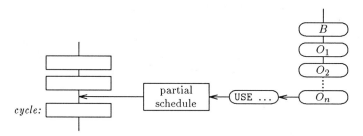

If some machine-operation jump J is copied into the join as O_i, its on-trace edge points at O_{i+1} (or the USE if $i = n$), and its off-trace edge points to $B_1 = OffTraceSucc(ICO(J))$. Then all the machine operations N_j originally between the join and the jump on the trace but now below the join in the schedule must be copied onto the off-trace edge of O_i:

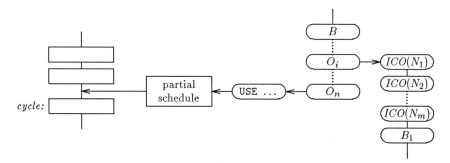

More formally, the machine operation N_j is copied if

$$TracePos(ICO(N_j)) \geq t$$
$$TracePos(ICO(N_j)) < TracePos(ICO(J))$$
$$Cycle(N_j) \geq cycle.$$

8. Incremental live analysis. The live-in and live-out sets of the new split and join copies are computed as described in the previous section.

9. Setting the execution counts. The execution-count estimates of the newly added machine instructions and split and join copies are computed using the same rules that were used for the original flow graph, with one minor addition to handle machine instructions with multiple jumps. Suppose a newly formed instruction contains the jump operations $J_1, J_2, \ldots, J_n$ with the corresponding exiting edges $e_1, e_2, \ldots, e_n$, where e_{n+1} is the fall-through edge. The multiple jumps are semantically equivalent to the following flow graph:

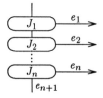

Let p_i be the probability of the off-trace edge of the original intermediate-code operation $ICO(J_i)$. Then the probabilities of the new instruction's edges e_i are:

$$\text{prob}(e_1) = p_1$$
$$\text{prob}(e_i) = p_i \prod_{1 \le j \le i-1} (1 - p_j)$$
$$\text{prob}(e_{n+1}) = 1 - \sum_{1 \le j \le n} \text{prob}(e_j)$$
$$= \prod_{1 \le j \le n} (1 - p_j)$$

10. Unbuffering the trace. The buffering nodes are removed from the flow graph.

Code Explosion

The intermediate-code copies created during the bookkeeping of a trace are selected and compiled as part of later traces. Conceivably, trace scheduling might never terminate for some programs—copies would be generated as fast as or faster than they are picked by traces. However, Nicolau shows that trace scheduling is correct and does indeed terminate [Nicolau 84].

But even though trace scheduling terminates, there can be an exponential number of copies generated [Fisher 79]. Figure 4.3 shows such an example. The first trace through the flow graph is shown at top, and next to it, a possible schedule. Notice that the jumps are scheduled in reverse order. The bottom half of the figure shows the flow graph after bookkeeping. All the joins from the operations B_i must be made to the end of the schedule after A_1. The off-trace edges of the copied jumps aren't shown—the off-trace edge of a copy of C_i leads to B_i.

There are $\displaystyle\sum_{1\le i\le n-1} 2i$ split copies and $\displaystyle\sum_{1\le i\le n-1} 2i$ join copies, for a total of $2n^2 - 2n$ copies on the first trace alone. The next n traces could well be:

trace 2:	$C_1, A_1, \ldots, C_{n-1}, A_{n-1}, B_n$
trace 3:	$C_1, A_1, \ldots, B_{n-1}, C_n, A_n$
...	
trace $n+1$:	$B_1, C_n, A_n, \ldots, C_2, A_2$

Each of these traces has $O(n-1)$ operations, and like the first trace could be scheduled in reverse order, giving rise to $O(n-1)$ new traces each with $O(n-2)$ elements. Each of those traces could give rise to $O(n-2)$ traces of $O(n-3)$ elements each. And so on until the remaining traces have length 1. Thus the total number of operations is proportional to:

$$n + n(n-1) + n(n-1)(n-2) + \cdots$$

which is $O(nn!)$ or roughly $O(n^n)$.

At least two critics have complained that this potential code explosion could make trace scheduling impractical [Linn 83, Lah 83]. But my benchmarks demonstrate that code explosion isn't a serious problem for much, maybe most, scientific code. The experiments reported in chapter 8 show that the amount of actual copying is usually quite acceptable.

Most scientific code has very simple control structures with few cascaded conditionals. However, sometimes the inner loops do contain an IF-THEN-ELSE or two; unrolling these loops 16 or 32 times could lead to exponential code explosion similar to the example above. Luckily, all of the inner-loop conditionals in the benchmarks that caused code explosion fell into two main classes, each of which could be rewritten to avoid code explosion.

One class of inner-loop conditionals looks like:

```
IF x˜=0.0 THEN
    y:=x*z
```

The only purpose of the conditional is to avoid an extra multiplication. On a scalar machine this might save time. But it is pointless in a highly parallel, pipelined VLIW unless x is almost always zero (in which case the algorithm can probably be rewritten, say, using sparse-matrix techniques). If x is frequently

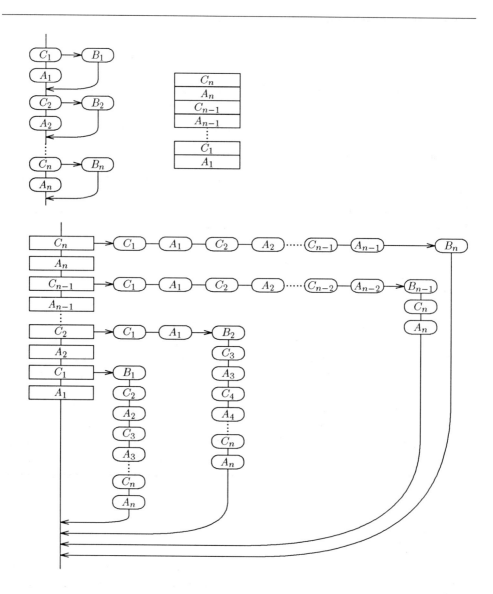

Figure 4.3. An example of code explosion

non-zero, then simply removing the conditional eliminates the possibility of code explosion when the loop is unrolled:

```
y:=x*z
```

The other class of conditionals looks like:

```
IF b THEN
     x:=e1
ELSE
     x:=e2
```

where the expressions `e1` and `e2` are very simple, often just constants or variables. Examples:

```
IF x>y THEN
     i:=j-1
ELSE
     i:=j+1

IF x~=0 THEN
     z:=z/x
```

To avoid potential code explosion in this class requires the introduction of a new Tinylisp, intermediate-code, and machine operation, SELECT.

```
SELECT( b, x1, x2 )
```

returns either `x1` or `x2` depending on whether `b` is true or false. So the above can be rewritten as:

```
IF b THEN              ⇒       x:=SELECT( b, e2, e1 )
     x:=e1
ELSE
     x:=e2


IF x>y THEN            ⇒       i:=j+SELECT( x>y, 1, -1 )
     i:=j-1
ELSE
     i:=j+1


IF x~=0 THEN           ⇒       z:=SELECT( x~=0, z/x, z )
     z:=z/x
```

(The last example assumes the machine doesn't signal exception on division by 0.)

The SELECT operator is easily implemented in hardware (the Numerix MARS-432 has a SELECT, and many vector machines have vector equivalents). Remember that the purpose of the ELI project was to develop a compiler and an architecture simultaneously; we're not concerned about compiling for other random machines. The disadvantage of SELECT is that both operands must be evaluated; but this isn't a problem if one assumes the operands are usually constants, variables, or simple expressions that can usually be evaluated in parallel.

An interesting example of the usefulness of SELECT arose when I decided to implement SIN and COS as functions that get expanded and compiled inline. On traditional machines these functions are implemented as a block of straight-line code (one or two dozen operations) followed by one or two very simple IFs testing the sign of intermediate results. When a simple loop containing a call to SIN using that implementation was unwound several times, there was massive copying after the first trace because each expansion of SIN was data-independent from the others, and the conditionals floated up towards the top of the schedule. Replacing the IF-THEN-ELSEs with SELECTs eliminated the code explosion without sacrificing performance.

Not all inner-loop conditionals cause code explosion. Conditionals that exit from a loop don't cause excessive copying:

```
LOOP
    . . .
    IF e1 THEN
        EXITLOOP
    . . .
    IF e2 THEN
        EXITLOOP
    . . .
```

(Actually, all loops look like this after they are unwound.) Because these conditionals don't have joins to the loop body like IF-THEN-ELSEs, the explosive copying is avoided. And as will be discussed in chapter 6, transformations needed for memory-bank disambiguation will result in many loops that iterate some multiple of the amount of unrolling. For these unrolled loops, only one exit test is needed; the others can be discarded, resulting in even less copying.

Data-dependent cascaded conditionals usually don't cause problems either:

```
IF b1 THEN
    x:=e1
ELSE
    x:=e2
IF x>0 THEN
    s1
ELSE
    s2
```

Because the second conditional uses the value of x produced by the first, the relative ordering of the conditionals in the schedule remains unchanged and the second conditional is prevented from moving above the join from the first, minimizing the number of split and join copies.

Other Ways to Control Code Explosion

There are several heuristics that may reduce the number of split and join copies.

The code generator can maintain the relative trace ordering of conditional jumps within the schedule. This is easy for the code generator—it won't place a jump any earlier in the schedule than all the jumps occurring previously in the trace. Thus no conditional jumps would ever be copied into splits, and fewer jumps would be copied into joins. Since copied jumps are responsible for the exponential factor in code explosion, reducing their number greatly reduces the total amount of copying. I haven't had time to run rigorous experiments, but based on a few casual experiments this heuristic appears to work well in scientific code, reducing copying without affecting the speed of the generated code. This is probably because the control structures are so simple. Many of the results reported in chapter 8 were produced using this heuristic.

There are some obvious generalizations. The code generator could limit the number of operations that moved past a split or join during code generation. Or it could limit the number of splits or joins any one operation is allowed to pass in the schedule. Or it could fiddle with the priority function used to pick which operation to place on the schedule next. The list-scheduling code generator forms the instructions of the schedule sequentially, packing as many eligible operations into the current instruction as will fit, considering eligible operations in priority order. The priority of an operation could be decreased by an appropriate amount according to how many copies would be generated by placing it in the current instruction. These heuristics could be applied solely to jumps instead of all operations. (I haven't implemented any of these heuristics.)

In drastic situations, the trace picker can simply limit its traces to single basic blocks; there will be no join copies and very few split copies, with no jumps copied at all. (The few split copies could be eliminated by forcing the jump at the end of the block to be scheduled in the last instruction.) Of course, this eliminates most of the potential parallelism as well.

Finally, the heuristics could be changed as compilation progressed. The first time-critical traces would be allowed to generate copies freely, while the space-saving heuristics would be turned on for later, less critical traces. The strength of the heuristics could be adjusted to the estimated execution frequency of the trace, or the number of copies already produced.

While we of the ELI project have mentioned such triggered heuristics in the past, I'm now doubtful as to their efficacy. Consider a loop body consisting of 64 operations, with two cascaded IF-THEN-ELSEs, each with 50% branch probability. (This could arise from two calls to SIN.) Unrolling the loop 16 times yields a loop body with 32 IF-THEN-ELSEs and 1024 operations. The schedule for the first trace through the loop could easily move all the conditionals near the bottom, producing roughly

$$992 + 960 + 928 + 896 + \cdots = 15872$$

join copies on the first trace alone. Any heuristic applied to later traces wouldn't be very useful, since an impractical number of copies were produced on the first trace. Even ignoring this, a heuristic triggered by the execution count of a trace wouldn't work, because all the possible execution paths through the loop body are equally likely, and the traces will have roughly the same execution counts. A heuristic triggered by number of copies wouldn't work well either, because then some of the traces would be compiled into highly parallel code (and produce a lot of copies) while the rest of the (equally likely) traces would be compiled into much less parallel code.

Improvements in Bookkeeping

Another way to reduce copying is to look for improvements in bookkeeping itself. The current algorithm sometimes copies operations unnecessarily, and with quite a bit of work the extra copies can be avoided.

An operation assigning x that has moved below a split need be copied only if x is live on the off-trace edge of the split. For example, consider this trace and schedule:

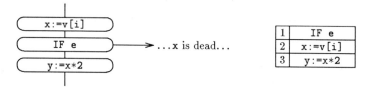

The operation x:=v[i] has moved below the IF, and the current bookkeeper would copy it onto the off-trace edge. But it really doesn't need to be copied, since the value of x is dead on that edge and won't be used.

To implement this, the bookkeeper must the update the set of variables live on the off-trace edge after each operation is copied onto the edge. To see why, consider this example:

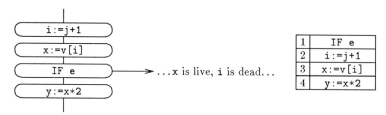

Both `i:=j+1` and `x:=v[i]` have moved below the `IF`. Originally, `i` is dead on the off-trace edge. But after `x:=v[i]` is copied onto the edge, `i` is now live on the edge, so `i:=j+1` must also be copied:

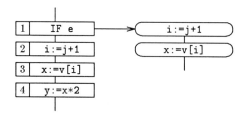

Nicolau describes further minor details of this enhancement. Implementing it in the current bookkeeper wouldn't be hard. But on the other hand, it probably wouldn't result in much saved copying, since such situations probably don't occur frequently in scientific code.

A more serious problem (which Nicolau doesn't address) is the excess copying that occurs at code motions past `IF-THEN-ELSE`s. Consider this trace:

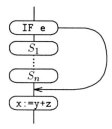

Currently, if the code generator moves `x:=y+z` up above the `IF`, it will get copied into the join:

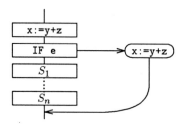

But the copy is redundant, since the original has moved completely above the IF.

How serious is this problem? Consider a trace through a flow graph that models two calls to SIN expanded in-line and the schedule for the trace:

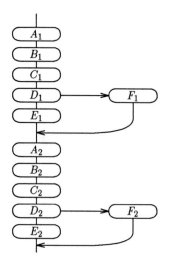

1	A_1	A_2
2	B_1	B_2
3	C_1	C_2
4	D_1	D_2
5	E_1	E_2

The two expansions of SIN are data-independent and can be done in parallel, so the code generator has done exactly that in the schedule. But now look at the flow graph after bookkeeping:

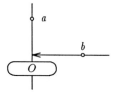

The entire second expansion of SIN has been needlessly duplicated on the off-trace edge of D_1 in cycle 4 of the schedule. Not only are extra copies created, but the program is slower than optimal as well. Assuming the branch probability of D_1 is 50%, then on half of all the executions through the flow graph, twice as many instructions will be executed than necessary. Thus on average the code is 1.5 times slower than it could be. The situation is much worse when an inner loop containing such an IF-THEN-ELSE is expanded 16 or 32 times. (Of course, SIN in particular can use the SELECT operator and avoid this problem, but it may not be possible to rewrite all critical IF-THEN-ELSEs that way.)

In general, suppose an operation O moves above a join to point a:

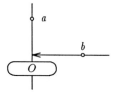

The operation needn't be copied into the join if:

1. Every path of execution from the program start to b first goes through a (that is, a dominates b).

2. On any path from a to b, none of the variables used by O are assigned.

Both of these conditions are easy to check in a static flow graph. Condition 1 uses the "dominates" relation normally used for loop optimization, and condition 2 uses "reaching copies," a slight generalization of the data-flow analysis used for copy propagation [Aho 77]. But trace scheduling changes the flow graph, so both the dominators and reaching copies analysis would have to be incrementally updated during bookkeeping, taking account of the reordered operations in the schedule and the new copies as they are added into splits and joins.

The analogous situation where an operation moves below an IF-THEN-ELSE could be handled by a generalization of Nicolau's suggested improvement for splits. For example, suppose the code generator moves the operation x:=y op z down to point a:

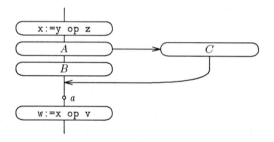

Assuming C doesn't reference x, x is now dead on the off-trace edge of A. By Nicolau's rule it isn't necessary to copy x:=y op z onto the off-trace edge. Unfortunately, the current incremental live analysis (and the one proposed by Nicolau) would report after bookkeeping that x is live on the off-trace edge. This is because the analysis doesn't proceed past the buffering nodes at splits and joins; so even though x would be reported dead at the join below C, that fact wouldn't be propagated up through C into the split. The analysis doesn't have to proceed past buffering nodes because of the current bookkeeping rules. Changing those rules would require the analysis to change. For the more sophisticated copying rules to work, a potentially much more expensive incremental analysis is needed that takes account of all the code at C, which could be arbitrarily complex (loops and conditionals) and include machine instructions from previous traces.

While feasible, the incremental reanalyses needed for detecting unnecessary split and join copying would complicate bookkeeping quite a bit more. Are the complications worth it? For that matter, are any of the heuristics and improvements previously discussed worth it? Maybe not, if the benchmarks reported in chapter 8 are representative of the time-critical control structures of scientific code; for most of those programs, the current compiler appears to perform adequately well. For the benchmarks on which the trace scheduler doesn't do well, the reasons are not due to unnecessary copying (see chapter 8).

On the other hand, if the benchmarks are not representative of most scientific code, or if one wishes to expand the domain of the trace scheduling to include other applications, then perhaps the improvements discussed above are necessary. But then it probably makes sense to junk the current algorithm and adopt a generalization of trace scheduling called "SRDAG compaction" [Linn 83]. SRDAG compaction cleanly and efficiently incorporates more general code motion, including motion past IF-THEN-ELSEs, without creating the unnecessary copies produced by trace scheduling.

Multicycle Jumps

Many pipelined machines, including the MIPS and the FPS-164, have conditional jump operations that take longer than one cycle. (Sometimes these are called "delayed jumps.") Transfer of control occurs on the last cycle of the jump if the test is true. Because the machines are pipelined, other operations can be executed while a jump is completing.

The current compiler only handles one-cycle jumps. This isn't an unreasonable architectural assumption. A number of microcoded machines machines (for example, the Numerix MARS-432) have large, fast instruction caches with high hit rates; given an address, the cache can deliver an instruction in much less than one cycle if it is in the cache. If multiple jumps are allowed in an instruction, the memory-bank-interleaving scheme Fisher proposed for implementing them [Fisher 80] could just as easily be applied to the cache as well. Branch conditions that take a long time to evaluate (floating point comparisons, for example) can be split up into two separate operations, a comparison that delivers a boolean result into a register and then the jump itself:

```
IF x>y THEN        ⇒        temp:=x>y
                            IF temp THEN
```

But suppose that for hardware reasons multicycle jumps turned out to be more practical. Could the compiler handle them? Yes, with only a few minor changes needed.

What would happen if multicycle jumps were treated like any other multi-cycle operation? Consider this trace and its schedule:

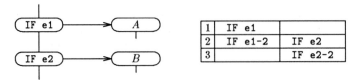

1	IF e1	
2	IF e1-2	IF e2
3		IF e2-2

The second cycle of the first jump overlaps the first cycle of the second jump; the split (the transfer of control) from the first jump actually occurs at the end of cycle 2 and bisects execution of the second jump. Applying the normal bookkeeping rules for multicycle operations yields the following flow graph:

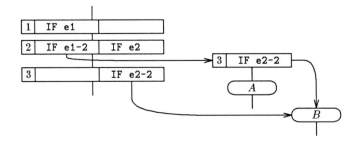

Because IF e2 was bisected by the split from IF e1, its tail end is placed in a partial schedule on the split. Note that the partial schedule is a placeholder only, indicating that instruction is occupied by the last cycle of an operation that was started in the main schedule.

But this machine code is wrong. Suppose the branch conditions of IF e1 and IF e2 are both true. In the original flow graph, control ends up at A. But in the new flow graph, control ends up at B. Here's the sequence of events:

cycle 1   IF e1 initiated
cycle 2   IF e2 initiated
           IF e1 completes, transfers control to partial schedule
cycle 3   IF e2 completes, transfers control to B

What to do?

The Easy Solution. The easiest solution is simply to prevent jumps from overlapping. So a valid schedule and flow graph for the above trace would be:

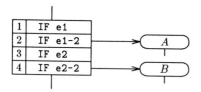

If a multicycle jump is bisected by a join, its first part is put into the join's partial schedule just like any other bisected operation:

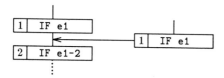

Thus, no matter which way control enters the schedule, the jump will be initiated and complete in cycle 2 of the schedule. (According to the definition of where joins are placed during bookkeeping, the only operations that could be bisected by a join are those that were originally below the join in the trace. So we're assured that it is correct to initiate the bisected jump if control enters from the join.)

This easy solution isn't so bad. (It's essentially the solution used for the MIPS [Gross 82].) Other multicycle operations can still overlap a jump, so most of the advantages of pipelined jumps are retained. And assuming the machine supports multiple jumps initiated per instruction, the machine is still able to execute a large number of jumps quickly.

Another Solution. A better solution allows multicycle conditional jumps to overlap, but requires a little extra architectural support. Assume jumps take d cycles to complete and that the hardware determines the result of the branch condition after the first cycle. When a branch condition for a jump J is true, the hardware will ignore any successive jumps initiated in the next $d - 1$ cycles needed for J to complete, even if the the successive jumps' branch conditions are true.

Consider the trace and resulting schedule and flow graph from the example above:

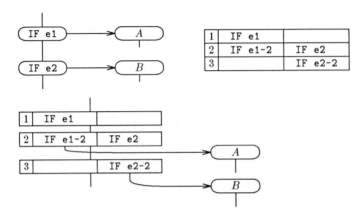

If e1 is true, the hardware will ignore IF e2 and control will transfer directly to A—we don't have to worry that one cycle after IF e1 jumps IF e2 might jump again. If IF e1 is false, then IF e2 will execute normally. Note that because IF e2 is ignored if IF e1 jumps, there is no reason to include the second cycle of IF e2 in a partial schedule at the split from IF e1.

Now consider an alternative schedule for the same trace:

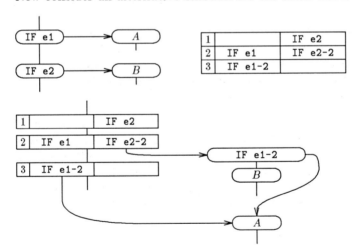

IF e1 has moved below IF e2 in the schedule, and the split from IF e2 bisects IF e1. Again, the second cycle of the bisected jump isn't included in a partial schedule at the split. But this time, because IF e2 will cause IF e1 to be ignored when IF e2 is true, IF e1 (which was originally above IF e2) is treated as if it were completely below the split and copied into the split. You can convince yourself that this is correct by trying all combinations of boolean values for IF e1 and IF e2.

The modified bookkeeping rules at splits are:

Conditional jumps bisected by a split are never put into the partial schedule.

A conditional jump J_1 is copied into a split from jump J_2 if J_1 was originally above the split but is now initiated below the split, that is, if $TracePos(ICO(J_1)) < TracePos(ICO(J_2))$ and $Cycle(J_1) > Cycle(J_2)$.

At joins, conditional jumps are treated like any other multicycle operation. The discussion about joins in the easy solution applies here as well.

How good is this second solution? Better than the first. It's not much harder to implement: Both the required hardware and the bookkeeper modifications are simple. Unlike the easy solution, this one allows multicycle conditional jumps to overlap freely, * and there is fully pipelined execution of overlapped jumps except in one infrequent case. In the example above, IF e1 moved below IF e2 in the schedule and was copied into the split; when IF e2 is true, the execution of IF e1 and IF e2 aren't pipelined. But this is a rare event in programs that can be handled well by trace scheduling, since the underlying assumption is that jumps usually don't branch off the trace. And if, as discussed in a previous section, jumps are always kept in trace order on the schedule, then this situation will never occur.

Efficiency of Partial Schedules

The job of partial schedules is to either fill or drain the pipelines at the boundaries of a schedule. The instructions of a partial schedule typically have many "holes"

---

* Gross, who helped design the optimization of multicycle jumps in the MIPS, told me that the people on the MIPS project didn't seriously consider overlapping jumps; they thought the problem was too hairy.

where other operations could be placed. For example, a partial schedule at a split might look like:

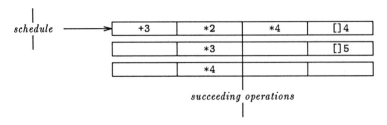

Most of each instruction in the partial schedule is not being used, even though it's likely that a smarter compiler could move some of the succeeding operations up into the holes, thereby producing faster, more parallel code.

How serious is this problem? The results reported in chapter 8 show that the benchmark programs are spending only a few percent of their time in partial schedules; even if partial schedules were somehow eliminated, it would make little difference. Of course, the inner loops of these programs are very simple and contain few conditionals, so this result isn't much of a surprise. The trace scheduler successfully picks long, likely traces of execution through the inner loops, and the time spent in the partial schedules at the boundaries is insignificant in comparison to the time spent in the main traces.

But what if the benchmarks are not completely representative of the time-critical control structures in scientific code? What if the inner loops of some important scientific code contain many IF-THEN-ELSEs, and contrary to the basic assumption of trace scheduling, many of the those conditionals are just as likely to go either way? If such is the case, trace scheduling probably wouldn't perform well for many other reasons; but just the same, I'll offer two potential improvements to partial schedules.

Improvement 1. One way to fill the holes in the partial schedules is to include the partial schedules in the traces handed to the code generator. At most one split partial schedule could occur at the beginning of the trace, and at most one join partial schedule at the end. The code generator would try to integrate the partial schedules into the newly formed schedule while obeying the constraints required by the nature of partial schedules. The partial operations in the partial schedule at the beginning must start in the first cycle of the schedule, while the partial operations in the partial schedule at the end must finish in the last cycle of the schedule.

It's easier to do this integration for the partial schedule at the beginning of the trace than for the join partial schedule at the end. Because the schedule's instructions are formed sequentially, the code generator could simply initialize the schedule and related data structures to contain the partial schedule at the beginning; the code generator would then form the rest of the schedule as usual. But the partial schedule at the end causes problems—the code generator can't possibly know exactly how to fit it onto the end of the schedule until the rest of the schedule is already formed. Probably the best the code generator could do practically is to merely place the partial schedule as early as possible on the schedule such that the partial operations still finish in the final cycle of the schedule (taking account of the register usage and resource contention).

Though the integration of partial schedules sounds conceptually straightforward, it would likely be a hairy mess to implement.

Improvement 2. A simpler approach to filling the holes in partial schedules is to use a peephole optimizer. The peephole optimizer would try to overlap partial schedules with the previous or following basic blocks of instructions, subject to the constraints of register usage and resource contentions. But the optimizer wouldn't attempt to rearrange the relative ordering of operations within the blocks.

For example, the peephole optimizer would merge the split partial schedule and succeeding basic block of instructions (shown on the left) into a single basic block that is shorter by one instruction (shown on the right):

*3	+3 (W r4)
*4 (W r1)	
	* (R r4)
	*2
+ (R r1)	*3

$\Rightarrow$

*3	+3 (W r4)
*4 (W r1)	* (R r4)
	*2
+ (R r1)	*3

The registers written by the partial-schedule operations and read by the basic-block operations are shown in parentheses. The basic block can start no earlier than the second cycle of the partial schedule, since its multiply reads the value in register r4, which isn't produced until the end of the first cycle.

The peephole optimizer would be pretty easy to implement, but how well would it perform? It might not be able to do much with split partial schedules, because the code generator generally tries to place operations as early in a schedule as possible; as a result, it's likely that an operation in the first cycle of the block following the split partial schedule reads a register written in the last cycle of the partial schedule, precluding any overlap. But the peephole optimizer might do better with join partial schedules, since the same "early as possible" policy of the code generator tends to leave the ends of schedules relatively empty; as a result, there is likely to be plenty of room in which to overlap a following partial schedule.

If the time wasted by partial schedules becomes significant (but I doubt it will), then the correct approach is to first implement the peephole optimizer, since it is quite simple. If that doesn't do the trick, only then should one consider the first suggestion of including partial schedules with the trace when it is given to code generator.

Chapter 5
Memory-reference Disambiguation

The problem of disambiguation is: Given two vector references v[i] and v[j], could they possibly refer to the same memory location? In order to get the most parallelism from traces of scientific programs, the code generator must disambiguate as many vector references as possible.

How does the disambiguator disambiguate two vector references v[i] and v[j]? Using the conventional flow analysis of reaching definitions, the disambiguator derives symbolic expressions e_i and e_j for the indices i and j in terms of the induction variables and loop invariants of the loops enclosing the two references. It then compares the two expressions symbolically to see if they could possibly be equal; that is, it sees if there are any integer-valued solutions to the equation $e_i - e_j = 0$

For example, suppose that for the following code the code generator asked about the two vector references v[j] and v[k]:

```
FOR i:=1 to n DO
    j:=i+m
    v[j]:=y
    k:=j+1
    x:=v[k]
```

The disambiguator derives the expressions $i + m$ for index j and $i + m + 1$ for index k. The two indices are equal if and only if $(i + m) - (i + m + 1) = 0$. The disambiguator simplifies that to $-1 = 0$ and concludes that j could not possibly equal k; therefore, v[j] and v[k] refer to different memory locations.

The code generator only asks about pairs of vector references from the same trace—it will never ask about two references that come from different traces. This simplifies disambiguation considerably.

Symbolic Derivations

As the first step in disambiguating two vector references v[i] and v[j], the disambiguator expresses the indices i and j in terms of loop invariants, loop induction variables, and other variable definitions. These symbolic **derivations** are produced by recursively following the use-definition chains resulting from the reaching definitions analysis [Aho 77].

First consider a straight-line code example:

```
1. IN m
2. IN n
3. j:=m*n
5. k:=m/3
6. l:=k
4. j:=j+4
7. i:=l+1
8. v[i]:=x
9. v[j]:=y
```

(IN m signifies that m is an input variable to the program.) Using use-definition chains, the disambiguator recursively produces a derivation for the use of j at operation 9:

$$(m_1 * n_2) + 4$$

(m_1 indicates the value assigned to m by operation 1.) Similarly, one might expect that the derivation for i at operation 8 would be:

$$(m_1/3) + 1$$

But as is explained later, the disambiguator is interested only in the integer operations $+$, $*$, and $-$, and it stops recursing when it encounters any other operators. So the actual derivation for i is:

$$k_5 + 1$$

The value produced by operation 5, a division, is treated as an atomic variable in the derivation.

Code with conditional jumps (but no loops) adds some complications, since more than one definition may reach a use of a variable. For example:

```
1. IN m
2. IF e THEN
3.     i:=m+1
   ELSE
4.     i:=m+3
5. v[i]:=x
```

There are two definitions of i reaching its use in operation 5, and the disambiguator must consider both of them. So an alternation operator $\vee$ is introduced into the derivation:

$$(m_1 + 1) \vee (m_1 + 3)$$

The $\vee$ operator means that the expression could have either one of the two values. In the presence of multiple conditional jumps, multiple levels of alternation may occur corresponding to the different possible paths of execution. For example:

```
1. IN M
2. IF e1 THEN
3.    i:=m*3
   ELSE
4.    i:=m*2
5. IF e2 THEN
6.    j:=i+1
   ELSE
7.    j:=i+3
8. v[j]:=x
```

To get the derivation for j at operation 8, the disambiguator first obtains:

$$(i+1) \vee (i+3)$$

Each use of i has two reaching definitions, and the derivation of both uses of i is:

$$(3 * m_1) \vee (2 * m_1)$$

So the resulting derivation for j is:

$$(((3 * m_1) \vee (2 * m_1)) + 1) \vee (((3 * m_1) \vee (2 * m_1)) + 3)$$

This represents the value that j could have resulting from each of the four different possible paths of execution.

More formally, derivations are produced as follows. The derivation of a constant is just the constant itself:

derivation$(c) \rightarrow c$, for a constant c

The derivation for a use of a variable **a** in some operation is:

derivation$(d_1) \vee$ derivation$(d_2) \vee \ldots \vee$ derivation(d_n)

where the d_i are the definitions of **a** reaching the use. The derivation of a reaching definition depends on the operator, and is expressed recursively as the derivation of the operands:

$$\text{derivation}(a := b) \rightarrow \text{derivation}(b)$$
$$\text{derivation}(\text{EQUIV } a, b) \rightarrow \text{derivation}(b)$$
$$\text{derivation}(a := b + c) \rightarrow \text{derivation}(b) + \text{derivation}(c)$$
$$\text{derivation}(a := b - c) \rightarrow \text{derivation}(b) - \text{derivation}(c)$$
$$\text{derivation}(a := b * c) \rightarrow \text{derivation}(b) * \text{derivation}(c)$$
$$\text{derivation}(a := -b) \rightarrow -\text{derivation}(b)$$
$$\text{derivation}(o) \rightarrow o, \text{ for any other operation}$$

Notice that EQUIV is handled the same as :=. EQUIV is described in detail in chapter 2; its purpose is to express a new induction variable a introduced by induction-variable simplification in terms of the original source variables (the expression represented by the variable b).

The last rule terminates the recursive derivation: Any operation producing a value by means other than integer $+$, $-$, or $*$ becomes a variable in the final symbolic derivation. Since program input variables are all defined at the beginning of the program with the special operator IN, the recursion is guaranteed to stop eventually.

But what about loops? The loop induction variables will produce cyclic use-definition chains, and the recursive derivation algorithm won't terminate. For example:

```
1. IN m
2. i:=1
   LOOP
3.    IF i>n THEN EXIT
4.    j:=i-2
5.    v[j]:=x
6.    k:=j+m
7.    v[k]:=y
8.    i:=i+1
```

The definition of i at 8 reaches the use of i at 8.

But remember that we want to produce symbolic derivations in terms of loop induction variables and loop invariants. In the example above, i is the loop induction variable; the derivation for the use of j at 5 should be:

$$i - 2$$

and the derivation for the use of k at 7 should be:

$$(i - 2) + m$$

To implement this efficiently, a trick is used that effectively prevents the derivation algorithm from following a use-definition chain across the back edge of a loop. Before code generation begins, all the induction variables of a loop are identified. Informally, an induction variable is a variable whose value is written in one iteration but used in a later iteration. More formally, an induction variable is any variable x that meets these conditions:

x is live on entry to the loop header (the top of the loop).

x has at least one definition in the loop that reaches the header.

Then for every induction variable, a dummy definition of the variable is inserted at the top of the loop. For example, in the previous example, i is an induction variable, and the dummy definition 2a would be inserted at the top of the loop:

```
1.  IN m
2.  i:=1
    LOOP
2a.     LOOP-ASSIGN i
3.      IF i>n THEN EXIT
4.      j:=i-2
5.      v[j]:=x
6.      k:=j+m
7.      v[k]:=y
8.      i:=i+1
```

Once all the loops have been processed, reaching definitions are recomputed. As far as the reaching-definitions algorithm is concerned, LOOP-ASSIGN i is equivalent to i:=i. In the example, the uses of i within the loop are now reached only by the LOOP-ASSIGN i definition. The derivation algorithm will terminate when it gets to a LOOP-ASSIGN, applying the last derivation rule:

derivation(o) → o, for any other operation

The effect of this trick is to break the use-definition chains with the LOOP-ASSIGNs at the point where the chains cross a loop back edge, removing the back edges from the flow graph as far as the disambiguator is concerned.

So in the example above, the derivation of the use of j in operation 5 is:

$$i_{2a} - 2$$

and the derivation of the use of k in 7 is:

$$(i_{2a} - 2) + m$$

That is, the uses of j and k have been expressed symbolically in terms of the induction variable i and the loop invariant m.

Before code generation begins, the derivations of all uses of index variables are precomputed and stored in the individual operations using the variables. Then the dummy LOOP-ASSIGNs are removed from the program.

Note that this trick will only work if traces don't cross the back edges of loops, that is, as long as a trace doesn't include operations from different iterations of the same loop. The disambiguator assumes that a loop induction variable has the same value when comparing derivations, and that assumption could be invalid if a trace crosses a loop back edge.

For example, consider this loop:

```
1. LOOP
2.     LOOP-ASSIGN i
3.         j:=i-1
4.         x:=v[j]
           ...
5.         v[i]:=y
6.         i:=i+1
```

The derivation of index j in operation 4 is $i_2 - 1$, and the derivation of index i in operation 5 is i_2, so the disambiguator concludes that operations 4 and 5 are to different locations. But suppose the trace handed to the code generator started at operation 5 and didn't stop at the back edge, but instead crossed it and included operations 3 and 4 at the end of the trace:

```
5.         v[i]:=y
6.         i:=i+1
3.         j:=i-1
4.         x:=v[j]
```

Even though the disambiguator thinks that operations 4 and 5 are to different memory locations, in this trace they refer to the same location. This is because operation 5 is from one iteration of the loop and operation 4 from the next iteration, and i in fact has different values in the two derivations.

As I discussed in chapter 4, allowing traces to cross the back edges of outer loops might yield some advantage. If so, the disambiguator must be modified. The simplest fix is to assume that two references on different sides of a loop back edge within a trace could possibly refer to the same memory location, regardless of their derivations. This would constrain vector references in such traces to be executed in source order. But remember that the motivation for allowing traces to cross the back edges of outer loops was to overlap the initial code of the outer loop with the final code, and much of that code doesn't contain vector references. Thus more sophisticated changes to the disambiguator that would handle vector references in such traces might not be worth it.

Comparing Derivations

To disambiguate two vector references, the disambiguator must compare the symbolic derivations to see if they could possibly be equal. That is, given two index variable derivations, e_i and e_j, it forms the difference $e_i - e_j$, simplifies it, and attempts to determine if the difference could possibly be zero for some integer values of the variables. In other words, if the equation $e_i - e_j = 0$ has any integer solutions, then the vector indices i and j could possibly be equal, and the memory references might refer to the same location during execution.

Many of the difference expressions encountered during disambiguation simplify to a constant, as in the first example in this chapter. But sometimes the equation doesn't simplify as neatly. For example, consider the following loop:

```
FOR i:=1 to n BY 2*m
    ...
    v[i]   := ...
    v[i-1]:= ...
    ...
```

Suppose the inner loop is unrolled 2 times. Then the vector references of the unrolled body are:

```
v[i]
v[i-1]
v[i+2*m]
v[i+2*m-1]
```

To disambiguate the first and last vector references, their index derivations are subtracted, yielding the equation:

$$2 * m - 1 = 0$$

Assuming m is integer-valued, there are no solutions to this equation no matter what value is chosen for m. Thus v[i] and v[i+2*m-1] could not possibly refer to the same location.

Answering the general question of whether an equation of real-valued variables has a solution is very difficult. But most index calculations in scientific programs are strictly integer-valued and linear; linear equations of integer-valued variables are called **linear diophantine equations**, and the algorithm for determining whether there is a solution is well known. This is why the derivation algorithm considers only the integer operations +, *, and −, treating values produced by other operations (for example, floating operations) as variables in the derivation.

A linear diophantine equation of one variable of the form

$$ax + c = 0$$

has solutions if and only if c is divisible by a. An equation of two variables

$$ax + by + c = 0$$

has solutions if and only if c is divisible by the greatest common divisor (gcd) of a and b. Equations of more variables can be reduced to the two-variable case. Checking these conditions is very simple and efficient.

For ease of manipulation, the difference of the derivations is first put into a normalized form as an alternation of sums of products. Internally, of course, the expressions are represented as Lisp s-expressions (prefix notation); the syntactic rules for normalized form are:

$$expr \rightarrow (\lor\ sum\ [sum \ldots sum])$$
$$sum \rightarrow (+\ product\ [product \ldots product])$$
$$product \rightarrow (*\ constant\ [var \ldots var])$$

That is, a normalized expression is an alternation of one or more sums; a sum contains one or more products; and a product contains a constant multiplying 0 or more variables (a variable is represented by the operation in the program producing the variable's value). The first product in a sum has no variables and looks like:

$$(*\ constant)$$

(*constant* may be 0). All the succeeding products in a sum have unique combinations of variables; that is, no two products can be combined.

The elementary algebraic identities plus some distributive rules for handling alternation are used to normalize derivations:

$$a + (b \lor c) = (a + b) \lor (a + c)$$
$$a * (b \lor c) = (a * b) \lor (a * c)$$

Alternation is also commutative and associative.

Once the difference expression is normalized, it has the form:

$$(\lor\ sum_1\ sum_2 \ldots sum_n)$$

The value of the expression could be the value of any of the sums, so each must be examined in turn using the method for linear diophantine equations described above. For each sum, there are three possible answers:

Yes—the sum will always be equal to zero for any values of the variables.

No—the sum will never be equal to zero for any values of the variables.

Maybe—the sum may or may not be equal to zero for different values of the variables.

The maybe answer results from linear equations that have been discovered to have solutions and from non-linear equations. To come up with a *yes-no-maybe* answer for the entire alternation expression, there are four cases:

At least one of the sum answers is maybe. One of the sums may be equal to zero for some variable values; therefore, the entire expression may be equal to zero for some variable values. Final answer: *maybe*.

All the answers are yes. Therefore the entire expression is known to be zero for all variable values. Final answer: *yes*.

All the answers are no. Therefore the entire expression will never be zero for any variable values. Final answer: *no*.

Some answers are yes, some are no. For some paths of execution, the expression is always equal to zero, for others it is never equal to zero. Final answer: *maybe*.

A *yes* answer for the entire expression means that the two vector references being disambiguated will always be to the same location. A *no* answer means that the two references will never be to the same location. A *maybe* answer means that it can't be determined for sure one way or the other, so the code generator will have to assume that they might refer to the same location.

Bookkeeper Copying

The disambiguator computes the derivations of index variables using the optimized intermediate-code flow graph produced before code generation begins. But, as described in chapter 4, the flow graph changes during code generation—copies of trace operations are inserted on the boundaries of a trace after code has been generated for it. At first glance, one might think that the disambiguator would have to compute the derivations on the fly during code generation, using the current flow graph as modified by the bookkeeper; this would entail a recomputation of reaching definitions after every pick-trace/generate code/bookkeep cycle.

Fortunately, however, the pre-code-generation flow graph is sufficient. The symbolic derivation of an operation copied by the bookkeeper is exactly the same as the derivation of the original. Intuitively, this is because the bookkeeper copying is intended to preserve program correctness by preserving the reaching definitions of the copied operations.

For example, consider the following fragment of a flow graph:

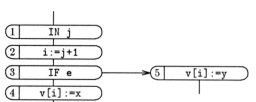

Suppose a trace includes operations 1–4 and that during code generation operation 2 gets moved below the conditional jump 3. The bookkeeper will place a copy of 2, 2', on the off-trace edge of the jump:

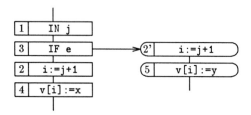

The derivation of the use of i in operation 5 is still the same even in the presence of the copy 2'; 2' was copied precisely to preserve the correctness of i's value.

A case-by-case analysis of the bookkeeper copying rules shows that each copying transformation preserves the symbolic derivations. Nicolau presents a more formal and detailed argument for this claim [Nicolau 84].

More Powerful Techniques?

The method of disambiguation described above is sufficient to disambiguate most vector references in most scientific programs. But this isn't good enough—if only two references in an inner loop were not disambiguated, parallelism could decrease by at least half. For example, consider the following simple loop:

```
FOR i:=1 TO n BY m
    v[i]:=v[i]+1
```

Assume m is an input variable. If the loop is unrolled two times, then the vector references in the unrolled body are:

```
read    v[i]
store   v[i]
read    v[i+m]
store   v[i+m]
```

Using the disambiguation method described, the read of v[i+m] would be constrained to follow the store of v[i], because i+m could equal i if m is zero; thus, without any knowledge about possible values of m, the disambiguator answers maybe and the references must be done sequentially. But obviously, m must be greater than zero if the loop is to terminate, and thus the vector references are actually to different locations; if the disambiguator only knew this, then the reads could be done in parallel and the stores in parallel.

To handle these situations, we considered using more powerful techniques such as symbolic range analysis [Harrison 77]. However, symbolic range analysis is reputed to be quite slow and fairly difficult to implement efficiently. The extra benefit didn't seem to be worth the costs, especially considering that no matter how powerful our techniques, there were still going to be programs that couldn't be disambiguated automatically. As a simple example, suppose that the above loop was embedded in an outer loop that fetched m from some array previously constructed:

```
FOR j:=1 to p
    m:=a[j]
    FOR i:=1 to n BY m
        v[i]:=v[i]+1
```

It would be a very smart (and slow) program analyzer indeed that could determine that m was non-zero. And if m is an input variable, then no automatic system could hope to handle the situation without additional programmer-supplied specifications for the inputs.

Programmer Assertions

So instead of pursuing ever more costly automatic techniques with diminishing returns, I decided instead to implement an assertion facility that the programmer can use to give hints to the disambiguator. In the example above, a single assertion about the variable m would be sufficient to disambiguate all the memory references:

```
FOR j:=1 to p
    m:=a[j]
    ASSERT m>0
    FOR i:=1 to n BY m
        v[i]:=v[i]+1
```

Only the arithmetic relations $<$, $\leq$, $\geq$, $>$, and $\neq$ can be asserted.

How does the programmer know when assertions are needed? The compiler tells him. On request, the compiler prints out every pair of vector references encountered during compilation that couldn't be disambiguated (that is, those pairs for which the disambiguator answered maybe). Along with the vector references the compiler prints out the simplified symbolic difference of the index-variable derivations. If, after examining his program, the programmer determines that the vector references are indeed to different locations, he can add the appropriate assertions and recompile.

Usually it is immediately apparent to the programmer exactly which assertions are needed, even if he isn't familiar with the underlying algorithm. The structure of loops in scientific code tends not to be very complicated. Our benchmark programs typically have needed only one or two assertions (or copies of the same assertion in similar loops) to completely disambiguate all memory references. To understand exactly how assertions are used, how simple they are, and their importance, we'll work through some examples.

FFT. The loops and vector references of FFT look like:

```
length:=1
WHILE 2*length<=n DO
    FOR j:=1 TO n BY 2*length DO
        FOR l:=1 TO length DO
            ASSERT l>=1
            ASSERT l<=length
            ...v[l+j-1]...
            ...v[l+j-1+length]...
    length:=length+length
```

Unrolling the inner loop 4 times would produce the following:

```
 1. IF l+0>length THEN EXIT
 2. ASSERT l+0 >= 1
 3. ASSERT l+0 <= length
 4. v[l+0+j-1]
 5. v[l+0+j-1+length]

 6. IF l+1>length THEN EXIT
 7. ASSERT l+1 >= 1
 8. ASSERT l+1 <= length
 9. v[l+1+j-1]
10. v[l+1+j-1+length]

11. IF l+2>length THEN EXIT
12. ASSERT l+2 >= 1
13. ASSERT l+2 <= length
14. v[l+2+j-1]
15. v[l+2+j-1+length]

16. IF l+3>length THEN EXIT
17. ASSERT l+3 >= 1
18. ASSERT l+3 <= length
19. v[l+3+j-1]
20. v[l+3+j-1+length]
```

Disambiguating vector reference 19, v[l+3+j-1], and reference 5, v[l+0+

`j-1+length]`, the disambiguator subtracts the index derivations, yielding $3 - length$. Without the assertions, the disambiguator would have to assume that *length* could equal 3, and thus that the references could be to the same location. But using assertions 2 and 18 the disambiguator proves that $3 - length \leq -1$, and thus that references 19 and 5 are to different locations.

Note that the assertions in the loop are context sensitive, applying only to the code that follows the assertion. For example, assertion 18, `ASSERT 1+3 <= length`, is not always true at vector reference 4 (specifically, when *length* < 4). The implementation of the assertion mechanism, described below, must keep track of where in the code assertions are valid.

SOLVE. In SOLVE (LU decomposition), a permutation vector `ps` is used to select rows of a two-dimensional array:

```
ASSERT ps[i]~=ps[k]
FOR j:=k+1 TO n DO
    ...lu[ps[i],j]...
    ...lu[ps[k],j]...
```

The difference of the index derivations is $ps[i] - ps[j]$; the disambiguator must be told via an assertion that the two index values are different.

Another fragment from SOLVE:

```
IF pividx~=k THEN
    ASSERT pividx~=k
    ...ps[k]...
    ...ps[pividx]...
```

Without the assertion, the disambiguator wouldn't know that on one branch of the `IF` only, `ps[k]` and `ps[pividx]` refer to different locations.

TRID4. From TRID4 (tridiagonal solver using cyclic reduction):

```
FOR i:=i0[l]+1 TO i0[l]+m,
    j:=j0[l]+1 TO j0[l]+m
DO
    ASSERT i-j>=10
    ...x[i]...
    ...x[j]...
```

The variables `i` and `j` are stepped in parallel beginning with `i0[l]+1` and `j0[l]+1`. The validity of the assertion depends on gory details of the algorithm, but it allows the inner loop to be unrolled up to 10 times while still completely disambiguating all the vector references.

The assertions in these three examples fall into two categories: Those that could be generated easily by the compiler from the source, and those that tell the compiler subtle facts about indices involving double indirection in the vector references. The assertions in the rest of the benchmark programs generally fall into these two categories as well.

The latter category, subtle facts usually arising from double indirection, demonstrate the true worth of these assertions. No practical automatic method of program analysis could possibly deduce these facts, but once alerted by the disambiguator, any programmer can formulate the required assertions in a few minutes. And as explained below, the assertions can be efficiently processed by the compiler.

As for the former category of assertions, obviously the compiler could automatically generate range assertions for simple loops:

```
FOR i:=m TO n DO
    ASSERT m<=i
    ASSERT i<=n
    . . .
```

And it could easily generate assertions for the different branches of an IF:

```
IF expression THEN
    ASSERT expression
    . . .
ELSE
    ASSERT ~expression
    . . .
```

In effect, these automatically generated assertions would be implementing a limited but useful and efficient symbolic range analysis. The only reason the current compiler doesn't generate the assertions is simply that I had more important things to do in my limited time.

Implementing Assertions

Before disambiguation begins, the compiler scans the program and collects all the assertions, converting them into a normal form that is easy to manipulate. In the intermediate code, assertions have the following form:

```
ASSERT var1 relop var2
```

where var1 and var2 are variables, and relop is one of the integer operators <, <=, >=, >, or ~=. Using the same derivation mechanism used for index variables in disambiguation, derivations are computed for var1 and var2. (See above and chapter 2 for a discussion of the EQUIV mechanism, which relates the derivations of assertions on original source-program variables to the derivations of the induction variables introduced by the front-end loop optimizations.)

Using elementary algebra, the assertions are put into normal form:

```
ASSERT expression > 0
```

or

```
ASSERT expression ~= 0
```

For example:

```
1. IN i
2. i:=i*2
3. j:=0
4. LOOP
5.     LOOP-ASSIGN j
6.     x:=i+3
7.     y:=j*4
8.     z:=y-2
9.     ASSERT z<=x
          . . .
```

First derivations are obtained for z and x in the assertion:

$$4 * \dot{j}_5 - 2 \le 2 * i_1 + 3$$

Putting the assertion into normal form yields:

$$2 * i_1 - 4 * \dot{j}_5 + 6 > 0$$

Note that, like index derivations, the variables in the normal-form assertions are actually value-producing operations in the program, not the original textual variables names like i and j.

If the normal-form expression for the assertion contains alternation, for example $(x - 3) \lor (x - 1)$, then the assertion is ignored. To see why, consider this example:

```
1. IN m
2. IN n
3. x:=m
4. y:=n
5. IF e THEN
6.     x:=x-1
7.     y:=y-1
8. ASSERT y>x
```

The derivations for x and y at the assertion are:

$$m_1 \lor (m_1 - 1)$$
$$n_2 \lor (n_2 - 1)$$

and the difference of the derivations is:

$$(n_2 - m_1) \vee (n_2 - m_1 + 1) \vee (n_2 - 1 - m_1)$$

yielding these possible normal-form assertions:

$$n_2 - m_1 > 0$$
$$n_2 - m_1 + 1 > 0$$
$$n_2 - 1 - m_1 > 0$$

Which of these should the disambiguator use? The last assertion is incorrect, since m_1 could be 6 and n_2 could be 7, but using the alternation mechanism, the disambiguator has no way to deduce this. The problem with alternation is that it doesn't take account of the execution paths used to produce the derivations; this general problem is discussed in a later section (page 135). Without knowing more about the execution paths, the disambiguator must ignore any assertion containing alternation. (The current compiler doesn't implement this, though it would be trivial to fix.)

When the disambiguator isn't able to disambiguate two vector references using the method of linear diophantine equations, it consults the collection of assertions to see if any might apply to the vector indices. To do this, it has to know which assertions might apply to the vector references; that is, it has to determine which assertions include the references in their **scope**.

Consider this example:

```
 1. ASSERT m>0
 2. FOR i:=1 TO n BY m
 3.      ASSERT i<=n
 4.      IF i>10 THEN
 5.          ASSERT i>10
 6.          s1
 7.          s2
 8.      ELSE
 9.          ASSERT i<=10
10.          s3
11.      s4
12.      s5
```

The scope of assertion 1 is lines 2–12, the scope of assertion 3 is lines 4–12, the scope of assertion 5 is lines 6–7, and the scope of assertion 9 is line 10.

To determine the scopes, the disambiguator uses the dominators flow analysis that is usually used for loop optimizations [Aho 77]. Operation A dominates operation B if and only if every path of execution from the program start to B includes A at least once. The scope of an assertion is those operations dominated by the assertion. To see why, suppose we had an assertion A dominating some operation B. Then any path of execution from the start to B must include the assertion; that is, the assertion will be executed no matter which path is taken to reach B. Remember that the loop back edges have been effectively removed from the flow graph by the insertion of the LOOP-ASSIGNs, so that every such execution path to B is loop-free.

Given two references v[i] and v[j] to be disambiguated, the corresponding sets S_i and S_j of dominating assertions might not be identical. Which of those assertions does the disambiguator use in trying to prove $i \neq j$? The intersection of the two sets? The union? Further, do the code motions and transformations of trace scheduling require that the dominators relation must be incrementally updated?

The current compiler's solution to these problems is simple but unintuitive. It relies on a minor restriction that vector stores are not allowed to move above conditional jumps during code generation. To try to prove $i \neq j$, the disambiguator uses the union of the dominating assertions, $S_i \cup S_j$, that is, all assertions that dominate either v[i] or v[j]; and the dominators relation does not have to be incrementally updated.

I'll sketch an informal argument for this solution; by no means should it be taken as a formal proof. There are four types of code motion performed on vector references during trace scheduling: motion in straight-line code, moving from above a split to below it, moving from below a split to above it, and moving from below a join to above it (moving below a join is disallowed by the bookkeeping rules). First, I'll show that for each of these motions, if an assertion A applies to a vector reference before the motion, then after the motion A still applies to the reference and any copy of it produced by bookkeeping.

Consider motion in straight-line code (a basic block). Because the assertion A and the index derivation are in terms of reaching definitions and not textual variable names, wherever the vector reference can be moved legally within the basic block (as constrained by the data dependencies), the assertion is still true.

Consider motion below splits. Suppose a vector reference moves below a split and thus is copied onto the other edge of the split. The assertion A still applies to both copies because A dominates the new locations of the copies and the conditional jump does not affect the truth of the assertion.

Consider motion above splits. The only way a vector reference x:=v[i] could move above a split is if x is dead on the off-trace edge of the split. For example:

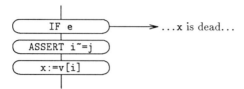

If `x:=v[i]` is moved above the split:

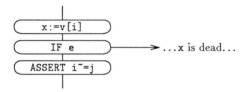

we can safely assume that `ASSERT i˜=j` still applies to it, since the only case that matters is when **e** is false; when **e** is true, it won't matter if x gets the wrong value. This argument doesn't apply to the motion of vector stores. For example:

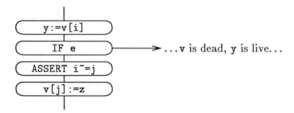

If `v[j]:=z` moved above the `IF` and the assertion continued to apply to it, the following should be correct:

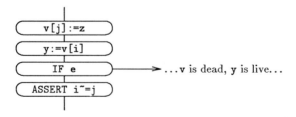

But now y could get the wrong value when **e** is true and `i=j`; that's why the motion of vector stores is restricted.

Consider motion above joins. Suppose a vector reference moves above a join and thus is copied into the join edge. As discussed previously, a variable in an applicable assertion must have exactly one reaching definition. So a definition used by both the assertion A and the vector reference must reach both edges of the join right before the join, and therefore the assertion applies to the vector reference and its copy after the motion.

Thus, no matter where a vector reference is moved or copied during trace scheduling, the assertions dominating it before trace scheduling began still apply. Incremental update of dominators isn't necessary. (This argument relies on Nicolau's demonstration that reaching definitions of an operation are in effect unchanged by trace scheduling.)

The only use the code generator makes of the disambiguator is to determine whether one vector reference can move past another on the trace. Conceptually, if the code generator is to move v[i] past v[j], it must first move v[i] and/or v[j] so that they are adjacent, and then it must swap them. If the code generator can't move v[i] and v[j] to be adjacent (because of data-dependency constraints) then it doesn't matter whether or not the disambiguator correctly disambiguates them—the data dependencies will force them to be done in original trace order. If the code generator can make them adjacent by legal code motions, then when they are adjacent any assertion that applies to one of the references obviously applies to the other. Thus, the disambiguator can use the union of the two sets of dominating assertions S_i and S_j when it attempts to prove $i \neq j$.

The restriction that vector stores can't move above splits isn't serious. Examining the benchmark library and the code generated for them, I didn't find any inner loops where there was even the possibility of a vector store moving up above a conditional jump (the vector must be dead on the other edge of the branch). And in scientific code, typically the conditionals of an inner loop all float to the top of the loop, and the vector stores occur at the end of the loop, after a bunch of computation.

Once the disambiguator finds the set $S_i \cup S_j$ of assertions dominating the two references in question, it then tries to use those assertions to prove that the normalized difference d of the index derivations is not equal to zero. In general, d is an alternation of several sums, and the disambiguator must prove each sum is not equal to zero.

First the disambiguator looks for an assertion $d \neq 0$; if none is found, it must then resort to the > 0 assertions, using a heuristic proof method. The method is based on the fact that if $x + y > 0$ and $y \leq 0$, then $x > 0$. The recursive procedure *Prove?* below tries to prove, given a set of assertions, that *sum* is not equal to zero by proving that *sum* is either greater than or less than zero.

Prove?(sum,assertions) $\rightarrow$

1. If *sum* is just a constant, return true if the constant is not equal to zero, return false otherwise.

2. Find the subset S of *assertions*. Assertion $A : e > 0$ is in S if e contains all the products of *sum* (except possibly for the constant of *sum*), that is, if *sum* has the form:

$$sum = constant_1 + prod_1 + prod_2 + \cdots + prod_m$$

and e contains $prod_1$ through $prod_m$:

$$e = constant_2 + prod_1 + prod_2 + \cdots prod_m + prod_{m+1} + \cdots + prod_n$$

3. For each such assertion A in S, try to recursively prove that $sum \geq e$ using the remaining assertions in S. That is, if

$$Prove?(1 + constant_1 - (constant_2 + prod_{m+1} + \cdots + prod_n), S - A)$$

then return true, because $sum > 0$. If trying all the assertions in S fails, then return false.

Prove? is not general; for example, given the assertion $4x + 4 > 0$ it can't prove that $3x + 4 > 0$. Nevertheless, *Prove?* appears to be quite sufficient for disambiguation because the index calculations and the assertions needed to disambiguate them tend to be quite simple. The worst that happens when *Prove?* fails is that two memory references can't be disambiguated. Because the number of assertions whose scope includes any two vector references on a trace is very small (typically less than 6), *Prove?* is quite fast and has allowed us to disambiguate all our benchmark programs.

The only extension that might be worthwhile is to add a second method: To prove $prod_1 + prod_2 > 0$, try to recursively prove $prod_1 > 0$ and $prod_2 \geq 0$. The assertions required by one of the benchmarks would have been slightly simplified if *Prove?* knew this method as well.

The general problem of trying to prove $e > 0$ given a set of assertions $e_1 > 0, e_2 > 0, \ldots, e_n > 0$, where all the expressions are linear expressions of some number of variables, is equivalent to integer programming, which is NP-complete. There are clever algorithms for solving integer programming problems, but they tend to be quite complicated with large overhead. Even if assertions are automatically generated for loop induction variables and IFs, the number of assertions valid at any point in the program will be very small, and the overhead of the general algorithm would not be worth the very little extra benefit.

Disambiguator Implementation Details

The disambiguator uses the same flow-graph data structure used by the intermediate-code optimizations. After the optimizations have been applied but before trace scheduling begins, the disambiguator identifies the loop induction variables and inserts the LOOP-ASSIGNs. Then it recomputes reaching definitions in the presence of the LOOP-ASSIGNs.

Next the derivation of each use of an index variable within a vector reference is computed. To avoid recomputation, the first time the derivation of the value produced by an operation is computed, it is stored away in the corresponding flow-graph statement representing the operation. Thus, the computation of all index derivations takes time linearly proportional to the size of the flow graph.

After the index variable derivations are computed, the assertions are collected. Then the disambiguator constructs a mapping, implemented by a hash table, of intermediate-code operations to the flow-graph statements representing the operations. This mapping is used to get from the operations supplied by the code generator to the corresponding statements in the flow graph. Finally, the LOOP-ASSIGNs are deleted from the flow graph. At this point trace scheduling begins.

The symbolic manipulations on derivations (normalization, diophantine equation solving, and proofs using assertions) are implemented as a separate module. This module is also invoked by loop induction variable simplification to simplify its symbolic expressions for induction variables. Because the derivations include only the operators $+$, $*$, and $-$, the symbolic manipulations are quite easy to implement. (Much easier in Lisp, however, than in an Algol-based language.)

The diophantine equation solver currently handles equations with at most two variables; extending it to handle more would be messy but not too hard. However, none of our benchmark programs contain diophantine equations with more than two variables; the few equations with more than two variables that did arise during disambiguation weren't linear and would have needed the assertion mechanism anyway.

The interface to the code generator was originally designed to aid the code generator in building an expression DAG from a trace as well as answer questions about vector references. To build the DAG, the code generator presents the operations of the trace one at a time in source order to the disambiguator. For each operation, the disambiguator returns the previously presented trace operations that should form the predecessors of the current operation in the DAG. With each predecessor, the disambiguator returns information identifying the edge type between the operation and the predecessor, for example, whether it represents a read-after-write of an operand or a write-after-write (these edge types are discussed more fully in chapter 7). The predecessors of a vector read include all the previous vector writes on the trace that could possibly be to the same location;

the predecessors of a vector write include all the previous vector reads and writes that could possibly be to the same location.

In retrospect, it would have been cleaner to have kept most of the details of DAG building out of the disambiguator/code-generator interface. As discussed in chapter 7, there are many subtleties to building a DAG for a trace, and the code generator can best handle them directly. In fact, the current code generator ignores all the information returned by the disambiguator except the disambiguation conflicts between vector references. So a cleaner interface that could easily be substituted for the current one would be simply a single procedure that takes two vector reference operations:

VectorConflict?(vector-reference-1,vector-reference-2)

and returns one of:

yes—the vector references are always to the same location

no—the vector references are never to the same location

maybe—the vector references may or may not be to the same location.

Shortcomings

The current disambiguator has two not-serious shortcomings.

When the disambiguator fails to resolve two memory references, its output informing the programmer is too cryptic because it is in terms of the intermediate code instead of the source code. Some sample output:

```
Possible vector index conflict:
  53: (IVSTORE PS $184 $183)          54: (IVLOAD %143 PS $111)
$184            =   (+ -1 PIVIDX)
$111            =   (+ -1 K)
$111 - $184     =?0 (+ K (* -1 PIVIDX))
```

Printing out the failures in terms of the original source is a "trivial" problem that in fact is quite hard to engineer simply. The compiler must maintain a mapping from the optimized intermediate code back to the source expressions, and updating that mapping during optimization isn't easy. The same sorts of problems occur in debugging optimized code [Hennessy 82b].

In retrospect, the mechanism used to handle multiple reaching definitions for index variables isn't too useful. In none of the benchmark programs was it actually used during disambiguation, and in one of the programs it actually interfered with the assertion mechanism. Consider:

```
1. IN m
2. i:=2*m
3. IF e THEN
4.      i:=i-1
5. j:=i+1
6. v[i]:=x
7. v[j]:=y
```

The derivations of i and j in the two vector references are

$$(2 * m_1) \vee (2 * m_1 - 1)$$
$$(2 * m_1 + 1) \vee (2 * m_1)$$

and their difference is

$$1 \vee 2 \vee 0 \vee -1$$

Because one of the sums of the alternation is zero, the disambiguator concludes that i and j might be to the same location even though clearly they are not. Adding in an assertion doesn't help because the difference of the derivations contains constants only, for which assertions are meaningless.

The root problem is that the disambiguator's alternation mechanism doesn't take account of the execution paths used to produce the alternate derivations; it will compare derivations produced via two or more paths that couldn't possibly be executed at the same time. Thus, in the example above the disambiguator compares the derivation $2 * m_1$ for i with the derivation $2 * m_1$ for j. But the derivation for i assumed the IF was not taken while the derivation for j assumed it was, impossible during actual execution.

One solution to this problem might be to separately consider each execution path to the two vector references, comparing the derivations of the index variables produced along each path (remember that the back edges of loops have been effectively removed from the flow graph by the insertion of LOOP-ASSIGNs). In the example above, there are two paths reaching the vector references: 1–2–3–5 and 1–2–3–4–5. Along the first path, i has derivation $2 * m$ and j has derivation $2 * m + 1$, and thus on this path, i and j are not equal. Along the second path, i has derivation $2 * m - 1$ and j has derivation $2 * m$, and again i and j are not equal. So we conclude that i and j could not be equal at the vector references.

In the limit, the number of paths reaching a point in a flow graph with no loops could be exponential in the number of nodes in the graph. In most scientific code this wouldn't matter, since index calculations tend to be short and rarely include few, if any, conditional jumps. But consider this fragment:

```
j:=1
FOR i:=1 TO n
    IF ... THEN
        j:=j-1
    ELSE
        j:=j+1
    ...v[j]...
    ...v[i]...
```

If this loop is unrolled 32 times, there would be 2^{32} different paths of execution reaching the last v[j] that the disambiguator would have to examine. An example like this doesn't arise very often in scientific code, but the disambiguator should at least be prepared to handle it gracefully (maybe by considering at most only some small number paths before giving up).

There is another alternative that, while not as effective as considering each path separately, is perhaps more practical and easier to implement. The current derivation algorithm could be modified so that when it reaches a use of a variable with more than one reaching definition, instead of recursively "forking" the derivation with the alternation operator $\vee$, it instead stops recursing and returns the set of reaching definitions as a derivation variable. For example:

```
1. IN m
2. i:=2*m
3. IF e THEN
4.      i:=i-1
5. j:=i+1
6. i:=i+4
7. v[i]:=x
8. v[j]:=y
```

Because the use of i in operation 5 has two reaching definitions, its derivation would simply be a single variable identified by the set of reaching definitions $\{i_2, i_4\}$. The derivations of the uses of i and j in 7 and 8 would be:

$$4 + \{i_2, i_4\}$$
$$1 + \{i_2, i_4\}$$

Since the difference of the derivations is 3, the disambiguator would conclude i and j were not equal at 7 and 8.

Intuitively, the sets of definitions uniquely capture the value of a variable at some point in the flow graph. More formally, suppose we have a flow graph with no back jumps (no loops), but arbitrary forward flow of control with several entrances and exits from the graph (remember that the LOOP-ASSIGNs inserted during disambiguation effectively remove the back jumps from the graph). Assume there are two operations in the graph, A and B. If A and B occur on one or more paths of execution through the flow graph, then either A always precedes B, or B always precedes A (otherwise there would be a loop).

> **Claim:** If the same definitions of i reach both A and B, then for every path of execution that includes both A and B, the value of i will be identical at A and B.

> **Proof:** Assume that A precedes B. Suppose the same definitions of i reach both A and B, but that on some path of execution i has a different value at B than at A. Then there must be an assignment to i on the path between A and B. According to the original assumption, the assignment (call it C) must reach A as well as B. But that would imply there is a loop, from A to C and back to A again. That contradicts the assumption that the flow graph has no loops.

Since the disambiguator compares the indices of vector references only if they are on the same path of execution (that is, a trace), this claim allows us to use the reaching definition sets as variables in derivations. In the implementation, hashing could be used to give the sets unique names for efficient comparison.

Because scientific code has so few index calculations involving conditionals, this derivation method would probably disambiguate better than the current method, correctly handling the one benchmark example where the current disambiguator fails. Though not as powerful as the compare-all-paths-separately method, it would be more efficient and easier to implement.

Chapter 6
Memory-bank Disambiguation

In addition to providing a slow, central memory controller, the VLIW architecture allows the individual interleaved memory banks to be addressed directly. The central memory controller is called the **back door**, and the ports to the individual banks are called the **front doors**. The back door handles only one request at a time, while the front doors operate in parallel. For example, if there were 8 memory banks, then 1 back-door and 8 front-door requests could be initiated every cycle.

If the compiler knows the bank of a particular memory reference, it will generate code to use the bank's front door; otherwise, it will be forced to use the slower back door. The goals of **memory-bank disambiguation** are to make as many memory references as possible through the front doors and to distribute the load on the front doors evenly. To accomplish these goals, the memory-bank disambiguator uses a symbolic analysis technique, similar to memory-reference disambiguation, combined with several classes of source transformations.

The Bulldog compiler implements the symbolic analysis and the simplest source transformation, loop unrolling. The other source transformations are much more complex and currently must be done by the programmer. Later I'll discuss the prospects for automating them.

Throughout this chapter, b designates the number of memory banks in the machine.

A Simple Example

To illustrate the problems of memory-bank disambiguation, consider this simple loop implementing vector addition:

```
i:=1
LOOP
    IF i>n THEN EXITLOOP
    a[i]:=b[i]+c[i]
    i:=i+1
```

Suppose the machine has 8 banks ($b = 8$). The bank of each of the vector references will be different on successive iterations through the loop. But by unrolling the loop 8 times:

```
i:=1
LOOP
    IF i>n THEN EXITLOOP
    a[i]:=b[i]+c[i]          /* bank 0 */
    i:=i+1
    IF i>n THEN EXITLOOP
    a[i]:=b[i]+c[i]          /* bank 1 */
    i:=i+1
    ...
    IF i>n THEN EXITLOOP
    a[i]:=b[i]+c[i]          /* bank 7 */
    i:=i+1
```

the vector references are now to the same banks on successive iterations. If the compiler knows the base address of the vectors, or at least the bank of the base address, it can easily determine the bank of each reference at compile time and generate code to use the front doors.

In general, such loops must be unrolled a multiple of b times.

Determining the Bank

The compiler uses the symbolic derivation techniques of memory-reference disambiguation (chapter 5) to discover the bank of a vector reference. Given a vector reference v[i], the compiler finds the symbolic derivation e_i for the index i; that is, it expresses i in terms of loop invariants and loop induction variables. The bank of v[i] is then

$$(e_i + \text{base}(v)) \bmod b = e_i \bmod b + \text{base}(v) \bmod b$$

where $\text{base}(v)$ is the base address of v. If the bank expression simplifies to a compile-time constant, the reference v[i] will always be to that bank, and the code generator can use the bank's front door for the reference. But if the bank expression doesn't simplify to a constant, v[i] may be to different banks during execution, and the code generator must use the back door.

For example, consider the intermediate code generated for x:=a[i,3], where a is a 256×256 array:

```
t1:=i*256
t2:=t1+3
x :=a[t2]
```

Assuming i is a loop induction variable, the derivation of the index t2 is $256*i+3$. If $b = 8$ and a begins in bank 0, then

$$(256 * i + 3 + \text{base}(a)) \bmod b = 3;$$

thus, the reference a[i,3] is always to bank 3.

Remember that index derivations may contain the alternation operator $\vee$, indicating the values corresponding to the different paths of execution that could be taken to reach the vector reference. Given a normalized derivation e of the form

$$sum_1 \vee sum_2 \vee \ldots \vee sum_n,$$

the disambiguator evaluates $m_i = sum_i \bmod b$ for each i. If all the m_i's are compile-time constants and all have the same value, then e has the same residue no matter which path is used to reach the vector reference, and the reference is to a single known bank; the bank's front door may be used for the reference. But if some of the m_is are not compile-time constants or if they aren't all equal, then the vector reference could be to many different banks during execution, and the back door must be used.

Simple algebra is used to simplify the residue of normalized sums and products:

$$(x + y) \bmod b = (x \bmod b + y \bmod b) \bmod b$$
$$jb \bmod b = 0, \qquad \text{for any integer } j$$

Assertions

As in memory-reference disambiguation, the programmer can supply assertions to help out the compiler. The assertions have the form:

```
ASSERT expression1 MOD b = expression2
```

Assertions are used mainly to tell the compiler about input variables and loop variables. In the simple loop unrolling example above, the derivations of the vector indices are in terms of the value of the loop variable i at the top of the loop. An assertion is needed to tell the compiler that after unrolling, $i \bmod 8$ is always 1 at the top of the loop:

```
i:=1
LOOP
    ASSERT i MOD 8 = 1
    IF i>n THEN EXITLOOP
    a[i]:=b[i]+c[i]              /* bank 0 */
    i:=i+1
    IF i>n THEN EXITLOOP
    a[i]:=b[i]+c[i]              /* bank 1 */
    i:=i+1

    ...
    IF i>n THEN EXITLOOP
    a[i]:=b[i]+c[i]              /* bank 7 */
    i:=i+1
```

The derivations for the vector references are $i, i+1, \ldots, i+7$. The compiler uses the assertion about i to compute the residues of the derivations modulo 8. For example, given $i + 3$, the disambiguator computes i mod 8 and 3 mod 8. Because i isn't a constant, the compiler consults the assertions and finds that i mod 8 is 1. Thus it concludes that $(i + 3)$ mod 8 is 4.

The same assertion-scoping mechanism used in memory-reference disambiguation is used here to find assertions applicable at a given point in the program. Assertions are stored in normalized form:

ASSERT *expression* mod $x = 0$

If the residue modulo b of a normalized sum s doesn't evaluate to a constant, the compiler consults the applicable assertions. Suppose s has the form $c + p_1 + \cdots + p_n$, where c is a constant and the p_i are normalized products. If there is an applicable assertion of the form

ASSERT $(a + p_1 + \cdots + p_n)$ mod $jb = 0,$ for any $j > 0$

then s mod $b = (c - a)$ mod b.

If there is no such assertion, the compiler recursively tries to find the residue of each product p_i. If p_i doesn't have a constant residue, the assertions are consulted again. Assume p_i has the form $c * v_1 * \cdots * v_m$, where c is a constant and the v_i are variables. If there is an applicable assertion of the form:

ASSERT $(a + p_i)$ mod $jb = 0,$ for any $j > 0$

then p_i mod $b = (-a)$ mod b. Or if there is an assertion of the form:

ASSERT $(a + v_1 * \cdots * v_m)$ mod $jb = 0,$ for any $j > 0$

then p_i mod $b = (-c * a)$ mod b.

As in memory-reference disambiguation, this proof method isn't general. For example, given:

ASSERT z mod $b = 0$
ASSERT $(x + y)$ mod $b = 0$

the method can't prove $(x + y + z)$ mod $b = 0$. Nevertheless, the method is quite sufficient for this application.

There is a messy interaction between programmer-specified loop unrolling and assertions. If an assertion is in a loop body, it will be unrolled (repeated) just like any other statement. But that is incorrect—the assertion is valid only in the first unrolling. For example, suppose this loop is unrolled 8 times:

```
FOR i:=1 TO n UNROLL 8
    ASSERT i MOD 8 = 1
    body
```

Not only will the assertion be untrue if the loop isn't unrolled a multiple of 8 times, but the unrolled loop will have **7** incorrect assertions:

```
i:=1
LOOP
    IF i>n THEN EXITLOOP
    ASSERT i MOD 8 = 1
    body
    IF i>n THEN EXITLOOP
    ASSERT i MOD 8 = 1
    body
    . . .
    IF i > n THEN EXITLOOP
    ASSERT i MOD 8 = 1
    body
```

The solution is to make the assertion dependent on the unrolling using a source-language construct:

```
1: FOR i:=1 TO n UNROLL 8
    ASSERT i MOD UNROLL(1) = UNROLL-INDEX(1)
    body
```

The expression UNROLL(label) evaluates to the amount of unrolling specified for the loop with the given label; UNROLL-INDEX(label) is expanded during loop unrolling and evaluates to the number of the current unrolling of the loop body (from 1 to UNROLL(label)). For example, the loop above unrolls into this intermediate code:

```
i:=1
LOOP
    IF i>n THEN EXITLOOP
    ASSERT i MOD 8 = 1
    body
    IF i>n THEN EXITLOOP
    ASSERT i MOD 8 = 2
    body
    . . .
    IF i>n THEN EXITLOOP
    ASSERT i MOD 8 = 8
    body
```

Now each assertion in the unrolled loop is correct, even if the programmer later on changes the amount of unrolling.

Source Transformations

Symbolic bank analysis alone isn't sufficient for memory-bank disambiguation; source transformations are also needed. We've already seen the simplest transformation, loop unrolling with an assertion at the top. Unrolling by itself works only if the loop variable has an initial value with known residue, the bases of the vectors referenced in the loop are known, and residues of the vector indices evaluate to compile-time constants.

Many inner loops in scientific code fit this mold. But many don't. Sometimes the initial values of loop variables are variables and don't have a known residue:

```
FOR i:=j to k
    ...v[i]...
```

Sometimes the base of an array doesn't have a known residue, as when arbitrary cross sections of arrays are passed as parameters. Sometimes all the vector references in an inner loop can be bank-disambiguated, but they are all to the same bank, restricting parallelism.

These situations require source transformations more complex than loop unrolling. The transformations fall into three broad classes: data, control, and algorithmic. Data transformations change the layout of aggregate data like arrays; control transformations globally reorder the loops and statements of the implementation without changing the abstract algorithm; algorithmic transformations make large-scale transformations in the abstract algorithm. The data and control transformations could probably be automated in the near future, whereas algorithmic transformations require very sophisticated reasoning.

The following catalogue describes the transformations needed for the benchmark library of programs. By no means is it intended as a complete list.

Data Transformations

The compiler assumes by default that arrays start in a known bank (usually bank 0). This isn't hard to arrange for statically and dynamically allocated arrays—they're simply allocated starting on b-word boundaries. Is this a serious restriction? For most time-critical scientific kernels, no. The only problem arises with arbitrary cross sections of arrays passed as input parameters, for example, passing a row of an array to a routine that expects a vector parameter. Luckily, this feature isn't crucial to most scientific code; but when it is, it can still be bank-disambiguated using some of the transformations below.

The way multidimensional arrays are laid out in memory is crucial to bank disambiguation. Inner loops of scientific code tend to access arrays by rows, by columns or by both rows and columns. If the time-critical accesses are predominantly by row or predominantly by column, then those references can be easily bank-disambiguated.

If time-critical access is primarily by row, then the array should be laid out in row-major order, and the rows should be a multiple of b elements long. Thus each row will start in bank 0, and a loop accessing a row can be trivially bank-disambiguated by simple unrolling. For example, consider this typical inner loop accessing a row of a 100×256 array (assume $b = 8$):

```
FOR j:=1 TO n UNROLL 8
    ...a[i,j]...
```

The intermediate code for the unrolled references `a[i,j]` looks like:

```
t1:=256*i
t2:=t1+j
x :=a[t2]
```

The index derivations for the 8 references have the form $256 * i + j + c$ where c is between 0 and 7. With the appropriate assertion at the top of the loop, $(256 * i + j + c) \bmod 8$ is c; thus the cth reference in the loop is to bank c.

Similarly, if the time-critical access to an array is by columns, then it should be laid out in column-major order, and the columns should be a multiple of b elements long.

Constraining the row- or column-length of arrays to be a multiple of b isn't a serious restriction for most applications. If the actual input sizes aren't divisible by b, it's usually a simple matter to pad out the inputs with appropriate dummy values (typically zeros).

Once an array is so constrained, it is possible to pass cross sections consisting of one or more entire rows to procedures (if the array is row-major). The cross sections are guaranteed to start in bank 0.

Simple unrolling and array padding can accommodate only one access direction, either by row or by column. If time-critical code accesses an array in both directions, then control transformations must be used to bank-disambiguate the accesses in the other direction.

Another layout trick is to merge several vectors that are accessed in parallel into a single array, each vector forming a column of the array. For example, in the routine EOS from the SIMPLE benchmark, the inner loop evaluates a polynomial whose 7 constants are drawn from the vectors a, b, c, d, e, f, and g, each of length n:

```
x[0]*a[j] + x[1]*b[j] + ... x[7]*g[j]
```

The index j is obtained indirectly from a table each time through the loop, so loop unrolling won't help here. But by laying out the 7 vectors as columns in an

$n \times 8$ array w (the 8th column is padding):

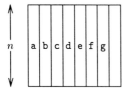

the bank of the vector accesses can now be predicted (assuming $b = 8$). All **a** elements are in bank 0, all **b** elements in bank 1, all **c** elements in bank 2, and so on. To evaluate a polynomial, the jth row (a[j], b[j], ..., g[j]) is fetched in parallel. Because each row starts in bank 0, the fetch of row j is completely bank-disambiguated regardless of the value of j.

Another way to think of this transformation is that the array w is a vector of records, each record having 7 fields **a** through **g**, with a dummy padding field to make the record fall on 8-word boundaries.

This trick was also used to bank-disambiguate QK61 (the kernel of an adaptive quadrature package) and the constant-table accesses of the inline SIN and COS library functions.

Of course, Fortran doesn't give the programmer any tools for controlling array layouts; the programmer is forced to implement different layouts by manually editing the program. One of the advantages of using a Lisp-embedded language like Tinylisp is that tools like macros and inline procedures make non-standard data layouts easy. For example, arrays in Tinylisp are always row-major; but a column-major array a is easily implemented by using a row-major array work_a and an inline procedure that expands a[i,j] into work_a[j,i].

Control Transformations

Reversing the loop. Suppose a loop has the form:

```
FOR i:=j TO n
    ...v[i]...
```

where $n \bmod b$ and base(v) are known, but $j \bmod b$ isn't. If the iterations of the loop are data-independent or if the loop implements an associative vector reduction (such as adding the elements of a vector), the iteration sequence can be reversed:

```
FOR i:=n TO j BY -1
    ...v[i]...
```

When normal loop unrolling is applied, $i \bmod b$ will always be 0 at the top of the unrolled loop, and the vector references will be completely bank-disambiguated.

Often n is the upper bound of the vector or array row being accessed. As discussed above, a few extra padding elements usually can be added to the vector to make n a multiple of b.

This transformation was used for SOLVE (LU decomposition) and SVD (singular value decomposition).

Adding a preloop. The worst-case loop has the form:

```
FOR i:=j TO k
    ...v[i]...
```

where either base(v) mod b or both j mod b and k mod b are unknown. To bank-disambiguate the references, a preloop can be added that executes a copy of the loop body at most $b - 1$ times until base$(v) + i$ hits a known bank; control then transfers into the main loop:

```
FOR i:=j TO k
    IF (BASE(v)+i) mod b = 0 THEN
        temp:=i
        EXITLOOP
    body

ASSERT (BASE(v)+temp) MOD b = 0

FOR i:=temp TO k UNROLL b
    body
```

The preloop can't be disambiguated, but the main loop can, using simple unrolling.

The problem with adding preloops is that there is significant overhead when the number of iterations is small. To get a feel for the problem, let's consider an 8-cluster machine with $b = 8$. Suppose that the loop implements a simple element-wise vector operation. Thus we can expect close to an 8-fold speed-up of the main loop compared to a sequential machine. But because the preloop is constrained to fetch one element per cycle through the back door, it won't be much faster than the sequential machine.

Assume that one iteration of the sequential version of the loop body takes c cycles and that the body is executed n times. Then the sequential version takes time:

$$s = nc$$

In the transformed version, the preloop body is executed about 3.5 times on the average before transferring to the main loop; the time of the preloop is:

$$p = 3.5c$$

The main loop takes time:

$$l = \frac{(n - 3.5)c}{8}$$

yielding a total time on the parallel machine of:

$$t = p + l = 3.5c + \frac{(n - 3.5)c}{8}$$

The following table shows, for an increasing number of iterations n, the speed-up of the transformed loop over the original sequential loop (s/t) and the percentage of time spent in the preloop relative to the total time of the transformed loop (p/t):

n	s/t	p/t (%)
8	2.0	.86
16	3.2	.69
32	4.5	.50
64	5.8	.32
128	6.7	.18
256	7.3	.10
512	7.6	.05
1024	7.8	.03

By these estimates, there is quite a bit of overhead for loops with less than 100 iterations, and 500 iterations are needed to approach full utilization of the machine. Unfortunately, the inner loops of many scientific programs originally written for scalar architectures often have less than 100 iterations. This is a problem with vector machines like the Cray-I as well; the same techniques used to increase the vector sizes on a vector machine can be applied here.

Because of its overhead, adding a preloop should be the transformation of last resort. In my library of benchmarks, only one program, EOS, required a preloop.

Merging with outer loops. A number of scientific programs access multi-dimensional arrays by both rows and columns. The row accesses can be bank-disambiguated by unrolling and padding, but some other transformation is needed for the column accesses. A preloop won't work for the column accesses, because all the elements of a column are in the same bank. However, the doubly and triply nested loops can often be rearranged to bank-disambiguate the column accesses with little overhead.

The typical example of mixed row and column accessing is matrix multiplication. The definition of $Z = XY$ is:

$$z_{i,j} = x_{i,*} \cdot y_{*,j} = \sum_k x_{i,k} y_{k,j}$$

where $x_{i,*}$ denotes the ith row vector of X and $y_{*,j}$ the jth column vector of Y. The common implementation of that on scalar machines is:

```
FOR i:=1 TO m
    FOR j:=1 TO o
        sum:=0
        FOR k:=1 TO n
            sum:=sum + x[i,k]*y[k,j]
        z[i,j]:=sum
```

The innermost loop moves across the ith row of x and down the jth column of y. Assuming the arrays are in row-major format and the rows are padded to have a multiple of b elements, unrolling the loop will bank-disambiguate the references to x but not y. Adding a preloop won't work here because all the elements of the kth column of y are in the same bank and thus must be fetched sequentially.

A general solution for bank-disambiguating column accesses is to process b columns at a time in the inner loop. In matrix multiply, that means forming b dot products in parallel:

$$z_{i,j+0} = x_{i,*} \cdot y_{*,j+0}$$
$$z_{i,j+1} = x_{i,*} \cdot y_{*,j+1}$$
$$\cdots$$

$$z_{i,j+b-1} = x_{i,*} \cdot y_{*,j+b-1}$$

The implementation of this is (assuming $b = 8$):

```
FOR i:=1 TO m
    FOR j:=1 TO o BY 8
        sum0:=0
        sum1:=0
        . . .
        sum7:=0
        FOR k:=1 TO n
            sum0:=sum0 + x[i,k]*y[k,j+0]
            sum1:=sum1 + x[i,k]*y[k,j+1]
            . . .
            sum7:=sum7 + x[i,k]*y[k,j+7]
        z[i,j+0]:=sum0
        z[i,j+1]:=sum1
        . . .
        z[i,j+7]:=sum7
```

The code assumes both arrays have rows with a multiple of b elements. Because j is now always a multiple of 8, the references to y in the inner loop are trivially bank-disambiguated. When the inner loop is unrolled 8 times, the references to x will also be bank-disambiguated, and there will be 8 references to each of the 8 banks.

This method of folding an outer loop into an inner one is often used on vector machines—the variables sum$i$ are stored in a vector register (which on the Cray-I has 64 elements). A nice side effect of the transformation on matrix multiply is that the number of memory references to x have been reduced by a factor of b (the compiler identifies the b occurrences of x[i,k] as a common subexpression).

A seeming disadvantage of the transformation is that the inner loop must be unrolled at least b^2 times: b times for x and b times for y. For $b = 8$ or $b = 16$ this isn't a major problem, but for larger values it is impractical. But for the larger values of b, the transformed inner loop doesn't really need to be unrolled an extra factor of b times. There would be 1 back-door reference to x and b front-door references to y, and the extra time needed for the back-door reference would be insignificant.

In addition to matrix multiply, this transformation was also used for SVD (singular value decomposition).

The transformation assumes that the initial or final column is in a known bank. If it isn't, then a preloop must be added that processes one column at a time until a known bank is encountered.

Skewing arrays. Another possible method for disambiguating arrays accessed by both rows and columns involves a data transformation as well as a control transformation. The rows of the array are padded so that their length is relatively prime to b. Thus, any successive b elements from a row or column will be in b different banks. This evens out the memory load for loops accessing an individual column, since b successive elements of a column can be fetched in parallel. But now neither the rows nor the columns necessarily start in bank 0, and preloops must be used for both row and column-oriented loops.

Given the overhead of preloops, loop merging is preferable for column access; skewing arrays should be used only when loop merging isn't possible, such as when both individual columns and rows are accessed "randomly" instead of successively. However, I don't know of a scientific program that accesses rows and columns like that; only two library programs, matrix multiply and singular value decomposition, have mixed row and column accessing, and loop merging is feasible for both.

Interesting aside: Memory architectures have been proposed for vector machines that have a prime number of banks. Most arrays in programs don't have dimensions that are divisible by, say, 17. Thus, there is a high probability that the memory references of most cross sections, whether by row, column, or diagonal, will be evenly distributed among the banks. In effect, the hardware is skewing the arrays automatically. Unfortunately, these architectures presuppose a central memory controller, which is precisely what VLIWs are trying to avoid.

There is little reason to have the hardware skewing if the compiler can do it instead, especially considering that when b isn't a power of two, special memory hardware is required. In practice, given an array, a value for b, and the small set of accessing patterns used on the array by a real program, it is likely that the array can be skewed by the programmer or compiler so as to bank-disambiguate all the memory references and fully utilize all the banks, while requiring only a little extra memory for padding the array.

Three Programs

Most of the programs in the benchmark library were easily bank-disambiguated using the techniques described above. However, three of the programs required special transformations.

TRID4. TRID4 is a tridiagonal solver using cyclic reduction. Its inner loops have the form:

```
FOR i:=1 TO l
    FOR j:=j0[i] TO m[i]
        ...v[j]...
```

At first glance, the inner loop appears to require a preloop, since both the initial and final values of the loop variable j are variable. But an examination of the algorithm reveals that the array j0 contains the following values:

$$j0[1] = n$$

$$j0[2] = n + \left\lfloor \frac{n}{2} \right\rfloor$$

$$j0[3] = n + \left\lfloor \frac{n}{2} \right\rfloor + \left\lfloor \frac{n}{4} \right\rfloor$$

$$\cdots$$

$$j0[l] = n + \left\lfloor \frac{n}{2} \right\rfloor + \left\lfloor \frac{n}{4} \right\rfloor + \cdots \left\lfloor \frac{n}{2^{l-2}} \right\rfloor + \left\lfloor \frac{n}{2^{l-1}} \right\rfloor$$

where n is the size of the input vector v and

$$\frac{n}{2^{l-2}} \geq c > \frac{n}{2^{l-1}}.$$

The constant c is specified in the implementation ($c = 20$ in the current version).

Assuming b is a power of two, the values in j0 will be divisible by b if the input size n is constrained to be a power of two and c is chosen such that $c \geq b$. Thus the initial value of j in the inner loop will always be divisible by

b, and simple loop unrolling and an assertion will bank-disambiguate the vector references.

(When n is a power of two, up to 2 times the actual input size is needed for the arrays. But if $c \geq 3b$, n needn't be a power of two; it could be either 2^i or $3 * 2^i$ for some i, and the values of j0 will still be divisible by b; in this case, at most only 50% extra space is needed. Similarly, if $c \geq 5b$, n may have any of the forms 2^i, $3 * 2^i$, or $5 * 2^i$, and at most 33% extra space will be needed. However, increasing c increases the running time of the algorithm somewhat.)

SVD. SVD computes the singular value decomposition of an $m \times n$ array u. Most of the time-critical array accesses can be disambiguated by unrolling and padding the rows. But one time-critical section of the original version of SVD accessed u by columns.

The column accessing performs the following operations:

$$u_{i:m,j} := u_{i:m,j} + ((u_{i:m,i} \cdot u_{i:m,j})/h) * u_{i:m,i}, \qquad \text{for } i < j \leq n$$

where $u_{i:m,j}$ represents the vector formed by taking elements i through m from the jth column of u. The original implementation of this did one column at a time:

```
FOR j:=i+1 TO n
    sum:=0
    FOR k:=i TO m
        sum:=sum + u[k,i]*u[k,j]
    f:=sum/h
    FOR k:=i TO m
        u[k,j]:=u[k,j] + f*u[k,i]
```

Loop unrolling and array padding won't work here, and a preloop will have too much overhead (especially considering that i goes from 1 to n-1).

But the loops can be rewritten to do row accesses instead. The vector expression is split into two parts, the first part doing the dot products for all the columns j and storing them in a temporary vector f[1:n]:

$$f_j := (u_{i:m,i} \cdot u_{i:m,j})/h, \qquad \text{for } i < j \leq n$$
$$u_{i:m,j} := u_{i:m,j} + f_j * u_{i:m,i}, \qquad \text{for } i < j \leq n$$

The first part can be implemented using loop merging, doing b columns at a time:

```
FOR j:=n TO i+1 BY -b
    ASSERT j MOD b = 0
    sum[0]:=sum[1]:= ... :=sum[b-1]:=0
    FOR k:=i TO m
        uki:=u[k,i]
        sum[0]:=sum[0] + uki*u[k,j-0]
        sum[1]:=sum[1] + uki*u[k,j-1]
        ...
        sum[b-1]:=sum[b-1] + uki*u[k,j-b+1]
    f[j-0]   := sum[0] / h
    f[j-1]   := sum[1] / h
    ...
    f[j-b+1] := sum[b-1] / h
```

All but one of the vector references are now to known banks. Notice that the outer loop has been reversed so that $j \bmod b$ is always 0; for this to work the array must be padded so that $n \bmod b = 0$. Also notice that the last iteration through the outer loop might overshoot the final value $i + 1$ and compute up to $b - 1$ extra dot products. But that's ok—the extra dot products will be computed in parallel with the ones actually needed and will be ignored later on.

The second part of the expression:

$$u_{i:m,j} := u_{i:m,j} + f_j * u_{i:m,i}, \qquad \text{for } i < j \leq n$$

is an element-wise array expression that can be done by rows just as well as by columns:

$$u_{k,i+1:n} := u_{k,i+1:n} + f_{i+1:n} * u_{k,i}, \qquad \text{for } i \leq k \leq m$$

The code for this is:

```
FOR k:=i TO m
    uki:=u[k,i]
    FOR j:=n TO i+1 BY -1 UNROLL b
        u[k,j]:=u[k,j] + f[j]*uki
```

All the vector references but one are now to known banks, and that one isn't in the inner loop. Notice that the inner loop has been bank-disambiguated by reversing it and unrolling it b times.

Finally, even though a temporary vector f has been introduced, the total number of memory references is less than the original implementation for most values of m and n. Assume $m = n$ (in many applications $m \approx n$). The variable i iterates from 1 to $n - 1$, so the total number of memory references done by the old and the new versions is:

$$r_{old} = \sum_{1 \leq i < n} 5i(i+1)$$

$$r_{new} = \sum_{1 \leq i < n} (4 + 1/b)i(i+1) + i + 1$$

Asymptotically, the new version does about 18% fewer memory references when $b = 8$.

FFT. Of all the programs, the Fast Fourier Transform required the most complicated transformations. For the following transformations to work, the input size n must be a multiple of b, both n and b must be powers of two, and $n \geq b^2$.

First let's consider the shuffle part of FFT:

```
FOR i:=0 TO n-1
    v[i]:=u[ BR(i,n) ]
```

`BR(i,n)` is the bit-reversal of the binary representation of i using a word of $\log n$ bits.

None of the techniques presented above could possibly bank-disambiguate this loop. Instead, we'll rewrite the loop, in the process unrolling it b^2 times. Let $d = n/b$; by the initial assumptions, $d \bmod b = 0$. For simplicity, assume $b = 4$; the transformation extends naturally to larger values. The loop will move 16 elements at a time from u into v, in 4 groups of 4:

```
v[i]     through  v[i+3]
v[i+d]   through  v[i+d+3]
v[i+2d]  through  v[i+2d+3]
v[i+3d]  through  v[i+3d+3]
```

The loop variable i will go from 0 to `d-1` in increments of 4:

```
FOR i:=0 TO d-1 BY 4
    FOR j:=0 TO 3
        FOR k:=0 TO 3
            v[i+j*d+k]:=u[ BR(i+j*d+k) ]
```

When the two inner loops are unrolled completely, all 32 vector references will have known banks:

Reference	Bank	Reference	Bank
v[i+0*d+0]	0	u[BR(i+0*d+0)]	0
v[i+0*d+1]	1	u[BR(i+0*d+1)]	0
v[i+0*d+2]	2	u[BR(i+0*d+2)]	0
v[i+0*d+3]	3	u[BR(i+0*d+3)]	0
v[i+1*d+0]	0	u[BR(i+1*d+0)]	1
v[i+1*d+1]	1	u[BR(i+1*d+1)]	1
v[i+1*d+2]	2	u[BR(i+1*d+2)]	1
v[i+1*d+3]	3	u[BR(i+1*d+3)]	1
v[i+2*d+0]	0	u[BR(i+2*d+0)]	2
v[i+2*d+1]	1	u[BR(i+2*d+1)]	2
v[i+2*d+2]	2	u[BR(i+2*d+2)]	2
v[i+2*d+3]	3	u[BR(i+2*d+3)]	2
v[i+3*d+0]	0	u[BR(i+3*d+0)]	3
v[i+3*d+1]	1	u[BR(i+3*d+1)]	3
v[i+3*d+2]	2	u[BR(i+3*d+2)]	3
v[i+3*d+3]	3	u[BR(i+3*d+3)]	3

You can convince yourself by writing out the values of the indices i+j*d+k and looking at the low order $\log b$ bits and the high order $\log b$ bits. But even with the two loops unrolled, there is no way the symbolic analysis could discover the residue of BR(i+j*d+k). So 16 assertions must be manually added:

```
ASSERT BR(i+0*d+0) MOD 4 = 0
ASSERT BR(i+0*d+1) MOD 4 = 0
...
ASSERT BR(i+3*d+3) MOD 4 = 3
```

A nice property of this transformation is that the memory references and the communication between banks are uniformly distributed among the banks.

The main loop of FFT looks like:

```
FOR i:=1, 2, 4, ..., n/2
    FOR j:=0 TO n-1 BY 2*i
        FOR k:=0 TO i-1
            ...v[k+j]...v[k+j+i]...
```

None of the standard techniques can bank-disambiguate this code. But look what happens when the first three iterations of the *outer* loop are unrolled (assume now that $b = 8$):

```
i:=1
FOR j:=0 TO n-1 BY 2 UNROLL 8
    k:=0
    ...v[k+j]...v[k+j+i]...

i:=2
FOR j:=0 TO n-1 BY 4 UNROLL 4
    k:=0
    ...v[k+j]...v[k+j+i]...
    k:=1
    ...v[k+j]...v[k+j+i]...

i:=4
FOR j:=0 TO n-1 BY 8 UNROLL 2
    k:=0
    ...v[k+j]...v[k+j+i]...
    k:=1
    ...v[k+j]...v[k+j+i]...
    k:=2
    ...v[k+j]...v[k+j+i]...
    k:=3
    ...v[k+j]...v[k+j+i]...

FOR i:=8, 16, ..., n/2
    FOR j:=0 TO n-1 BY 2*i
        FOR k:=0 TO i-1 UNROLL 8
            ...v[k+j]...v[k+j+i]...
```

At the top of each unrolled inner loop, $(k + j) \bmod b = 0$ and $(k + j + i) \bmod b$ is known. Thus all the vector references now have known banks. This special unrolling also eliminates the large overhead due to the many short iterations of the inner loop. Experiments showed that this unrolling increased the available parallelism by a factor of 4. Rodrigue [Rodrigue 82] discusses other methods for eliminating the overhead for vector machines.

Automating the Transformations

Of all the bank-disambiguating transformations presented, the compiler implements only loop unrolling, and even there the programmer must specify how much to unroll and the corresponding assertions. All other transformations must be done manually by the programmer. What's the prospect of automating them?

It would be easy to change the compiler to allocate all array rows in multiples of b elements. And it wouldn't be too hard to automatically detect the situations where simple unrolling, possibly aided by loop reversal, would suffice. The compiler could even add in preloops when no other transformation is applicable.

But one of the most valuable control transformations, rewriting nested loops that manipulate arrays, is very hard. Allen and Kennedy [Allen 84] have implemented a system for applying similar sorts of transformations to code intended for vector machines. Most likely many of the same techniques could be modified for use here. But they are complicated, and not very general.

As I'll discuss in the last chapter, perhaps a better long-term approach is to forget low-level languages like Fortran, and instead use a notation like APL that expresses the array operations directly. It would then be much easier for the compiler to choose loop structures for implementing the array operations of an expression; by construction the array references would be automatically bank-disambiguated.

Non-vectors

What about data structures other than vectors? There is no clear answer. Dynamically allocated objects can have any size and can fall on any bank. However, if objects are allocated in sizes that are multiples of b, then clearly every object begins on a known bank. Whether this is practical for many programs, I don't know, since I've only fully investigated scientific applications, whose data structures are usually large arrays.

Chapter 7
Code Generation

The code generator gets a trace of operations as input and produces parallel machine code as output, treating the trace as if it were one very large basic block. There are three main phases: representing the trace as a DAG (directed acyclic graph), functional unit assignment, and list scheduling.

As in many traditional code generators, the intermediate-code operations of the trace are converted into a DAG. The nodes of the DAG represent operations, and there is an edge between two nodes if one node uses the value produced by another. To prevent illegal code motions past jumps and undisambiguated memory references, new edges are introduced to prevent one node from being evaluated before another.

The assignment phase performs operation placement, picking functional units for each of the intermediate-code operators in an attempt to get maximum utilization of the machine. It is analogous to the register allocation of traditional compilers, and in fact was inspired by the top-down-greedy register-allocation algorithm [Barrett 79]. Traditional register allocation tries to assign a limited set of registers to the operations of the DAG, minimizing the movement of data between registers and memory. Analogously, the assignment phase allocates functional units to intermediate-code operations, minimizing the costly movements of data between distant functional units and the delays caused by contention for heavily used units.

The list-scheduling phase actually generates machine instructions, using a first-fit algorithm that originated in processor scheduling but has since been widely used for compilation [Sites 78, Fisher 79, Touzeau 84]. The list scheduler forms a **schedule** of instructions by enumerating the DAG nodes in some topological order, packing operations into machine instructions.

The interface to the trace scheduler makes code generation more complex. A trace may give locations of the live variables at the beginning of the trace or at the end of the trace or both. If locations for the live variables at the beginning are given, the code generator must use them as the initial variable locations; otherwise the code generator is free to assign registers to variables. Similarly, if locations for the live variables at the end are given, then the code generator must ensure that the variables end up in those locations, moving them if necessary; if no locations are given, then the code generator may leave the live variables wherever convenient.

After it forms the schedule of machine instructions, the trace scheduler will splice the schedule back into the flow graph. To aid the trace scheduler in its

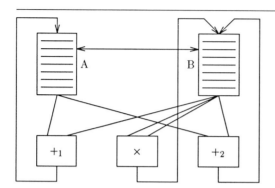

Figure 7.1. An example machine model.

bookkeeping, the code generator must maintain a map between intermediate-code operations and the corresponding machine operations in the schedule. At the boundaries of the trace (at the beginning, the end, conditional jumps, and joins into the middle) the code generator must also report the locations of live variables, so that adjoining traces will know where to find them.

An Example

Before describing code generation in detail, let's consider a simple example that illustrates some of the complexity of code generation. Suppose that the compiler is compiling for the (unrealistic) machine model shown in 7.1.

There are two register banks A and B, two adders (denoted +1 and +2), and a multiplier. Each adder can read its operands from either or both register banks but must write its result in one particular bank. The multiplier reads its operands and writes its result to bank B only. Additions and multiplies take 2 cycles. If necessary, a value can be moved directly from one bank to the other. Two values can be read and one written to each bank every cycle.

Figure 7.2 shows a sample trace of intermediate-code instructions, the DAG constructed from the trace, and a possible schedule for the machine model. The leaves of the DAG are at the top and the roots at the bottom. (Unlike most academics, I draw DAGs this way because they are easier to read: Evaluation of the DAG proceeds naturally from top to bottom, just like the linear code the DAG represents.)

Variables m, n, and q are live on entry to the trace, and t, u, q, and s are live on exit. The nodes are labeled with their variable name, the functional unit chosen for the node by the assignment phase, and the register chosen for the node during list scheduling. Note that at least 4 cycles will be needed for any

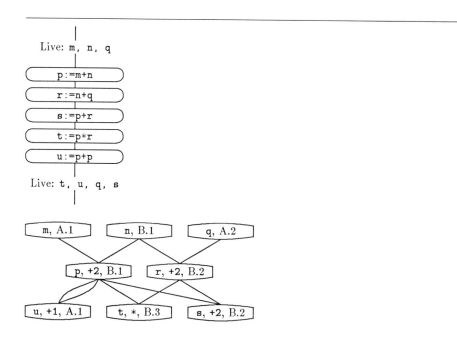

USE m A.1, n B.1, q A.2

1	r(B.2):=n(B.1) +2 q(A.2)		
2	+2-2	p(B.1):=m(A.1) +2 n(B.1)	
3		+2-2	
4	t(B.3):=p(B.1) * r(B.2)	s(B.2):=p(B.1) +2 r(B.2)	u(A.1):=p(B.1) +1 p(B.1)
5	*	+2-2	+1-2

DEF s B.2, t B.3, u A.1, q A.2

Figure 7.2. An example trace and the corresponding DAG and schedule produced by the code generator.

schedule, since the longest path from an entrance to an exit of the DAG contains 2 operations.

The schedule shown is 5 cycles long and is optimal. Four cycles are not enough, because the multiplier requires both of its operands to be in bank B—p and r must either be computed using +2 or else one or both of them computed using +1, requiring an extra cycle to move the results from bank A to bank B. If the compiler had mistakenly chosen +1 for both of the first two additions instead of +2, the schedule would have been one cycle longer. Note that in cycle 4, only 2 values are read from the banks even though three operations are initiated; a value appearing on a bank's output port can be read by many functional units.

The USE pseudo-op at the beginning of the schedule records for later traces the registers chosen to hold the trace's input variables. The DEF pseudo-op at the end records the registers where the output variables were left.

Building the DAG

The trace scheduler supplies the code generator with a trace of intermediate-code operations from which the code generator builds a DAG. The DAG-builder uses techniques similar to those used by traditional compilers for basic blocks [Aho 77]. You should be familiar with these techniques before reading any further in this chapter.

Supplied with the trace are the set of variables live on entrance to the beginning of the trace and the set of variables live on exit at the end. With each conditional jump in the trace is the set of variables live on the off-trace branch of the jump. These sets completely define the variables live at the boundaries of the trace. (The live variables at joins into the middle of the trace can be inferred from the operations below the join and the live-on-exit variables.) If a variable is live at some exit (either the end or at a conditional jump), then the code generator must preserve its value in some location until the exit.

At the beginning of the trace there may be an optional DEF pseudo-op that specifies initial register or memory locations for all the live-on-entry variables. At the end of the trace there may be a optional USE pseudo-op that specifies the required final locations for all the live-on-exit variables. The DEFs and USEs indicate the locations of variables assumed by earlier-compiled traces abutting the current trace. (Chapter 4 describes DEFs and USEs in detail.)

If a DEF isn't present, the code generator is free to assign initial locations to variables however it wishes (presumably minimizing data movements). If the DEF is present, the code generator must use the initial locations it specifies. Similarly, if a USE isn't present, the code generator may leave live-on-exit variables lying around wherever convenient; if the USE is present, then the code generator must guarantee that the variables end up in the final locations specified.

If a trace variable is live on entry and live on one of the exits (either at the end or at a conditional jump), and there are no initial locations for live-on-entry variables (that is, there is no DEF), then the code generator is responsible for assigning a location that will hold the variable for the duration of the trace. Even if the variable isn't read by any of the trace operations, the code generator must still assign a location to the variable. Later traces abutting this trace will then have a known place in which to find or store the variable.

Nodes and Edges

As in a traditional basic-block DAG, every operation in the trace becomes a node in the DAG. There are operand edges from an operation node to each of the nodes representing the operands.

Each live-on-entry variable is represented by a special DEF node, which represents the variable's initial value. Operations that read the entry-value of a variable will have an operand edge to the DEF node of the variable. If one or more initial locations for the variable are given for the variable in a DEF pseudo-op at the beginning of the trace, those locations are recorded in the variable's DEF node.

Each live-on-exit variable is represented by a special USE node. For each USE node there is an operand edge to the node for the operation that last assigned the variable in the trace. If no operation in the trace assigns the variable, then there is an edge directly from the USE to the DEF representing the variable's initial value. If one or more final locations were given for the variable via a USE pseudo-op at the end of the trace, those locations are recorded in the USE.

USE nodes have two purposes: to record the final locations of a variable and to keep that variable "alive" through the entire trace. Normally, after all nodes reading some node's value have been scheduled, the register holding the node's value can be deallocated and used for some other purpose. But USE nodes are never scheduled, so the register holding the corresponding value will never be deallocated.

As an example, figure 7.3 shows a sample trace and its corresponding DAG.

Constants

There are three types of constants in the intermediate code: numbers, vector bases, and addresses. A vector base, notated VBASE(v), is the address of the first element of a vector v; vector bases are often parameters to subroutines, so they are run-time, but not compile-time, constants. An address of a variable x is notated ADDRESS(X), and an address of the constant 3.5e-2 stored in memory is notated ADDRESS(3.5e-2).

Constants are further differentiated as immediate and non-immediate. Immediate constants are always produced by constant generators (usually fields

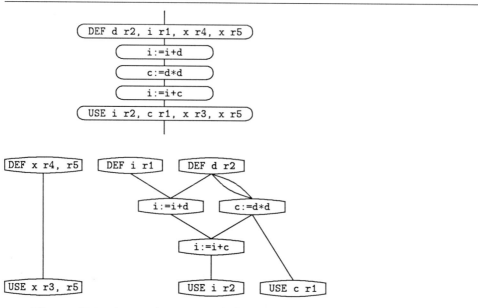

Figure 7.3. A sample trace and the corresponding DAG.

within the instruction word). They are either used directly by an operation (if the functional unit is connected to the constant generator) or kept in one or more registers during the trace until their last use. Every distinct immediate constant on the trace gets a separate DEF node in the DAG, and an operation node reading the constant has an operand edge to the DEF node.

Every non-immediate constant on the trace is loaded from memory before its first use and then kept in one or more registers for the duration of the trace. So a non-immediate constant c gets expanded into two nodes, a DEF for the memory address of c (which is itself an immediate constant) followed by a memory load.

For example, this trace fragment:

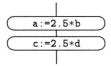

would get transformed into this DAG:

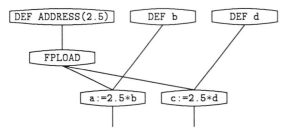

The `FPLOAD` operator takes a single operand, an address, and fetches the float stored at that address.

A constant never has a final `USE` node, and its value in registers is discarded immediately after the last use. (Loading a constant from memory for each trace that uses it may sound inefficient; a later section discusses this.)

Variables and Constraining Edges

During execution a variable x takes on a sequence of many values, $x_1, x_2, x_3, \ldots$ The current value of a variable often resides in many different locations at one time in the machine. For reasons presented in a later section, the lifetimes of a variable's values cannot overlap; that is, x cannot be assigned both x_i and $x_i + 1$ at the same time. Intuitively, a variable can have only one value at a time, and its value cannot be changed until all the uses of the current value have been evaluated.

For example, in the following trace fragment:

```
1. x:=y-z
2. a:=b+x
3. c:=x-d
4. x:=e+f
```

operation 4, which writes x, must not be executed until after operations 2 and 3 have read the previous value of x. Even if the two different values of x are kept in separate registers, operation 4 must still follow 2 and 3.

To implement this restriction, special constraining edges are added to the DAG. For every operation that assigns x, there is a **write-after-read** constraining edge from that operation to each operation that reads the previous value of x; there is also a **write-after-write** constraining edge to the previous operation assigning x. For the example above, the DAG looks like:

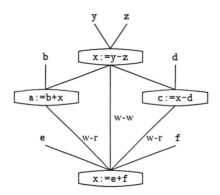

The write-after read edges are marked "w-r" and the write-after-write edges "w-w."

Because registers are read at the beginning of a cycle and written at the end, an operation assigning x can occur in the same cycle as the last use of the previous value of x. In this example:

1. a:=b+x
2. x:=c+d

operation 2 could be executed in the same cycle as 1 or later but no earlier. That is, a write-after-read edge constrains the writing node to be executed no earlier than the reading node. (Fisher called these write-after-read edges "equal edges" [Fisher 79] because the nodes were allowed to be executed in the same cycle.)

You might think that the write-after-read edges could restrict parallelism unnecessarily. Consider this trace:

1. x:=a+b
2. c:=x+1
3. d:=x*2
4. x:=e+f
5. g:=x+1
6. h:=x*2

Intuitively, operations 4–6 could be done in parallel with operations 1–3. But the write-after-read edges will constrain 4 to be done after both 2 and 3, reducing the amount of available parallelism. However, variable renaming (see chapter 2) will rename x in operations 4–6 to be a new variable x1:

1. `x:=a+b`
2. `c:=x+1`
3. `d:=x*2`
4. `x1:=e+f`
5. `g:=x1+1`
6. `h:=x1*2`

In this optimized fragment, there are no edges from operations 4–6 to operations 1–3, and the two groups could be executed in parallel.

Variable renaming can not eliminate all write-after-read edges. For example, part of a trace of the body of an inner loop might look like:

1. `j:=i/3`
   `...`
2. `i:=i+1`

Assuming i is a loop induction variable, the definition of i by operation 2 could not be renamed, since it is directly used by 1 and itself. So there must be a write-after-read edge from 2 to 1; that is, the increment of i must occur after all the operations that read the previous value of i.

Assignment Means Copy

No two variables can share the same physical location at the same time. In general, the assignment operation must physically move the value being assigned into a new location. To see why actual copying is necessary, consider this fragment of a flow graph:

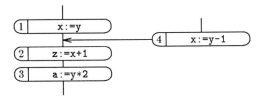

Suppose a trace included operations 1, 2, and 3, and assume that the code generator didn't actually generate a copy for `x:=y` but merely updated its variable-location information to indicate that x and y were located in the same location for operations 2 and 3. That would be incorrect, since on the execution path 4–2–3, x and y have different values and hence must have different locations.

So the assignment `x:=y` must be implemented by the code generator as a copy of the value of y into some new location. The assignment is represented by a special DAG node called a COPY node, with an operand edge to the node corresponding to y. COPY nodes are treated specially during the later phases of code generation.

Implementing assignment as copying contrasts with basic-block code generators, which can implement an assignment x:=y merely by attaching the label x (signifying the current value of x) to the node currently representing y. But as the example above shows, trace-based code generators must worry about joins into the middle of the sequence of operations, whereas basic-block code generators don't.

Fortunately, copy propagation and dead-code removal eliminate useless assignments from a program [Aho 77]. The only assignments left in a program after these optimizations are those that really must be implemented as a copy to a new location. As an example of these optimizations, the basic block

```
x:=y
z:=x+1
a:=x*2
```

would be transformed by copy propagation into

```
x:=y
z:=y+1
a:=y*2
```

and then the assignment x:=y would get deleted by dead-code removal:

```
z:=y+1
a:=y*2
```

Conditional Jumps

Basic-block code generators are guaranteed that a block contains at most one conditional jump and that it will be at the end of the block. But a trace may have several conditional jumps occuring anywhere in the trace; such jumps require further constraints on the evaluation order of DAG nodes.

Consider this fragment of a flow graph:

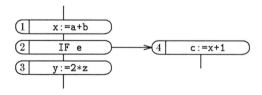

Assume that the current trace includes operations 1–3 and that x is dead on entry to 3. If 1 is evaluated before 2 in the generated schedule, then the register holding the value of x must remain allocated to x until after the conditional jump is evaluated, because the value of x is live on the off-trace edge of the jump, read by operation 4. After the jump executes, though, the register can be reused.

So in some sense the jump "reads" the value of x because x is **off-live** at the jump (live on the off-trace edge). By adding an operand edge from 2 to 1 in the DAG, we could guarantee that the register holding x will remain allocated to x until after the jump is executed. But such an edge would be too restrictive because there is no reason why 1 couldn't be scheduled after 2:

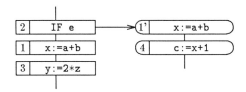

(The bookkeeper would place the copy 1' on the off-trace edge after code generation.) If an operand edge were placed from 2 to 1, this possibility would be disallowed, since the code generator would then be forced by topological ordering to schedule 2 after 1.

Instead of an operand edge, another edge type is used. An **off-live edge** is placed from every conditional jump to each operation producing a value that is live on the off-trace edge of the jump. Off-live edges are ignored for the purposes of topological ordering during scheduling; their only use is to inform the code generator when registers holding the values of off-live variables may be reused.

Another complication of conditional jumps is illustrated below:

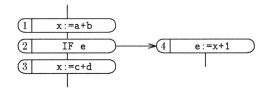

Assume the trace includes operations 1–3; because 4 reads x, x is off-live at the conditional jump. Operation 3 must not be scheduled before 2, since its execution before the jump would cause 4 to read the wrong value of x. So a **write-after-conditional-read** constraining edge must be added from 3 to 2 that will ensure that 2 is evaluated first; in effect, the jump "reads" the off-live value of x.

Write-after-conditional-read edges are like write-after-read edges, except that the writing node must be evaluated strictly after the conditional jump; if it were evaluated in the same cycle, the off-live variable would still get the wrong value. As with write-after-read edges, variable renaming will eliminate superficial write-after-conditional-read conflicts by renaming disparate uses of variable names.

Vector References and the Disambiguator

Vector operations include the vector address as one of their operands. For example, v[i]:=x would be represented in the DAG as:

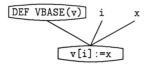

In addition to the normal operand edges, constraining edges must be added to force undisambiguated pairs of vector references to be evaluated in source order. For example:

1. x:=v[i]
2. v[j]:=y

If the disambiguator reports that v[i] could possibly refer to the same location as v[j], the DAG-builder will add a **vector-conflict** edge from operation 2 to operation 1 that will constrain 2 to be evaluated after 1:

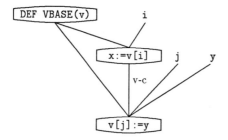

(If 2 were evaluated before 1, x could get the wrong value if j happened to equal i.) However, if the disambiguator reports that v[i] and v[j] refer to different locations, then they can be evaluated in any relative order, and no constraining edge is needed.

When building a node for a vector reference, the DAG-builder looks at each previous reference on the trace to the same vector such that one of the references is a vector store. (That is, if the current reference is a store, it looks at previous stores and loads; if the current reference is a load, it looks only at previous stores.) For each such pair of vector references, the DAG-builder asks the disambiguator if they could be to the same location; if the disambiguator answers *maybe* or *yes*, it adds a vector-conflict edge from the current reference to the previous one.

You might guess that if the answer is *yes*, the two references are to the same location, then the disambiguator might be able to eliminate one of the references. For example, given the following trace:

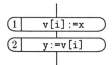

the code generator would ask the disambiguator about references 1 and 2, and the disambiguator would answer *yes*. So the code generator would be tempted to transform the second reference:

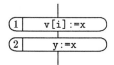

But this would not always be correct—there might be a join from off the trace between 1 and 2:

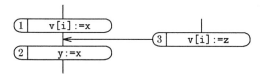

In this case, y would not get the correct value when control flows from operations 3 to 2.

But common-subexpression elimination at the intermediate-code level eliminates these situations before code generation begins. The current compiler only does it within basic blocks, though it wouldn't be hard to do it globally [Aho 77]. So the code generator can treat *yes* and *maybe* answers from the disambiguator identically without affecting the quality of code generated.

A vector as well as a scalar can be off-live at a jump:

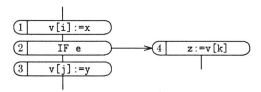

Because an element of v is read by 4, 3 cannot be allowed to move above the jump, since j and k might be equal and 3 could give v[k] the wrong value. So for these purposes, the vector v is considered live on the off-trace edge of the jump, and an off-live edge is added from the node for 3 to the node for 2 in the DAG.

To determine which vectors are off-live at a jump, the live analysis treats vectors as one large aggregate. Any load or store to the vector, for the purposes of live analysis, is considered to "read" the vector. Stores aren't added to the "kill" sets of the live-analysis algorithm, because in general it is impossible to tell exactly which vector references are killed by a vector store. By treating all vector references as "reads," the live algorithm will produce live sets that include all vectors that could possibly be live at a jump.

This approach to off-live vectors is extremely conservative (but simple to implement). Take the example above: It might be "easy" to prove that the store into v[j] by 3 couldn't possibly reference the same location as the reference to v[k] by 4, and therefore that 3 should be allowed to move above the jump. But a more sophisticated approach which attempts to determine exactly which vector references are off-live at a jump probably isn't worth it. Looking at the programs in the benchmark library, there doesn't seem to be any time-critical loops where the current conservative approach degrades performance; that is, there are no instances where a vector reference prohibited from moving above a jump causes a degradation in performance.

Summary of Edges and Nodes

At this point, let's summarize the types of nodes and edges created by the DAG-builder.

The DAG-builder uses four types of nodes: DEF nodes, operation nodes, COPY nodes, and USE nodes. (Two other types, DEF1 and USE1 are created by later phases of the code generator.)

A DEF node represents the initial value of a variable that is live on entry to the trace. It also represents the value of a constant used on the trace. If the trace gives initial locations for a live-on-entry variable, they will be recorded in the corresponding DEF node.

An operation node represents intermediate-code operations of the trace.

A COPY node represents an assignment operation of the form x:=y.

A USE node represents the final value of a variable that is live on exit from the trace. If the trace gives final required locations for a live-on-exit variable, they will be recorded in the corresponding USE node.

The previous sections described many different kinds of edges, but the implementation has only three kinds: operand edges, off-live edges, and constraint edges.

An *operand edge* goes from some operation reading variable x as an operand to the operation or DEF node producing the value of x being read.

An *off-live edge* goes from a conditional jump that has variable x live on its off-trace edge to the operation or DEF node that produces that value of x. Off-live edges help the code generator determine when registers holding off-live variable values can be reused for other purposes.

A *constraint edge* with associated delay d from node A to node B constrains A to be scheduled no earlier than d cycles after B (not quite true, but I'll explain later). Write-after-read edges are constraint edges with $d = 0$. Write-after-write, write-after-conditional-read, and vector-conflict edges are constraint edges with $d = 1$.

Constants Again

Constants are handled differently from variables—why? Some constants are immediate, capable of being generated from thin air by constant generators (such as the immediate field of an instruction), and others are stored in memory. A constant in a register can be discarded if there is a shortage of registers, since it can always be reloaded later on, while a variable must be spilled to memory. For these reasons, constants are excluded from live-variable analysis and don't show up in the trace's live-variable sets or in the DEF and USE pseudo-ops.

As described in a previous section, loading constants afresh each trace, either by constant generators or by reading memory, is not always the best thing to do, since constant generators may be a scarce resource and memory references are expensive. For example, in an inner loop it is often faster to keep a heavily used constant in a register than it is to load the constant at the beginning of every iteration. It would be nice if such constants were treated like variables and considered to be live for segments larger than an individual trace. On the other hand, one doesn't want to clog up the registers with constants referenced only a few times on the trace that could easily be produced by constant generators.

An intermediate-code transformation extends the lifetime of certain loaded constants past single traces. The machine model defines, via a predicate function, exactly which constants get transformed into variable references. Every use of such a constant is replaced by a new temporary variable; immediately preceding the use the temporary is assigned the constant. For example:

```
x:=a+3.0
```

gets transformed into:

```
temp:=3.0
x:=a+temp
```

Loop-invariant motion moves the constant assignments out of loops, and common-subexpression elimination and copy propagation then identify all the temporaries that get assigned the same value. As an example of the net effect, this code:

```
FOR i:=1 TO n
    v[i]:=3.0
    w[i]:=3.0
```

would get transformed into:

```
temp:=3.0
FOR i:=1 TO n
    v[i]:=temp
    w[i]:=temp
```

Without the transformation, the constant 3.0 would have been loaded from memory once every time through the loop; with the transformation, the constant is loaded into the variable temp before the loop starts, and temp is kept in a register for the duration of the loop.

Is the transformation worth it? Keeping a non-immediate constant in a register instead of reading it from memory each time will eliminate a memory reference at the expense of a register dedicated to the constant for the entire loop. But for inner loops, the time saved by eliminating an extra memory reference is often insignificant. These loops are usually unwound 16 or more times, and a constant used in all 16 unrollings is loaded just once at the top of the unwound loop; that memory fetch can often be fitted into a "hole" in the schedule where the memory units are otherwise idle. In a few casual experiments with the benchmark programs and model described in chapter 8, transforming non-immediate constants speeded some programs up just a few percent. Transforming immediate constants also had little effect (the model has one immediate constant generator for each integer ALU).

Actually, the current code generator has a lot more options for handling constants, none of which appear to make much difference in performance. It can treat constants much like variables, propagating their register locations across trace boundaries using DEFs and USEs, loading them on demand if they aren't to be found in a register; the disadvantage of this is that registers tend to get filled with constants, since one constant can be live across a large segment of the program. If a future code generator adopts this strategy, it will have to be very careful when it comes time to kick a constant out of a register because of a shortage of registers; the code generator should prefer to keep non-immediates over immediates, and it should try to discard constants that can be regenerated later without making the schedule longer.

The current scheme of transforming expensive constants into loop-invariant variables is simpler, with more manageable heuristics; given that the preliminary evidence indicates that little is to be gained by even the current transformation method, fancier methods don't seem worth it.

Variable Renaming and Write-after-read Edges

In a previous section I claimed that the lifetimes of a variable's values cannot overlap. That is, if x takes on the values $x_1, x_2, x_3, \ldots$ during execution, x cannot be assigned both x_i and x_j at the same time, for any $i \neq j$. To implement this restriction, the DAG builder adds write-after-read and write-after-conditional-read edges.

But how could a variable possibly be assigned two different values at once? By keeping the different values in different registers. For example, consider this fragment:

```
1. x:=a+b      /* register 4 */
2. y:=x+1
3. x:=c+d      /* register 5 */
4. z:=x+1
```

The value produced by operation 1 could be kept in register 4, and the value produced by operation 3 could be kept in register 5. The code generator would have to ensure that operation 2 reads the x in register 4 and operation 3 reads the x in register 5. In effect, the code generator would be renaming the different uses of x at code-generation time:

```
1. x1:=a+b
2. y:=x1+1
3. x2:=c+d
4. z:=x2+1
```

Assuming this could be done correctly all the time, what advantage is there in doing renaming like this at the trace and register level? Variable renaming at the intermediate-code level catches most, but not, all of the opportunities to increase parallelism. For example, in this source loop:

```
log:=0
FOR i:=1 TO n
    some expensive operations
    IF e1 THEN EXITLOOP
    log:=v[i]
    IF e2 THEN EXITLOOP
    log:=v[i+1]
x:=log+1
```

the two different assignments to **log** can't be renamed since they both reach the use of **log** after the loop. As a consequence, a trace of the loop body would look like:

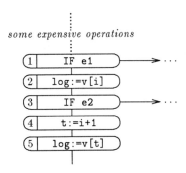

Since **log** is off-live at each of the jumps, there will be write-after-conditional-read DAG edges from 2 to 1, from 5 to 3, and from 5 to 1. If the initial part of the loop body is expensive to evaluate, the code generator might well be able to produce a shorter schedule by moving 2 and 5 above the IFs, overlapping them with the earlier computations. But the write-after-conditional-read edges force 2 and 5 to be evaluated after the IFs, resulting in less parallelism.

However, if the code generator could do a little register-level renaming, the vector loads of 2 and 5 could be moved above the IFs. For example, the code generator could put the first load into register **r1** and the second in register **r2**, reporting the location of **log** on the off-trace branch of operation 3 as register **r1** and the location at the end of the trace as register **r2**.

Unfortunately, such renaming doesn't always work, because sometimes at trace exits the code generator is forced to report locations for two different values of the same variable. For example, consider this fragment of a flow graph:

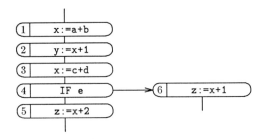

Suppose the trace consisted of operations 1–5, and that in the absence of write-after-read edges the code generator produced a schedule that looked like:

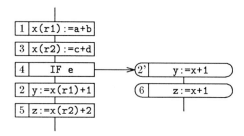

The value of x produced by operation 1 is put in register **r1**, and the value produced by operation 3 is put in register **r2** (each use of x is annotated with its register). Because operation 2 moved below the IF, the bookkeeper placed a copy 2' on the off-trace edge.

The code generator is now faced with a dilemma: Which register does it report for the location of x at the off-trace edge of 4? If it reports **r1**, then operation 6 will get the wrong value; if it reports **r2**, then 2' will get the wrong value.

The root cause of this problem is that the DEF-USE mechanism reports variable locations by name only; it has no way of associating different locations of a variable with different uses. One could probably think up solutions to this problem, such as reporting location by reaching uses (sets of operations in the flow graph reading a variable) instead of by live-variable name.

But is such complication worth it? I think not. Variable renaming at the intermediate-code level catches almost all of the potential renaming possibilities. I've examined all of our benchmark programs, and there was only one with a loop like that above with variables that couldn't be renamed to eliminate write-after-read conflict, and that loop wasn't time critical. It was easily rewritten to allow the renaming and avoid the conflict. For example:

```
log:=0
FOR i:=1 TO n
    some expensive operations
    IF ... THEN EXITLOOP
    log:=v[i]
    IF ... THEN EXITLOOP
    log:=v[i+1]
x:=log+1
```

could be rewritten as:

```
log2:=0
FOR i:=1 TO n
    some expensive operations
    IF ... THEN
        log:=log2
        EXITLOOP
    log1:=v[i]
    IF ... THEN
        log:=log1
        EXITLOOP
    log2:=v[i+1]
x:=log+1
```

Now the two vector loads can float freely above the IFs and be overlapped with the computation the top of the loop.

It wouldn't be hard to expand intermediate-code variable renaming to identify these situations and transform the code automatically.

Some Definitions

Before proceeding further, here are some basic definitions:

Delay(fu). The number of cycles needed to execute an operation on functional unit *fu*. Integer ALUs typically have a delay of 1, floating multipliers a delay or 3 or 4.

Distance(me1,me2). If both *me1* and *me2* are machine elements (functional units, register banks, or constant generators), the result is the number of cycles needed to move a value from the output of *me1* to the input of *me2*; this is equivalent to the number of register banks on the shortest path between the output of *me1* and the input of *me2*.

If both *me1* and *me2* are sets of machine elements, the result is the minimum distance between some element of *me1* and some element of *me2*:

$$\min_{\substack{i \in me1 \\ j \in me2}} Distance(i,j)$$

If either *me1* or *me2* is the empty set, the result is 0. If one is a single machine element but the other is a set, the former is assumed to be a singleton set.

FeasibleLocations(node). If *node* represents an intermediate-code operation, this returns the set of functional units that implement the operation of *node*. When looking for a functional unit to implement an intermediate-code operation, the code generator need only consider the units in this set.

If *node* is a DEF node, the result is the set of initial register bank locations currently assigned to the node.

Height and Depth

Simple ordering heuristics often improve results of the non-optimal DAG-manipulation algorithms used by compilers. This code generator uses the **height** and **depth** of nodes to place nodes in order of importance.

In an abstract DAG the height of a node is the length of the longest path from the node to an exit of the DAG, and the depth is the length of the longest path from an entrance to the node. In the context of expression DAGs, height and depth become more useful by weighting the path lengths with the execution times of the associated operations. The depth of a node is the earliest time that it could be executed, and the height is the minimum time needed to execute the node and the rest of the DAG dependent on the node.

Height and depth are recursively defined in terms of a node's operands and readers:

$$Depth(n) = \max_{o \in O(n)} Depth(o) + Delay(o)$$
$$Height(n) = \max_{r \in R(n)} Height(r) + Delay(n)$$

where $O(n)$ is the set of operands of n and $R(n)$ is the set of nodes reading n, that is, the nodes having n as an operand. The delay of an operation o is defined here to be the delay of the functional unit that executes the operator fastest. These definitions only account for operand edges; the actual definitions also look at the constraining edges (a node can't execute until all of its constraining predecessors have executed).

The **critical path length** of an abstract DAG is the longest path through the DAG, equivalent to the maximum depth or the maximum height. In this context, the critical path length l is the maximum height over all the nodes; any machine-code schedule for the DAG must take at least l cycles.

Functional-unit Assignment

After the DAG has been built from the trace, the next phase of the code generator assigns functional units to operations and initial locations to live-on-entry variables. The goal, of course, is to produce the shortest possible schedule for the trace. In pursuit of this goal, the code generator tries to get the fullest utilization of all the functional units while minimizing the costly movement of data between units.

To get a feel for the problem, let's look at a simple example. Here is an expression and its corresponding DAG:

```
x:=(v[i+1](1) * (a1+b1)) + (v[i+2](2) * (a2+b2))
```

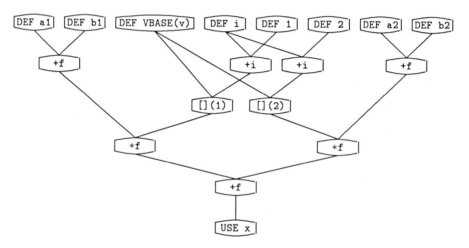

The vector references must be done in specific banks, notated (1) and (2). Integer operations are marked with **i** and floating operations with **f**.

Suppose that we have a very simple machine model consisting of two clusters connected by a narrow-bandwidth bus; each cluster has a memory bank, an integer ALU, a floating adder, and a floating multiplier, all connected to a multiported register bank. Each operation takes one cycle.

Because the vector references are tied to particular banks, they determine where the other operations should be executed in an optimal schedule. The operands of a vector reference should be computed in the same cluster as the reference, and the result of the reference should be used in the same cluster. An optimal schedule assigns the left half of the DAG to the first cluster and the right half to the second cluster, which would result in this schedule:

```
Cycle   Cluster 1                Cluster 2
1       t1 := i +i 1             t2 := i +i 2
        u1 := a1 +f b1           u2 := a2 +f b2
2       v1 := v[t1](1)           v2 := v[t2](2)
3       w1 := u1 *f v1           w2 := u2 *f v2
4       copy w2 to cluster 1
5       x1 := w1 +f w2
```

Notice that even though the critical path length of the DAG is 4, the optimal schedule takes 5 cycles, because at some point a value must be copied between clusters. Also, each cluster's register bank starts out with a copy of the input variables i and VBASE(v); if they were in only one bank, an extra cycle would be needed to copy them to the other bank.

It's easy for us humans to eyeball the DAG and come up with a good assignment of functional units to operations, but what about an algorithm?

One thought is to find clusters of nearby operations in the DAG (operations closely connected by operand edges) and assign them to functional units close to each other in the hardware. The assignment algorithm has to notice particular operations tied to particular functional units, such as vector references to specific banks. Since these operations could be in the middle of a DAG, a simple one-pass algorithm, either top-down or bottom-up, wouldn't work very well.

The assignment algorithm also has to notice the initial and final locations of variables if they were specified on the trace, avoiding excessive data movements of variables to functional units. If some input variable starts out in a given register bank (as specified in a DEF), it makes sense to try to assign operations reading that variable to nearby functional units. Similarly, if a variable must end up in a given register bank (as specified in a USE), it makes sense to assign the operation producing the variable's value to a nearby functional unit.

The example above shows that a simple one-pass algorithm, either top-down or bottom-up, couldn't do this clustering very well. A top-down algorithm would miss the fact that the index calculations should be computed near the corresponding memory banks; a bottom-up algorithm wouldn't know to compute the multiplies in banks near the corresponding references. A top-down algorithm wouldn't notice USEs until it was too late, while a bottom-up algorithm wouldn't notice DEFs.

The clustering algorithm must keep track of how busy functional units are. If a functional unit is very busy, it sometimes pays off to move the operands of some operations to a distant cluster of functional units that's idle, compute over there for a while, and then move the results back.

Bottom-up Greedy

The assignment algorithm used by the code-generator is called bottom-up greedy (BUG), after the top-down greedy register allocation paradigm [Barrett 79]. Both algorithms start at the roots of the DAG and recurse towards the leaves, but because academics draw their DAGs upside down with the roots at the top, they call their algorithm "top-down."

BUG makes a major simplifying assumption: Functional units are the only limiting resource in the machine, and conflicts due to scarce register-bank ports or buses are ignored. Is this a reasonable assumption? Probably, since in a well-balanced architecture the bandwidth of the register banks and buses matches that of the memories and other functional units. That is, if the code generator decides to use a functional unit in some cycle, there will be a high probability that there will be enough register ports to service the unit. If there weren't enough ports, then the machine is improperly designed: The functional units are underutilized, and removing one would improve the price/performance ratio.

This is all intuitive speculation, though. The final test of whether the assumption is correct is the overall performance of the code generator. I'll report on that later, of course, but suffice it to say that I'm pleased with the results.

BUG recursively propagates from the roots of the DAG to the leaves estimates of where each operation can best be computed. When it reaches the leaves, BUG works it way back to the roots, making final assignments of functional units to operations along the way. To make a final assignment to a node, BUG estimates the cycle in which the functional unit can compute the operation, and both the functional unit and the cycle get recorded in the node (notated *node.fu* and *node.cycle*). BUG also keeps a table that shows for each cycle the functional units still available during that cycle; when an assignment is made, BUG updates the table to mark the functional unit as unavailable during that cycle. BUG uses this table to decide which functional unit could earliest compute an operation.

The core of BUG is the recursive procedure *Assign*:

proc *Assign*(*node*,*destinations*)
      if *node* is a leaf **or** *node* is already assigned a functional unit
    then
        return

      for each *operand* of *node* **do**
          estimated-fus, *estimated-cycles* := *LikelyFUs*(*node*,*destinations*)
          Assign(*operand*,*estimated-fus*)

      estimated-fus, *estimated-cycles* := *LikelyFUs*(*node*,*destinations*)
      node.fu := **first**(*estimated-fus*)
      node.cycle := **first**(*estimated-cycles*)
      available?[*fu*,*cycle*] := **false**

Assign takes two arguments, *node* and the set *destinations*, a set of functional units that are likely places where the value produced by *node* might be used. First, *Assign* recursively calls itself to make assignments to each of the operands of *node*. Then, based on where the operands are assigned, it picks a good functional unit and estimated cycle for *node*, marks the functional unit unavailable during that cycle, and returns. The measure of goodness of a functional unit is how early the operands can be moved to the unit, the operation computed, and the result moved to one of the units in *destinations*.

Before recursively assigning each operand, *Assign* recomputes a best-guess set *estimated-fus* of functional units that could likely be assigned to *node*; this best-guess is used as the set of likely destinations for the operand in the recursive call to *Assign*. As each operand is assigned, the recomputed *estimated-fus* gets more and more accurate. After all the operands have been assigned, a final best-guess set is computed, and one of the functional units from it is chosen arbitrarily as the unit to be assigned to *node*.

Clustering information is passed up through the DAG via these best-guess sets (the *destinations* parameter of *Assign*). The actual assignments pass clustering information back down. For example, consider what happens at a vector reference tied to a particular memory bank:

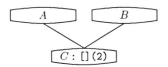

Because node *C* must be executed in the second bank, the initial best guess for *C* will consist only of that bank. That bank will be passed as the *destinations* parameter to the recursive *Assign* calls for *A* and *B*, biasing the selection of functional units for *A* and *B* towards ones near the bank.

The procedure *LikelyFUs* is called by *Assign* to compute the best-guess set of good functional units for *node* based on the feasible functional units for *node* and the existing assignments to the operands of *node*. *LikelyFUs* returns two corresponding lists, *estimated-fus* $= fu_1, fu_2, \ldots$ and *estimated-cycles* $= c_1, c_2, \ldots$, where fu_i is a good functional unit for *node* and c_i is the earliest cycle such that fu_i could be scheduled to compute the operation of *node*.

I'll present *LikelyFUs* from the bottom-up. But first, let's introduce another definition:

> *AvailableCycle(node)*. Returns the cycle when the value of *node* is produced and stored in a register ba..k (the last cycle of the operation); the value can't be read by other nodes until the succeeding cycle at the earliest. For leaf nodes, the result is 0. For operations, the result is defined only if *node* is already assigned a functional unit; the result is *node.cycle* + *Delay(node.fu)* − 1.

The procedure *StartCycle* returns an estimate of the earliest cycle that the functional unit *fu* could be used to compute the value of *node*:

proc *StartCycle(node,fu)*
    if any operands of *node* are assigned functional units **then**
        $c :=$ max, over each assigned *operand* of *node*, of
            AvailableCycle(operand) + *Distance(operand.fu,fu)*
        return the smallest $c1 \geq c$ such that *available?[fu,c1]* is **true**
    else
        $c :=$ max, over each *operand* of *node*, of
            Depth(operand) + *Distance(FeasibleLocations(operand),fu)*
        return c

StartCycle considers two cases: Some of the operands are already assigned functional units, and none are assigned units.

Suppose some of the operands of *node* are already assigned. For these operands, the estimated cycle in which they will be executed has already been computed and stored in their *.cycle* slots. The earliest possible arrival time of an operand at the inputs of *fu* is the cycle when the value is computed plus the time needed to move the value to *fu*. The maximum arrival time (over all assigned operands) is the first possible cycle *fu* could be scheduled; starting with that cycle, the result is the first in which *fu* is available.

In the other case, none of *node*'s operands are assigned. The arrival time of an operand is the depth (as described above) plus the minimum distance to *fu* from the set of feasible functional units for the operand. Since none of the operands have been assigned, this call to *StartCycle* is only a very rough estimate, so the per-cycle availability of the functional unit is ignored; the result is the maximum arrival time over all the operands.

The procedure *CompletionCycle* returns an estimate of when the operation of *node* could be computed on functional unit *fu* and its value moved to the nearest functional unit in the set *destinations*:

> **proc** *CompletionCycle*(*node*,*fu*,*destinations*)
>   **return** *StartCycle*(*node*,*fu*) + *Delay*(*fu*) − 1 + *Distance*(*fu*, *destinations*)

The completion cycle is computed by estimating the cycle in which node could be executed on *fu*, adding the execution time of *fu*, and then adding the time to move the result from the output of *fu* to the nearest unit in *destinations*.

Finally, here is the definition of *LikelyFUs*:

> **proc** *LikelyFUs*(*node*,*destinations*)
>   e := min, over each *fu* in *FeasibleLocations*(*node*), of
>   *CompletionCycle*(*node*,*fu*,*destinations*)
>   **return** *estimated-fus*, *estimated-cycles* **where**
>   *estimated-fus* is the list $fu_1, fu_2, \ldots$ and
>   *estimated-cycles* is the list $c_1, c_2, \ldots$, such that
>   – $fu_i \in$ *FeasibleLocations*(*node*),
>   – c_i = *StartCycle*(*node*,fu_i), and
>   – e = *CompletionCycle*(*node*,fu_i, *destinations*).

Remember that *LikelyFUs* returns a best-guess list of functional units that would be good choices on which to execute *node* and move its value to one of the units in the set *destinations*. Also returned is a corresponding list of cycles when the functional units could be scheduled. The implementation examines each functional unit capable of executing *node*, calling *CompletionCycle* to determine the earliest the functional unit could execute *node* and the result moved to one of *destinations*. The functional units with the minimum completion cycles are returned.

Here's some speculation: The definition of *StartCycle* only considers operands already assigned functional units, if any are assigned; if none are assigned, it doesn't consider functional-unit availability. My intent was to be conservative when not all of the operands have been assigned yet, returning a large set of likely functional units that will be used as the potential operand destinations in the recursive calls to *Assign*. Though the current definition of BUG appears to be doing a decent job, perhaps *StartCycle* could be improved slightly:

> **proc** *StartCycle(node,fu)*
> $\quad$ c := max, over each *operand* of *node*, of *ArrivalCycle(operand,fu)*
> $\quad$ **return** the smallest $c1 \geq c$ such that *available?[fu,c1]*

> **proc** *ArrivalCycle(operand,fu)*
> $\quad$ **if** *operand* is assigned a functional unit **then**
> $\quad\quad$ **return** *AvailableCycle(operand)* + *Distance(operand.fu, fu)*
> $\quad$ **else**
> $\quad\quad$ **return** *Depth(operand)* + *Distance(FeasibleLocations(operand), fu)*

The main differences in this version are that all the operands are always used to estimate the starting cycle and that the availability of *fu* is checked even if none of the operands are assigned. This version seems more intuitive, but intuition in such matters is often wrong—experimentation must be the final arbiter.

Priorities

The top level of BUG looks like:

> **for** each *node* that is a root **do**
> $\quad$ *Assign(node,∅)*

The top-level call to *Assign* assigns functional units to *node* and all of its predecessors that aren't already assigned. The empty set passed as the *destinations* parameter signifies that no particular destinations are desired for *node*. (The distance between the empty set and any functional unit or set of units is always zero.)

In what order should the root nodes be processed? For that matter, what order should the operands of a node be processed? Intuitively, nodes along the critical paths of the DAG should receive highest priority, since they are the primary bottleneck in the computation. If an operation on a critical path is delayed a few cycles waiting for a busy hardware resource, the length of the entire schedule for the DAG increases. But it doesn't matter as much if an operation not on the critical path is delayed a little, since by definition the value of that operation isn't needed right away; these non-critical operations can fit into the "holes" in the schedule between the critical operations.

The depth of a node indicates how critical it is compared to others. As defined above, the depth of a root node is the length of the longest path from a DAG entrance to the node. The larger the depth, the more time-critical the node and its predecessors. So the top level of BUG processes roots in decreasing depth order, calling *Assign* on the roots of critical paths first.

Similarly, the operands of a node are processed by *Assign* in decreasing depth order. Given two operands A and B of a node C such that $Depth(A) > Depth(B)$,

A is more time-critical. Any delay in the computation of *A* and its predecessors will most likely delay the computation of *C*, whereas the computation of *B* and its predecessors could probably be delayed a little while still delivering its value to *C* by the time *A* completes.

At this point, the reaction of most computer scientists is, "Yes, but have you tried other ordering heuristics?" No, I haven't. Long experience with DAG algorithms in compilers and other scheduling applications shows that the particular heuristic matters very little, as long as some reasonable heuristic is used. Height and depth are no worse than others examined and are sometimes slightly better [Fisher 79, Ruttenberg 85, Touzeau 84, Hennessy 83]. Finding the bounds and average performance of heuristics in simplistic DAG algorithms is a favorite game of theorists. But in a practical compiler, the differences in heuristics are mostly irrelevant—improvements made to other parts of the compiler can result in much larger gains.

Other Node Types

So far I've only discussed handling operation nodes. But BUG must handle DEF, COPY, and USE nodes as well. The procedure *Assign* actually looks like:

> **proc** *Assign*(*node,destinations*)
> > **case** *node.type* **of**
> > > *Def*:   *AssignDef*(*node,destinations*)
> > > *Operation*: *AssignOperation*(*node,destinations*)
> > > *Copy*:   *AssignCopy*(*node,destinations*)
> > > *Use*:   *AssignUse*(*node,destinations*)

We've already discussed assignment of operations.

USE nodes represent variables that are live on exit from the DAG. *AssignUse* is defined as:

> **proc** *AssignUse*(*node,destinations*)
> > *operand* := the one operand of *node*
> > *Assign*(*operand,node.final-locations*)

Any final register locations specified on the trace for the variable represented by the USE are stored in the node's *.final-locations* slot. They are passed on as the *destinations* parameter for the recursive assignment of the operand of the USE. This will bias the assignment towards functional units nearby the final locations. If no final locations were specified, *node.final-locations* is the empty set, and the variable value will end up wherever the operand leaves it.

COPY nodes represent intermediate-code assignments, for example x:=y. *AssignCopy* is defined as:

> **proc** *AssignCopy*(*node,destinations*)
>   *operand* := the one operand of *node*
>   *Assign*(*operand,destinations*)

That is, the destinations for the COPY are passed on to the destinations of the operand of the COPY. The actual assignment itself can be implemented anywhere in the machine as a register transfer, so its location doesn't really matter.

DEF nodes represent the initial locations of the trace's input variables and immediate constants. If initial locations for a variable are specified on a trace, BUG doesn't have to worry about picking locations; but the given initial locations should influence BUG's selection of functional units for operations that read the variable. If no initial locations are specified, however, BUG is responsible for picking one or more based on the functional units assigned to operations reading the variable. This decision is distributed between the main phase of BUG (the calls to *Assign* that pick functional units for operations) and a second phase that handles just DEF and USE nodes.

The procedure *AssignDef* is defined simply as:

> **proc** *AssignDef*(*node,destinations*)
>   **return**

That is, when *Assign* reaches a DEF node, it does absolutely nothing. All the work is done elsewhere.

First, let's consider the simpler case when a DEF node has initial register locations specified on the trace. BUG only has to make sure that these initial locations influence the assignments to operations reading the DEF. For example, if variable i has an initial location in some register bank, BUG should try to find an integer ALU near that register bank for the operation j:=i+1. This biasing is already handled by the definition of *LikelyFUs*. To obtain a good guess about where to place an operation, *LikelyFUs* (via *StartCycle*) calls *FeasibleLocations*(*operand*) to determine where each operand is likely to be placed. Since *FeasibleLocations* returns the set of initial locations for a DEF node, *LikelyFUs* will be influenced to seek functional units near the initial locations of an operand DEF.

The harder case is when a DEF node has no specified initial locations—BUG must choose some locations for the variable or immediate constant represented by the node. But how many locations should be chosen? A naive approach might be to add a new location whenever convenient. For example, consider this fragment:

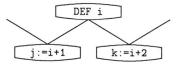

The naive approach would reason there should be two copies of i, one for each register bank servicing an integer ALU; that way, the two additions could be performed in parallel.

But there is a cost to introducing multiple locations for a DEF. Some later trace that joins to the top of the current trace will have to copy the variable into all its multiple locations, and that copying is not free. In the above example, suppose that BUG decided i should live in both register 2, bank 1, and register 5, bank 2. After generating code for this trace, the code generator would leave a USE pseudo-op at the entrance recording the locations of i and other variables. Some later trace will pick up that USE as its last operation, and that trace will have to copy i into both locations. So maybe one cycle was saved on the current trace by allowing the two additions to be done in parallel, but a cycle might have been added on a later trace to do the copying of i.

Sometimes this deferred copying pays off, and sometimes not. It all depends on whether the deferred copying can be overlapped with already-existing operations of later traces. If it can, then making up multiple locations is a win; if it can't then there is a net benefit only if the cost of deferred copying is cheaper than the extra cycles that would otherwise result by allowing only one initial location. Judging the net benefit is extremely difficult, since the code generator has no information about the contents of later traces (which might well be affected by what's generated for the current trace).

Suppose there is a trace consisting of the body of an inner loop and that there is some induction variable i that is read many times and then incremented at the bottom of the loop:

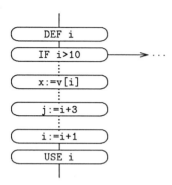

If there are many uses of i, it might be tempting to choose multiple locations for it, one close to each functional unit that reads its value. But because i is incremented after all the uses, only one location for i would be alive at the end of the trace. So after code has been generated for the trace, the flow graph would look like:

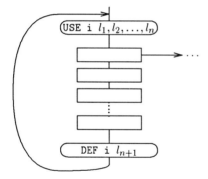

A later trace will traverse the loop back edge, consisting solely of the DEF and the USE. To satisfy the USE for i, the code generator would have to copy i from the location l_{n+1} to all the locations $l_1, l_2, \ldots, l_n$, which could take several cycles. The copying couldn't be overlapped with other operations since there are none on the back edge. The resulting flow graph would look like:

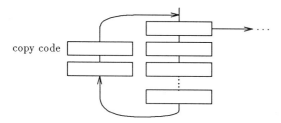

For tight inner loops with several induction variables, the copying on the back edge could increase the running time of the loop considerably.

On the other hand, suppose there was some loop invariant k referenced several places in the loop. Choosing multiple locations for k is almost always a clear win. Because k is live on entrance and live on exit from the loop-body trace, any initial locations chosen for k will be live on exit from the trace as well. The DEF and USE locations on the back edge will match up, so there won't be any copying of k on the back edge. The USE left at the entrance to the loop's machine code will cause code to be generated in a later trace that copies k into all the locations needed by the loop body. Assuming the loop is executed many times, this copying in the loop header is usually worthwhile, especially since it can probably be overlapped with other code in the loop header.

This loop example suggests a simple heuristic for BUG: When choosing locations for a DEF, allow multiple locations only if the variable isn't a loop induction variable (any variable whose value is computed on one iteration of a loop but is used on later iterations). Of course, when generating code for a trace the code generator is free to copy an induction variable from its initial DEF location to anywhere in the machine, but that copying will be done only if BUG determines that it is worthwhile, that is, if the increased parallelism of the operations reading the variable outweighs the cost of copying. BUG is pretty good about making such decisions. In the above example:

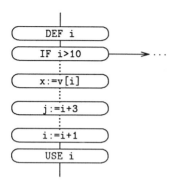

i would be restricted to a single initial location. If the many uses of i were time-consuming and could be done in parallel, BUG would decide that there would be a net gain from copying i to where it was needed. (BUG accounts for the cost of copying on the trace via the calls to *Distance* made by *StartCycle*.)

The current version of BUG uses an even simpler heuristic, though: Multiple locations are allowed for a DEF only if the variable isn't assigned on the trace; whether or not the variable is an induction variable doesn't matter. Almost all time-critical traces result from inner loops, and almost all the live-on-entry variables assigned on those traces are induction variables. Based on the experiments and examination of the code produced, this heuristic appears to be quite adequate.

BUG handles DEFs with no specified initial locations differently according to whether or not they are allowed multiple locations.

The *Assign* phase of BUG does nothing with DEFs allowed multiple locations. It implicitly assumes that the DEF will not affect the choice of functional units, that is, no matter which functional units are chosen for operations reading the DEF, a good set of initial locations can be found later. (The result of *Feasible-Locations* for such a node is the empty set, and the distance from the empty set to any functional unit is zero.) After the *Assign* phase has assigned functional units to operations, a later phase (described below) then picks the actual locations for multiple-location DEFs. For example, suppose that i is allowed multiple locations:

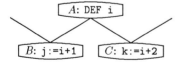

Because *FeasibleLocations*(A) returns the empty set, *Assign* could well place B on one integer ALU and C on another. Assuming that the two ALUs are serviced by different banks, the later phase would pick two initial locations for the DEF, one for each bank.

For DEFs allowed only a single location, *Assign* must do some more work. To see why, assume in the example above that the DEF was restricted to a single location and that node B is assigned a functional unit by *Assign* before C. Because B is assigned first, it is presumably more time-critical than C, so the location chosen for the DEF should be close to B's functional unit. We'd like to choose a location for the DEF immediately after choosing B's unit, so that later on when C is assigned, BUG can make its choice for C based on the location of the DEF (which was based on the location of B).

Towards this end, *Assign* is a little more complicated than presented previously:

> **proc** *Assign*(*node,destinations*)
>   **case** *node.type* **of**
>   *Def*:   *AssignDef*(*node,destinations*)
>   *Operation*: *AssignOperation*(*node,destinations*)
>   *Copy*:   *AssignCopy*(*node,destinations*)
>   *Use*:   *AssignUse*(*node,destinations*)
>   **for** each *operand* of node **do**
>   **if** *operand* is a *Def* with no initial locations and it must have a
>   single location
>   **then**
>   *ReassignDef*(*operand,node*)

After assigning a functional unit to *node*, the operands are examined. If a DEF operand has no initial locations yet but must have a single location, *ReassignDef* is called to pick a location. *ReassignDef* finds a register bank with free registers that is closest to the functional unit assigned to *node* and assigns it to the initial locations of *operand*. Subsequent calls to *FeasibleLocations* for that DEF will return the chosen register bank, thus influencing the functional unit selection of other operations reading the DEF.

BUG, Phase II

After *Assign* chooses functional units for all of the operations in the DAG, a second, smaller phase of BUG attacks the DEF and USE nodes. This second phase has two purposes: to choose locations for those DEF nodes that don't yet have any, and to prepare the DEF and USE nodes for list scheduling.

DEF nodes that still don't have initial locations are of two types:

> Nodes for variables that didn't have locations specified by the trace and that are allowed to have multiple register locations.

Nodes for immediate constants. One or more constant generators should be chosen for these nodes.

For each variable DEF node, BUG picks a set of register banks for the DEF by examining the operations that read the value of the DEF. For each such operation, BUG picks a register bank with free registers that is closest to the operation's assigned functional unit. If there is a choice, BUG prefers a register bank already picked for the DEF for some other operation; if there is still a choice after that, BUG prefers a register bank with the fewest assigned registers, in an attempt to even the load on the register banks. Finally, if a USE with specified locations reads the value of the DEF, those locations are merged with the locations picked for the operations. By including the final locations in the set of initial locations, no copying will have to be done on this trace to satisfy the USE. The final set of locations is assigned to the *.initial-locations* slot of the DEF.

For each immediate-constant DEF node, BUG picks a set of constant generators for initial locations using a similar method. The operation and USE nodes reading the DEF are examined, and a constant-generator closest to each is picked; if there is a choice, a constant-generator already picked for another reader is preferred.

To make life simpler, the list scheduler assumes that every node represents one location for one value. If a variable in the DAG has several locations, there should be a separate node for each location. To help meet this requirement, a final pass of BUG splices new nodes next to the DEF and USE nodes.

First, each USE node that has specified final locations gets new USE1 nodes spliced between the USE and the operand of the USE. There is a separate USE1 for each final location. For example:

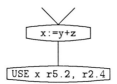

gets transformed into:

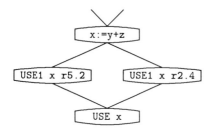

(The notation r5.2 indicates register 5 in bank 2.)

Next, each DEF node gets new DEF1 nodes spliced between the DEF and its readers, one DEF1 node per initial location. Each reader of the DEF gets attached to the particular DEF1 containing the location closest to the reader's functional unit or register bank. For example:

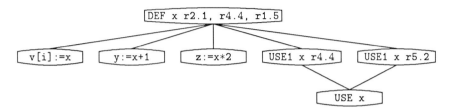

Assume the vector reference and the multiplication are closest to bank 5 and the addition is closest to bank 4. These nodes would then be transformed to:

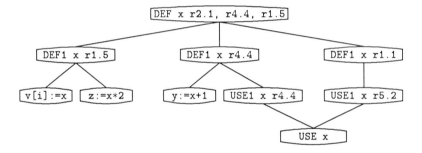

Notice that one of final locations of x (bank 2) doesn't have a corresponding initial location in the DEF, so BUG picks the closest initial location (in this case, bank 1). During list scheduling, a register transfer will be needed to move x into that final position.

Finally, a USE1 is spliced between each USE that has no specified final locations and its single operand. For example:

gets transformed into:

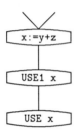

Sometimes a USE has a DEF1 operand, as in the following example:

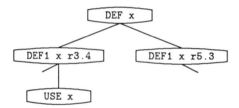

(The USE gets randomly attached to one of DEF1s when they are spliced in.) This situation occurs only if the variable x isn't assigned anywhere on the trace. We'd like to keep all the locations of x alive until the exit from the trace, not just one location, so in this special case USE1s get spliced between the USE and all the DEF1s:

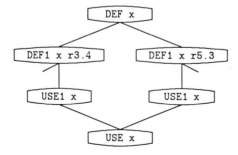

Time Complexity of Bug

To derive upper bounds on the time used by BUG, let:

n be the number of nodes in the DAG.

f be the maximum number of feasible functional units for any one operation; f is constant for any machine model.

Note that the number of operands of an operation is bounded by a small constant (typically 3).

I'll derive the time bounds from the bottom-up. First consider the procedure *StartCycle*:

proc *StartCycle*(*node,fu*)
1. **if** any operands of *node* are assigned functional units **then**
2. $c :=$ max, over each assigned *operand* of *node*, of
            AvailableCycle(*operand*) + *Distance*(*operand.fu*, *fu*)
3.   **return** the smallest $c1 \geq c$ such that *available?*[*fu,c1*] is **true**
4. **else**
5. $c :=$ max, over each *operand* of *node*, of
            Depth(*operand*) + *Distance*(*FeasibleLocations*(*operand*), *fu*)
6.   **return** c

If the condition tested on line 1 is true, the only non-constant cost is from line 3, finding the first cycle a functional unit is available. Currently, this is implemented as linear search, which in the worst case could take $O(s)$ where s is the size of the schedule.

However, Ruttenberg ingeniously uses the union-find algorithm instead of linear search, essentially reducing the worst-case time to be a constant [Ruttenberg 85]. Every functional unit has its own union-find universe. Each set in the universe is a maximal range of cycles $i{:}j$ such that the functional unit is unavailable in cycles i through $j-1$ and is available in cycle j. *Find*(*c*) returns the set $i{:}j$ containing c; by definition, j is the first cycle at or after c in which the functional unit is free, so *Find*(*c*) can replace the linear search at line 3. Then to mark the functional unit unavailable at cycle j, the set containing $j+1{:}k$ is found by calling *Find*(*j+1*), and the two sets $i{:}j$ and $j+1{:}k$ are merged (unioned) into a single set $i{:}k$; that is, the functional unit is now unavailable from cycles i to $k-1$ but is available in cycle k. Initially, the universe is initialized to the singleton sets $i{:}i$ for every cycle i in the schedule; that is, the functional unit is available in every cycle and unavailable nowhere.

Thus the worst-case cost of line 3 can be reduced to almost-constant time. BUG doesn't use union-find however, because in practice only a small number of cycles past *c1* need be examined to find one in which the functional unit is free. The not-insignificant overhead of union-find might make linear search the better choice on average.

Getting back to our analysis, if lines 5–6 are executed, the time used is the cost of finding the minimum distance between a single functional unit and a set of feasible functional units, which can be no larger than f. So the time cost is $O(f)$ times the number of operands (bounded by a constant).

Thus the time cost of *StartCycle* is $O(f)$.

CompletionCycle invokes *StartCycle* and then computes the distance from the functional unit to the *destinations* set passed to *Assign*. The size of *destinations* can be no larger than the set of feasible functional units, so the time for *CompletionCycle* is $O(f)$. In practice, the size of the *destinations* parameter is much smaller than f because of the restrictions imposed by vector references tied to particular banks.

LikelyFUs invokes *CompletionCycle* on each feasible functional unit for a node's operation, so it takes time $O(f^2)$.

Assign invokes *LikelyFUs* for each operand and then once more, so it also takes time $O(f^2)$.

Finally, *Assign* is called on each node of the DAG, so the total time of BUG is $O(nf^2)$. Since f is constant for any machine model, the time of BUG is linear in the size of the DAG.

The Complete Algorithm for Assign

For easy reference, here is the complete algorithm for the assignment phase of BUG:

```
for each node that is a root do
    Assign(node,∅)


proc Assign(node,destinations)
    case node.type of
        Def:        AssignDef(node,destinations)
        Operation:  AssignOperation(node,destinations)
        Copy:       AssignCopy(node,destinations)
        Use:        AssignUse(node,destinations)
    for each operand of node do
        if operand is a Def with no initial locations and it must have a
                single location
        then
                ReassignDef(operand,node)


proc AssignDef(node,destinations)
    return
```

proc *AssignCopy*(*node,destinations*)
    operand := the one operand of *node*
    Assign(*operand,destinations*)

proc *AssignUse*(*node,destinations*)
    operand := the one operand of *node*
    Assign(*operand,node.final-locations*)

proc *AssignOperation*(*node,destinations*)
    if *node* is a leaf **or** *node* is already assigned a functional unit
    then
        return

    for each *operand* of *node* **do**
        estimated-fus, estimated-cycles := *LikelyFUs*(*node,destinations*)
        Assign(*operand,estimated-fus*)

    estimated-fus, estimated-cycles := *LikelyFUs*(*node,destinations*)
    node.fu := **first**(*estimated-fus*)
    node.cycle := **first**(*estimated-cycles*)
    available?[*fu,cycle*] := **false**

proc *LikelyFUs*(*node,destinations*)
    e := min, over each *fu* in *FeasibleLocations*(*node*), of
        CompletionCycle(*node,fu,destinations*)
    return *estimated-fus, estimated-cycles* **where**
        estimated-fus is the list $fu_1, fu_2, \ldots$ and
        estimated-cycles is the list $c_1, c_2, \ldots$, such that
            $- fu_i \in$ *FeasibleLocations*(*node*),
            $- c_i = $ *StartCycle*(*node,fu_i*), and
            $- e = $ *CompletionCycle*(*node,fu_i, destinations*).

proc *CompletionCycle*(*node,fu,destinations*)
    return *StartCycle*(*node,fu*) + *Delay*(*fu*) − 1 + *Distance*(*fu, destinations*)

proc *StartCycle*(*node,fu*)
    if any operands of *node* are assigned functional units **then**
        c := max, over each assigned *operand* of *node*, of
            AvailableCycle(*operand*) + *Distance*(*operand.fu, fu*)
        return the smallest *c1* ≥ *c* such that *available?*[*fu,c1*] is **true**
    else
        c := max, over each *operand* of *node*, of
            Depth(*operand*) + *Distance*(*FeasibleLocations*(*operand*), *fu*)
        return *c*

List Scheduling Overview

Once functional units have been assigned to operations of the DAG, the list-scheduling phase emits actual machine code by enumerating the nodes in a topological order and filling in the schedule of machine instructions. The instructions are formed in order: first cycle 0, then cycle 1, then cycle 2, etc. To form the next instruction, the list scheduler considers all nodes that are **data ready**, that is, nodes all of whose predecessors have already been scheduled. It fills the instruction with as many of the data-ready operations as possible using first-fit; when no more can be squeezed into the current instruction, it is emitted and a new instruction started.

During list scheduling the code generator is often faced with a choice of several nodes. For example, at each step in list scheduling there are many data-ready nodes, only some of which will fit into the current instruction. In such cases, the code generator orders the nodes by height (maximum distance to an exit of the DAG), on the assumption that the nodes of greatest height are the most time-critical and should take priority.

The destination register bank and register for a value produced by an operation are chosen on the fly when scheduling the operation. The list scheduler looks for an available register bank on the shortest path between the functional unit producing the value and the functional units that will be using the value.

Data movements between distant register banks are also scheduled on the fly during list scheduling. As soon as a value-producing operation is scheduled, the list scheduler looks at all the operations reading the value. If any are more than one register bank away, the list scheduler inserts COPY nodes into the DAG between the producing node and the distant reading nodes that will move the value to the distant functional units. These COPY nodes will be scheduled just like normal operations, getting the values to the reading functional units as early as free hardware resources will allow.

Top Level

The top-level of list scheduling looks like:

```
Initialize(data-ready-queue)
current-cycle := 0

for each Def1 node do
    Schedule(node)

while data-ready-queue is not empty do
    node := DeleteFirst(data-ready-queue)
    current-cycle := node.earliest-cycle
    Schedule(node)
```

To manage the set of data-ready nodes efficiently, the list scheduler keeps them in a priority queue. Nodes in the queue are ordered according to the earliest cycle that they could be scheduled; nodes with the same earliest cycle are ordered according to DAG height.

The queue is initialized to contain all the successors of DEF1 nodes in the DAG. The main scheduling loop repeatedly removes a node from the queue and attempts to place it in the current machine instruction by calling *Schedule*. If the node can't fit in the current machine instruction, *Schedule* increments the node's *.earliest-cycle* slot and requeues it. If the node does fit, *Schedule* adds all the successors of the node that are now data ready to the queue. The *.earliest-cycle* of a newly added data-ready node is computed based on when the value of each of the operands is available and when any constraining predecessors were scheduled.

All the nodes in the DAG will eventually be added to the queue and then scheduled later; when the queue is empty, all the nodes have been scheduled.

The global variable *current-cycle* contains the current cycle being scheduled; because nodes are ordered in the queue by earliest cycle, its value increases monotonically. A vector of resource sets keeps track of which resources are used in each cycle; an operation can be scheduled in the current cycle only if the resources it needs are available. When an operation is scheduled, the resources it uses are marked unavailable during the appropriate cycles (remember that a resource request can extend over several cycles). Another vector indexed by cycle contains the machine instructions of the schedule.

Nodes

To aid in list scheduling, nodes have the following slots:

.predecessors-left is the number of unscheduled predecessors of the node. When a node's *.predecessors-left* count reaches 0, it is data ready, and it is added to the data-ready queue to be scheduled.

.earliest-cycle is the earliest cycle that the node could be scheduled. It is set when the node is added to the data-ready queue and is computed based on when the operands are available and when the constraining predecessors were scheduled.

.cycle is the cycle the node was actually scheduled.

.register-bank and *.register* give the register location of the value of this node after it has been scheduled.

.register-cycle is the first cycle that the node's value can be read from its register location. This is usually *node.cycle* + *Delay*(*node.fu*).

.read-cycle is the most recent cycle that the value of the node was read from its register location (or from the constant generator, if the node is a DEF1 for an immediate constant). In any cycle, once a register is

read out onto a port of the register bank, one or more machine elements connected to that port can read its value that cycle. This slot tells the code generator whether the value of the node is already being read by another operation in the current cycle; if it is, the code generator doesn't need to schedule the resources needed to read the register. Similarly, a constant generator can generate the same constant for many different machine elements in the same cycle.

.readers-left is the number of unscheduled nodes reading the value of this node. When this count reaches 0, the register containing this node's value can be freed for other uses. The count includes the number of conditional jumps for which this value is live on the off-trace edge. For example, in this trace:

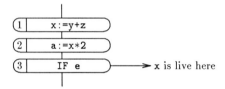

the *.readers-left* count of the node representing operation 1 starts out at 2. This guarantees that the register holding x will not be reused until after both operations 2 and 3 have been scheduled. If the conditional jump weren't included in the count, then the register containing x might be reused (and x's value lost) before operation 3 is scheduled; operations on the off-trace edge of the jump reading x wouldn't get the correct value.

If a USE1 is a reader of a node, that node's register will never be freed for other uses, since a USE1 is never scheduled. That is, the register will remain alive until the end of the schedule (exactly what we want).

Scheduling an Operation Node

The procedure *Schedule* takes the following steps trying to schedule an operation node:

1. The resources needed for the functional unit assigned to the operation are scheduled.

2. The resources needed to read the operands are scheduled.

3. A good destination register bank is found and the resources needed to write it are scheduled.

If any of steps 1–3 fail because the necessary resources aren't available in the current cycle, *Schedule* undoes any resources that were successfully scheduled for this node, sets the *.earliest-cycle* of the node to be *current-cycle* + 1, requeues the node in the data-ready queue, and returns.

4. The operands are marked as having been read this cycle.

5. The registers of operands for which this node is the last scheduled reader are freed.

6. A destination register is allocated from the chosen register bank and assigned to the node; copy nodes are inserted if necessary.

7. Any successors of the node that are now data ready are added to the data-ready queue.

8. The machine operation for this node is added to the current instruction.

Step-by-step details:

2. The resources needed to read the operands are scheduled.

Each operand is examined. If the operand's *.read-cycle* is the current cycle, that means the operand, in a register bank or a constant generator, already appears on the output port of the bank or generator because some other operation scheduled in this cycle is already reading that operand; no new resources are needed by the current operation to read the operand. Otherwise, the resources needed to read a value from the register bank or to use the constant generator are scheduled. Finally, whether or not *.read-cycle* equals the current cycle, the resources needed to move a value from the output of the operand's bank or generator to the input of this node's functional unit are scheduled (these resources are specified in the point-to-point connection table of the machine model).

3. A good destination register bank is found and the resources needed to write it are scheduled.

A functional unit may have several register banks connected to its output, and one must be chosen. Because those banks may have their outputs connected to different sets of machine elements, it pays to pick a bank that is closest to the inputs of the functional units that will be reading the value of this node, thereby reducing the need to move the value later on.

Let *destination-me* be the machine element location of the successor node of maximum height that reads the current node. If the maximum height reader is an operation, the location is the assigned functional unit; if the reader is a USE1 with a specified final register bank, the location is that bank. To find a good destination register bank, *Schedule* considers all banks that

– are connected to the output of the functional unit;

– are on the shortest path from the functional unit to *destination-me*;

– have a free register;

– can be written in this cycle (that is, the resources needed to write the register bank and the point-to-point resources needed to move the value from the functional unit to the register bank are available in the current cycle);

Of these, *Schedule* then finds one with the minimum number of register-bank reading conflicts (reading conflicts are described later) and schedules the required resources.

4. The operands are marked as having been read this cycle.

The *.read-cycle* of each operand is set to the current cycle. Any later operations being scheduled this cycle that also read the operand will then know that the resources needed to read the operand have already been scheduled.

5. The registers of operands for which this node is the last scheduled reader are freed.

The *.readers-left* count of each operand and each off-live predecessor is decremented. If a node's count reaches 0, that node's register is freed for other uses. The details of register allocation and deallocation are described later.

6. A destination register is allocated from the chosen register bank and assigned to the node; copy nodes are inserted if necessary between the node and its successors.

More on this later.

7. Any successors of the node that are now data ready are added to the data-ready queue.

The *.predecessors-left* count of each of the successor nodes (including constraining-edge successors) is decremented. If the count reaches 0, the successor is now data-ready; its *.earliest-cycle* is computed as described later, and it is added to the data-ready queue for scheduling.

Data Movements and Copy Nodes

For several reasons, the register bank chosen to hold a node's value may not be directly readable by some of the successor nodes reading the value.

The most common situation is that the inputs of a successor operation's functional unit may not be directly connected to the register bank. For example, consider these nodes:

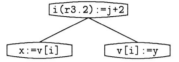

Suppose that the node for i was just scheduled and its value assigned to a register in bank 2. Further, the memory unit assigned to the left vector reference is directly connected to bank 2, while the unit assigned to the right reference isn't. Somehow the list scheduler must copy the value of i to some bank connected to the right reference's memory unit.

Immediately after i's node is scheduled and assigned a register bank, the list scheduler notices that the right reference can't read the value of i from bank 2, so it splices a COPY node into the DAG:

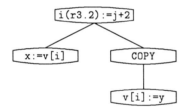

When it gets scheduled, this COPY node will copy the value of i from bank 2 to a bank nearer the memory unit. The COPY node receives a height-based priority in the data-ready queue just like any other node; a time-critical COPY will be scheduled early, and a not-so-critical COPY will be delayed in favor of more critical nodes.

Another reason that a value stored in a register bank may not be directly readable by a successor is that there are not enough output ports on the register bank. For example:

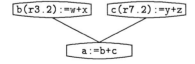

Suppose that the functional unit assigned to a:=b+c is connected to register banks

1 and 2, and that each bank has only one output port. As it stands, the addition can't execute because both its operands are in the same bank. This situation is called **register-bank reading conflict** and occurs whenever the number of bank output ports required by an operation exceeds the number of ports on the bank.

When choosing a destination register for a node, *Schedule* looks for banks with the least number of reading conflicts with its successor nodes, but it isn't always possible to avoid conflict. So when a destination register is assigned to a node, *Schedule* looks at its successors to see if any now have reading conflict. If so, *Schedule* splices a COPY node into the DAG that will copy the value into a non-conflicting bank.

For example, suppose that in the DAG above c:=y+z was scheduled after b:=w+x. When *Schedule* picks bank 2 for c:=y+z, it notices that a:=b+c now has reading conflict, since it can't read both its operands from bank 2. So a COPY node is spliced in:

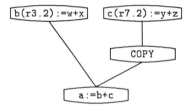

When the COPY gets scheduled it will copy the value of c into bank 1, at which point the addition will be schedulable.

The final situation where the list scheduler needs to splice in COPY nodes occurs at USE1s with specified final locations. Consider this example:

The initial location for x may have been specified on the beginning of the trace, or BUG may have chosen that location because a time-critical operation needed x as an operand in bank 3. In any case, the list scheduler must splice a COPY node between the two nodes so that x ends up in its required location. This situation also arises with operations:

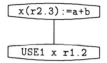

Note that if the two locations of x were in the same bank but in different registers, a COPY would still be needed.

The general strategy for splicing COPY nodes is as follows: Immediately after choosing a register for a node, *Schedule* finds all the successors that need a COPY node spliced in for one of the reasons described above. It then groups these successors such that each successor in a group has the same first register bank on the shortest path from the node to the location of successor. A COPY node is spliced between the node and each group. Grouping the nodes according to the first hop on the shortest path minimizes the amount of copying needed. *Schedule* then computes the height of the COPY nodes and the earliest cycle they could be scheduled and inserts them into the data-ready queue.

As an example of the grouping, consider this DAG:

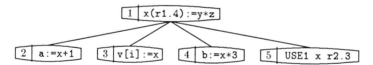

Suppose that only node 3 could read x directly from bank 4, that the first register bank on the shortest path from bank 4 to the functional units of nodes 2 and 4 is bank 2, and that the first register bank on the shortest path from bank 4 to bank 3 is bank 3 itself. The DAG would look then look like:

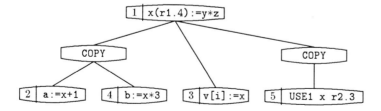

A COPY node moves a value only one register bank closer to its eventual destination. If after a COPY has been scheduled its value is still not directly readable by some of its successors, the process is repeated: One or more new COPYs are spliced between the original COPY and the successors and are added to the data-ready queue for scheduling. This continues until all of the successors have access to a copy of the value that they can read directly.

Scheduling a Copy Node

Scheduling a COPY node is very similar to scheduling an operation, except that the "operation" of a COPY node is simply a register transfer. The steps are:

1. The resources needed to read the operand from its register bank or constant generator are scheduled.

2. A good destination register bank is found and the resources needed to move the operand to the bank and write the register are scheduled.

   If steps 1 or 2 fail because the necessary resources aren't available in the current cycle, *Schedule* undoes any resources that were successfully scheduled for this node, sets the *.earliest-cycle* of the node to be *current − cycle* + 1, requeues the node in the data-ready queue, and returns.

3. A destination register is allocated from the destination bank. If the desired destination register is occupied by some other node, special action must be taken (described below).

4. The operand is marked as having been read this cycle.

5. If this node is the last scheduled reader of the operand, the operand's register is freed.

6. The destination register is assigned to the node and copy nodes are inserted if necessary.

7. Any successors of the node that are now data ready are added to the data-ready queue.

8. The machine operation for this node is added to the current instruction.

I'll only discuss the steps that are different from scheduling an operation:

2. A good destination register bank is found and the resources needed to move the operand to the bank and write the register are scheduled.

The same procedure used to pick a bank for operation nodes is used here. But instead of considering banks connected to the operation's functional unit, *Schedule* consider's banks connected to the register bank or constant generator of the operand.

3. A destination register is allocated from the destination bank. If the desired destination register is occupied by some other node, special action must be taken (described below).

A special case arises when the maximum-height reader of the COPY is a USE1 with a specified final location in the register bank selected for the COPY. For example:

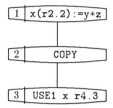

If bank 3 is directly connected to the output of bank 2, then bank 3 will be chosen as the destination bank of the COPY. Normally, any free register in the destination bank is as good as any other, but in this case it makes sense to copy only into the register specified for the USE1 (register 4 in the example). The register allocator recognizes this special case and will try to allocate the specific destination register of the USE1.

But what if the register is occupied by the value of some other node? For example:

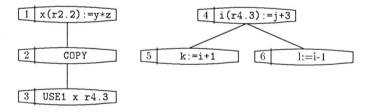

The COPY can't be scheduled until all the successors of node 4 are scheduled; at that point, register 4 in bank 3 will then be unused. If node 4 isn't a descendent of the COPY, then the list scheduler just adds constraining edges from the COPY to all the unscheduled successors of 4. The list scheduler won't attempt to schedule the COPY again until all the successors of 4 have been scheduled.

However, adding in the constraining edges won't work if some of the successors of 4 are descendents of the COPY. For example, if the COPY were an operand of node 5:

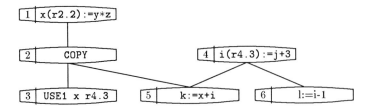

then adding a constraining edge from the COPY to the successor would create a circularity in the DAG—5 couldn't be scheduled until 2 was, and 2 couldn't be scheduled until 5 was.

The solution is to copy the value of node 4 from its current register to some other register, thus freeing up register 4, bank 3 for use by the COPY. To do this, the list scheduler splices a new COPY between 4 and its successors:

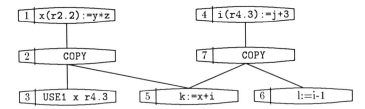

In addition, a constraining edge is added from node 2 to the new COPY 7, so that the list scheduler won't attempt to schedule 2 again until the new COPY has moved the value of 4 out of the way.

Scheduling Def1 Nodes

If you recall from the description of list scheduling's top level, the data-ready queue is initialized by scheduling all the DEF1 nodes, which causes their successors to be added to the data-ready queue. The steps taken to schedule a DEF1 node are:

1. A register is allocated for the node (if it isn't an immediate constant).

2. The register is assigned to the node and copy nodes are inserted if necessary.

3. Any successors of the node that are now data ready are added to the data-ready queue.

Details:

1. A register is allocated for the node (if it isn't an immediate constant).

If the DEF1 has an initial register location specified on the trace, that register is allocated. Otherwise, the bottom-up-greedy phase allocated a register bank to the node but not a register; *Schedule* just picks any free register in the bank.

2. The register is assigned to the node and copy nodes are inserted if necessary.

As for operations and COPY nodes, new COPY nodes are inserted between the DEF1 and all the successors that can't read the assigned register directly.

3. Any successors of the node that are now data ready are added to the data-ready queue.

The *.predecessors-left* count of each successor is decremented, and if it reaches zero, the successor is added to the queue.

Scheduling Use1 Nodes

Schedule does nothing when called on a USE1 node except, for debugging, verify that the node's value has indeed ended up in the required location.

Constraining Edges

As discussed previously, constraining edges are added to the DAG to enforce several types of ordering constraints. Associated with each constraining edge e is a delay d_e; for example, write-after-read edges have $d_e = 0$, and vector-conflict edges have $d_e = 1$. I fudged earlier and said that if operation B has a constraining edge e to operation A, then B can be scheduled no earlier than d_e cycles after A. However, multicycle operations and partial schedules impose an additional requirement: The last cycle of operation B must also occur at least d_e cycles after the last cycle of operation A.

To see why, consider this trace fragment:

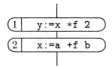

Because operation 1 reads x and operation 2 writes x, there is a constraining edge with delay 0 from 2 to 1. Assume that multiplies take 4 cycles and additions 2

cycles, and that the requirement about last cycles wasn't being enforced. Then the following would be a possible schedule:

1	y:=x *f 2	
2	*f-2	x:=a +f b
3	*f-3	+f-2
4	*f-4	

That is, the addition is started 1 cycle after the multiply. But suppose the trace scheduler decided to place a join originally above operations 1 and 2 in between cycles 3 and 4 of the schedule, bisecting the multiply. The trace scheduler would splice a partial schedule and a copy of operation 2 between the join and the schedule:

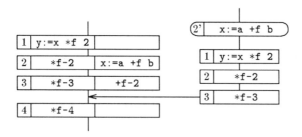

But now the copy of operation 2 is executed before the multiply, not after as it should, giving the multiply the wrong value of x.

That's the reason for the requirement that the last cycle of a constrained operation be at least d_e cycles after the last cycle of the constraining operation. Applying the rule to the example, the addition must be scheduled at least 2 cycles after the start of the multiply:

1	y:=x *f 2	
2	*f-2	
3	*f-3	x:=a +f b
4	*f-4	+f-2

Now, no matter where the trace scheduler makes a join, the correct partial schedule and operation copies will be generated at the join. For example, if the join were made between the third and fourth cycles, we'd get the following:

The addition properly executes after the multiply.

Rather than constrain the last cycles, a slightly better solution might be to include the addition in the partial schedule with the multiply, preventing the trace scheduler from copying the addition above the partial-schedule multiply at the join. (A similar technique could be used at splits, where the same situation arises.) It wouldn't be hard to implement this, since the situation can easily be identified using the constraining edges. The advantage would be that constrained operations could be scheduled slightly earlier. But I've examined several inner loops where this problem occurs, and in none of them did the current strategy (aligning last cycles) delay a critical-path operation; I would guess that using the enhanced partial-schedule solution would pay off little, if at all.

Computing the Earliest Cycle

When all of a node's operands and constraining predecessors have been scheduled, *Schedule* inserts the node into the data-ready queue. The queue is ordered primarily by the earliest cycles that the nodes could be scheduled, based on when the operands and constraining predecessors are scheduled.

The *.earliest-cycle* of a data-ready *node* is formally defined as:

$$\max(c_1, c_2)$$

where

$$c_1 = \max_{o \in O(node)} (o.cycle + Delay(o.fu))$$

$$c_2 = \max_{p \in C(node)} (p.cycle + CD(p, node) + \max(0, Delay(p.fu) - Delay(node.fu)))$$

$O(node)$ is the set of operands of *node*,

$C(node)$ is the set of constraining predecessors of *node*, and

$CD(n, m)$ is the maximum delay (0 or 1) associated with any constraining edges from nodes n to m.

That is, *node* can be scheduled only after all the operands have finished execution and after all the delays specified by the constraining predecessors. The expression

$$\max{(0, Delay(p.fu) - Delay(node.fu))}$$

used in the computation of the constraining delays guarantees that the last cycle of *node* is scheduled no earlier than the last cycle of predecessor p (as discussed above).

Dead Code Due to Conditional Jumps

Sometimes dead code is created during scheduling because operations move below conditional jumps. Consider this sample trace:

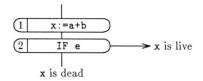

The variable x is live on the off-trace edge of the jump but dead immediately after the jump on the trace. Nodes 1 and 2 can be scheduled in any relative order; the only edge between them is an off-live edge indicating that x is off-live at 2, but this edge doesn't impose any scheduling constraints. The only purpose of the edge is to maintain the *.readers-left* count of node 1.

Suppose that node 1 is scheduled before 2. When 1 is scheduled, its *.readers-left* count is 1, indicating there is 1 unscheduled reader (node 2). Thus the register holding x remains allocated until node 2 is scheduled; at that point, the *.readers-left* count of node 1 is decremented and reaches 0, so x's register is deallocated, available for use in the next cycle.

But now suppose that node 1 is scheduled after node 2:

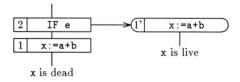

(After code generation, the trace scheduler will place a copy of 1 on the off-trace edge of 2.) When node 2 is scheduled, the *.readers-left* count of node 1 is decremented from 1 to 0 (because of the off-live edge from 2 to 1). Then when node 1 is scheduled, its *.readers-left* count is already 0, indicating that there are no unscheduled readers. In other words, the value produced by node 1 is now dead because 1 has moved below its only reader, the conditional jump. The code generator doesn't have to generate an actual machine operation for 1. Note that the copy 1' still computes the value of x on the off-trace edge of the jump.

In general, when *Schedule* gets a node with a zero *.readers-left* count, it assumes the value of the node is useless because it moved below a conditional jump, and it doesn't schedule a machine operation. Instead, it just adds a no-op to the schedule (the interface to the trace scheduler requires that every source operation have a representative machine operation in the schedule).

Allocating Registers

Because the schedule of machine instructions is formed in sequence, the list scheduler doesn't need a temporal data structure telling which registers are available during which cycles. It only needs to know whether or not a register is free in the current cycle being formed. Associated with each register is the cycle c when that register will next be free for use; if $c \leq$ *current-cycle* then the register can be allocated for an operation in the current cycle. When an register is allocated to a node, c is set to infinity.

When can a register be reused? Roughly, a register holding a node's value must remain allocated to that node until all the node's readers have completed execution. More precisely, a node's register can be reused in the cycle defined by

$$\max(c_1, c_2)$$

where

$$c_1 = \max_{s \in R(node)} LastCycle(s)$$

$$c_2 = \max_{s \in OL(node)} \left(LastCycle(s) + 1 \right)$$

$$LastCycle(node) = \begin{cases} node.cycle + Delay(node.fu) - 1, & \text{for operation nodes;} \\ node.cycle & \text{for COPY nodes.} \end{cases}$$

$R(node)$ is the set of readers of *node*, and

$OL(node)$ is the set of those conditional jumps for which the value of *node* is live on the off-trace edge (the conditional jumps which "off-live read" the value of *node*).

That is, a node's register cannot be reused until the last cycle of each successor that reads the register and until the succeeding cycle after each off-live successor.

To understand this requirement, suppose an operation takes one cycle and that it is the last scheduled use of one of its operands. Because a write into a register takes effect at the end of the cycle, the operand's register can be reused (written into by some other operation) in the same cycle as the operation. If instead the operation takes two or more cycles, you might think that the operand's register could still be reused in the operation's first cycle (as opposed to its last cycle), since its value will be latched by the functional unit's inputs. But consider this section of a trace:

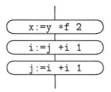

and the corresponding machine instructions that might be generated under such a policy:

1	x(r1):=y(r2) *f 2	i(r2):=j(r3) +i 1
2	*f-2	j(r4):=i(r2) +i 1
3	*f-3	
4	*f-4	

The registers assigned to variables are indicated in parentheses; assume the multiply takes 4 cycles. Notice that register 2, originally holding the variable y, was reused in the first cycle to hold i. Suppose the trace scheduler decides to place a join to the trace between cycles 1 and 2; the multiply is bisected by the join, so the trace scheduler creates a partial schedule between the join and the trace:

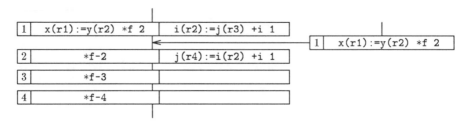

Because the addition i:=j +i 1 isn't bisected by the join, it isn't included in the partial schedule. Notice that on entry to the partial schedule from the join, both i and y should be in register 2, an impossibility.

The code generator avoids this situation simply by keeping a register allocated until the last cycle of each of the operations reading it. In the example, register 2 wouldn't be available for reuse until cycle 4, so another register would have been chosen for i.

An analogous situation occurs with destination registers and splits from the trace. Suppose we had a trace and schedule similar to the above, except that i is kept in r1 and an IF is also scheduled in the first cycle:

1	x(r1):=y(r2) *f 2	i(r1):=j(r3) +i 1	IF e
2	*f-2	j(r4):=i(r1) +i 1	
3	*f-3		
4	*f-4		

Because register 1, the destination register of the multiply, isn't written until cycle 4, you might think that register 1 could be also used for i, the result of the addition, as shown above. But the split from the trace caused by the IF bisects the multiply, resulting in a partial schedule between the trace and the split:

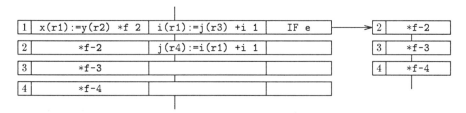

On exit from the partial schedule, both i and x are supposed to be in register 1. But by allocating the destination register of the multiply at the beginning of the multiply, this problem is avoided.

In summary, a register is allocated to hold a value starting on the first cycle of the operation producing that value. The register isn't deallocated until the last cycle of all the operations that read the register and until the succeeding cycle of all the jumps for which the value is live on the off-trace edge.

This strategy makes life easier for the compiler but wastes registers. In general, $2(d-1)$ extra registers are needed for a pipeline of d stages. Experiments with the benchmarks show that the compiler can rarely keep the pipelines full, so this wastage might not be important. However, if it turns out to be significant, the code generator could be smarter about what goes into partial schedules, including more than just bisected operations when necessary. In the last example, if j(r4):=i(r1) +i 1 were included in the partial schedule, then there wouldn't be any problem, since then only x would need to be in register 1 at the exit from the partial schedule. It wouldn't be hard to implement this smarter strategy, but it would add hair to an already hairy interface.

Choosing Good Registers

Choosing a good register bank for a node has already been described—BUG chooses banks for DEF1s, and *Schedule* chooses banks for operation and COPY nodes. Once the bank has been chosen, though, *Schedule* must choose a free register within the bank.

The procedure *AllocateRegister(bank,cycle,node)* selects a register in *bank* that is free no later than *cycle*, for use by a DAG node. A trivial implementation of *AllocateRegister* would simply look for some register such that its first cycle free is less than or equal to *cycle*. While trivial, this strategy results in excess copying of values between registers. For example, consider a trace of an inner-loop body; the final locations of the induction variables would probably be different from the initial locations, and copying on the loop back edge would be needed to move the variables' final values into the initial locations at the top of the loop. Experience with Ruttenberg's code generator, which only implemented the trivial strategy, showed that this back edge copying could be expensive (sometimes 10% or more of total execution time). But some simple heuristics can virtually eliminate that copying.

The list scheduler keeps a table that gives for each variable name any final locations specified by USE1s for that variable. When allocating a register from bank *b* for a node that assigns x, *AllocateRegister* consults the table and prefers any register *r* such that *r.b* is a final USE1 location for x. For example:

If bank 4 was chosen for the addition, then *AllocateRegister* would chose register 3 if it was free, since register 3, bank 4 would be recorded in the table under x. Assuming register 3 was available, no extra copying would be needed to satisfy the USE1. Another example:

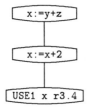

If bank 4 was chosen for node x:=y+z, *AllocateRegister* would try to allocate register 3 for the node, thus keeping x in the same register for both additions.

When looking for a register for variable x, *AllocateRegister* tries to avoid registers preferred for other variables. That is, a register preferred for y won't be selected for x unless there are no other free registers in the bank. This improves the chances that a preferred register will be allocated to a variable.

Traces of inner-loop bodies require special attention. For example, if this was an inner-loop trace:

```
(  DEF1 i   )
(  j:=i*2   )
(  i:=j+1   )
(  USE1 i   )
```

we'd like the initial and final location of i to be the same so that the final value of i wouldn't need to be copied into its initial location on the loop back edge. (BUG picks register banks, but not registers, for the initial locations but ignores the final locations.)

To get DEF1s and USE1s to match, *Schedule* takes special action after choosing a register for a DEF1 x. If x is a loop induction variable, *Schedule* looks for a USE1 x node. (For these purposes, an induction variable is one assigned in the loop whose value is live on entrance to the top of the loop; an induction variable will have only one USE1 node.) If the USE1 x has no specified final location, *Schedule* sets the location to be the register just chosen for the DEF1 x and records this new location in the USE1 preference table described above.

For example, consider the inner-loop trace above. When *Schedule* picks some register for the DEF1 i, it will simultaneously set the location of USE1 i to be that same register:

```
(  DEF1 i r3.4  )
(   j:=i*2      )
(   i:=j+1      )
(  USE1 i r3.4  )
```

When i:=j+1 gets scheduled, the USE1 preference mechanism causes *AllocateRegister* to try to pick register 3, bank 4 as the destination, thus avoiding the need to move i on the loop back edge. Even if the preferred register isn't available (because it's allocated to some other node), the copying needed to put the final value of i into its initial loop location will be incorporated on the trace, where it most likely can be overlapped with other computation.

AllocateRegister uses one more heuristic which is usually redundant with the previous ones. If the operation being assigned a register has the form x:=x op y, x:=y op x, or x:= op x, and the required destination bank is the same as the bank currently holding x, *AllocateRegister* returns the register holding x. That is, the assignment to x will be done in place in the register.

At this point you might be worried that heuristics based on variable names might get confused by different uses of the same variable name. But remember that variable renaming has given unique names to the different uses of a source variable.

Together, these simple heuristics eliminate the copying that would otherwise be needed on loop back edges. They also reduce the copying at other boundaries between traces. Execution profiles of the benchmarks show that almost all the time is spent in the inner loops; since the heuristics handle these loops just fine, attempting to adapt more sophisticated register-allocation algorithms (such as the graph coloring now in vogue [Chow 84]) could well be a waste of effort.

Spilling Registers

When a compiler runs out of available registers, it must **spill** some into memory. The current compiler doesn't implement spilling—it assumes that the machine model provides enough registers. If a node can't be scheduled because there isn't a free register in its chosen destination bank, the node is simply requeued for scheduling in the next cycle; in the meantime, the scheduling of other nodes may free up registers in the full bank (for example, the operands of such a node may be in the full bank while the destination is in another).

This delaying strategy will only work well when the number of registers required for parallel execution of the trace is close to (or less than) the number supplied by the hardware. If many more registers are needed, then the compiler must spill to memory. (The current compiler will blow up if delaying doesn't free up registers—it will just keep delaying data-ready nodes until it exceeds the maximum allowed schedule length.)

It wouldn't be hard to implement spilling in list scheduling, using a method like that used in the FPS-164 compiler [Touzeau 84]. The code generator looks for a low-priority node occupying a register in the full bank, and it splices a memory store and memory load between the node and its unscheduled successors. A constraining edge is added from the memory load to the node that couldn't find a register originally, guaranteeing that the memory load won't be scheduled until at least one new node has been allocated a register and scheduled.

The code generator could also look for variables live on entrance and exit from the trace but that weren't referenced during the trace. Currently these variables are assigned register locations to hold their values throughout the trace. If the code generator runs out of registers, it can simply pick memory locations for these variables instead, freeing the assigned registers for immediate use. (Of course, this forces later adjoining traces using the variables to do memory references.)

Finally, the code generator can look for constants occupying registers and simply appropriate the registers. Because a constant can be regenerated on demand, the code generator simply splices the nodes necessary for regeneration in between the node representing the constant and its unscheduled successors.

Ruttenberg claims that an operation scheduler could perform spilling better than a list scheduler. When it runs out of registers, the operation scheduler can look back up into the schedule already generated and schedule the spilling as early as possible; whereas the list scheduler is always constrained to schedule newly generated nodes after the current cycle being scheduled. Would the operation scheduler be better in practice? Who knows—it all depends on how time-critical are the traces in which spilling occurs, how many non-critical nodes are available for spilling, etc. My intuition, based on experience with both code generators, says that the operation scheduler wouldn't be much better.

But in the context of designing hardware and compiler simultaneously, minor differences in spilling ability shouldn't matter one bit in choosing a code-generation paradigm. If there aren't enough registers to service the time-critical inner loops of scientific code, the machine is improperly designed. Most of the inner loops are memory bound, and spilling will decrease performance drastically due to the excess inner-loop memory references. Either more registers should be added to the machine, or else some functional units removed (or their bandwidth decreased).

Time Complexity of List Scheduling

All of *Schedule*'s actions take constant time. Though a node may have arbitrarily many successors, all of the work done on them by *Schedule* (splicing copies, decrementing predecessor counts, etc.) can be charged to the individual successors. Because the number of operands of a node is bounded by a constant, that work takes constant time. Splicing a copy between a node and one of its successors takes $O(r)$ time, where r is the maximum number of register banks connected to the output of a functional unit.

Inserting and deleting a node from the data-ready queue takes $O(\log n)$ time, where n is the size of the DAG. So the list scheduling time is bounded by:

$$O\left(\sum_{node \in \text{DAG}} Q(node) r \log n\right)$$

where $Q(node)$ is the number of times a node is inserted in the data-ready queue.

A node can be requeued at most $O(n)$ times. For example, suppose a node P has successors $S_1, S_2, \ldots, S_n$, and that each of the S_i requires the same resource. After P is scheduled, all of the successors S_i are inserted in the data-ready queue. All n successors are considered for the next instruction but only one can be scheduled; the rest are requeued for the next instruction because of the restricted resource. The $n-1$ requeued nodes are considered for the next instruction, and only one can be scheduled while the $n-2$ others are requeued. This continues until all the nodes are scheduled, resulting in a total of $n(n+1)/2$ insertions.

So the worst-case time for list scheduling is $O(n^2 r \log n)$. Since r, the maximum number of register banks connected to a functional unit's output, is constant for any machine model, the worst-case time is $O(n^2 \log n)$.

The easy way to improve this upper bound is by having a separate data-ready queue for each functional unit. To form an instruction, the list scheduler removes the head of each queue and fits it into the instruction; when all the heads have been removed and placed, the instruction is emitted and a new one started. Assuming that the only resources required by nodes are functional units, nodes would never be requeued, and thus list scheduling would take $O(n \log n)$ time. Of course, if nodes require more than one resource (such as register ports and buses as well as functional units), then this scheme wouldn't work as well (though it would help).

But does the $O(n^2 \log n)$ worst-case time matter? Not with a realistic machine and realistic source programs.

I measured the number of times each node was inserted and the data-ready queue sizes for all of the traces of three typical programs on the 8-cluster machine model. (The programs and the machine model are described in chapter 8.) The inner loops were unrolled 8, 16, and sometimes 32 times:

	Insertions/node			DRQ Size		
Unrolling	8	16	32	8	16	32
FFT	1.5	1.7	–	30	53	–
TRID4	1.7	1.9	–	62	85	–
SOLVE1	1.2	1.3	1.3	20	29	33

"Insertions/node" is the total number of insertions into the queue divided by the total number of nodes scheduled. On average, a node is inserted in the data-ready queue less than two times; that is, *Schedule* is called on a node less than two times. *Schedule* usually does very little work to determine that an operation doesn't fit in the current instruction; before doing anything else it checks that the resources needed to read the operands and schedule the functional unit are available.

"DRQ Size" is the sum of the queue sizes before each insertion into the queue divided by the total number of insertions. (Remember that the queue can include nodes that are first ready to execute in the next several cycles, not just the current cycle.) In terms of $\log n$, these average sizes are in the realm of small numbers where constant factors can be more important than the asymptotic behavior. For example, to insert an item in a heap of size 60 takes 6 probes, and the insertion is probably much cheaper than the other work done by *Schedule*.

On casual examination, the other benchmark programs all look similar to those measured above, at least in terms of traces and the size of individual expressions. I think it's safe to say that the observed average behavior of list scheduling is quite linear, $O(nr)$.

Reporting Back to the Trace Scheduler

Once a schedule is generated for a trace, the code generator returns the schedule to the trace scheduler, which then integrates the machine instructions into the flow graph. The trace scheduler inserts partial schedules, DEFs and USEs recording live-variable locations, and copies due to code motion between the schedule and the rest of the flow graph. As described in chapter 4, the code generator provides several interface procedures to aid the trace scheduler in these tasks— the trace scheduler cannot access the schedule's data structures directly. The implementation of the algorithms and data structures supporting this interface is non-trivial.

Schedule:length(*schedule*) simply returns the length of the schedule.

Schedule:[](*schedule*,*cycle*) returns the contents of a machine instruction in the schedule as a list of pairs, each pair of the form <*machine-operation*, *intermediate-code-operation*>, where the intermediate-code operation is the source operation giving rise to the machine operation. COPY operations (register transfers) due to intermediate-code assignments have an associated intermediate-code operation, but COPY operations generated during list scheduling merely to move operands where they are needed in the machine have no associated intermediate-code operation. A *d*-cycle multicycle operation is represented as *d* successive machine operations, each associated with the original source operation.

To implement *Schedule:[]*, the list scheduler maintains the schedule as a vector of lists indexed by cycle, each list containing pairs of the form <*machine-operation*, *node*>. The DAG nodes contain the original intermediate-code operations as supplied by the trace scheduler.

Schedule:split(*schedule*,*cycle*) returns the partial schedule and live-variable locations at a jump off the schedule at the given cycle. Likewise, *Schedule:join*(*schedule*,*cycle*) returns the partial schedule and live-variable locations for a join to the schedule between *cycle* − 1 and *cycle*. The live-variable locations at a split are represented by a DEF pseudo-op, at a join by a USE pseudo-op. The join to the beginning of the trace and the exit from the end are handled just like other splits and joins.

Constructing the partial schedule at a split or join isn't hard. The code generator scans the schedule backwards and forwards from the given cycle, looking for operations that span the cycle.

The hardest part of the interface is computing the live-variable locations at a split or join. The reported locations are not what is live at the given cycle in the schedule, but rather what is live on exit from the constructed partial schedule (for splits) or on entrance (for joins). That is, a split with a partial schedule looks like:

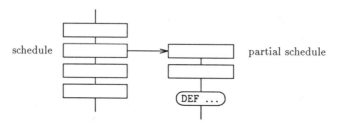

and a join looks like:

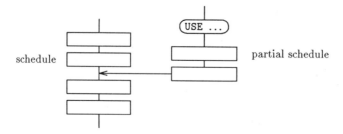

The variable locations reported at the DEF and USE points are slightly different from the locations at the actual split and join to the schedule.

A machine instruction may have many conditional jumps, each jumping to a different off-trace location:

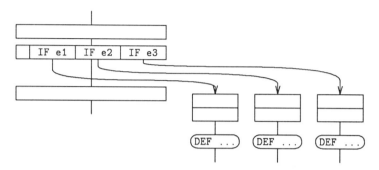

Though the partial schedules at the jump destinations are the same, there may be different sets of variables live at the destinations. But the interface to the code generator doesn't need to distinguish between the different jumps; instead, it returns a single DEF that is the union of all the variables live at each of the destinations. It doesn't matter that some variables will be reported live at a jump that really aren't. The trace-scheduler's incremental live analysis only looks at the contents of USEs, which are accurate, and it will propagate correct live variable sets up to the DEFs. When the code generator is given a DEF on some trace, it uses the live-on-entrance set also supplied with the trace to weed out variable-location pairs from the DEF that aren't really live.

To compute the live-variable locations, the code generator uses a live-dead analysis on the nodes of the DAG. Because a node represents one value in one location over one contiguous period of time, it's straightforward to compute a vector *live* such that $live[i]$ is the set of nodes whose value is live on entry to cycle i. To report the live-variable locations at the beginning of a cycle, the code generator merely enumerates the nodes in $live[i]$ and examines their variable name and recorded location. (There may be several nodes with the same variable name that are live in a cycle; they each represent a different location for the variable.)

The vector *live* is computed from two auxiliary vectors, *gen* and *kill*. The vector $gen[i]$ gives the set of nodes whose value first becomes live on entry to cycle i, and $kill[i]$ gives the set of nodes whose value first becomes dead at the end of cycle i. The vectors *gen* and *kill* are constructed by enumerating the nodes and computing their *gen* and *kill* cycles; a node whose value becomes available in cycle i is added to $gen[i]$, and a node whose value is last used by its successors in cycle j is added to $kill[j]$. The vector *live* is recursively defined in terms of *gen*, *kill*, and itself:

$$live[i] = (live[i-1] - kill[i-1]) \cup gen[i]$$

That is, the nodes live on entry to cycle i are the nodes live on entry to cycle $i - 1$, minus the nodes that became dead at the end of cycle $i - 1$, plus the nodes that are newly live in cycle i.

The sets of nodes are represented using bit vectors. Assuming constant time bit vector operations, the vectors *gen* and *kill* can be constructed from the DAG in time linear in the number of nodes, and *live* can be constructed in time linear in the size of the schedule.

Actually, I've been fudging. To account for the partial schedules, two separate live analyses are needed, one for splits and one for joins. At a split, we're interested in the variables live on exit from the split's partial schedule; similarly, at a join we're interested in the variables live on entrance to the join's partial schedule. Using the general techniques described above, two sets of vectors are computed: *splitGen*, *splitKill*, and *splitLive*, and *joinGen*, *joinKill*, and *joinLive*. The vector *splitLive* is used to report live-variable locations at splits, and *joinLive* at joins. The only difference between the sets of vectors is the way the *gen* and *kill* cycles of nodes are computed.

First, let's consider splits. Because a jump at cycle i takes effect at the end of the cycle after all values have been computed and stored, the interface looks at $splitLive[i + 1]$, the nodes live on entry to the next cycle, to determine those live at the split.

To compute *splitGen*, each node is added to the set $splitGen[node.cycle + 1]$. That is, a node's value is live on entry to the cycle immediately after the cycle the node is scheduled, even if the node is a multicycle operation. To see why, consider this schedule fragment:

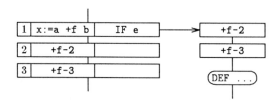

A conditional jump occurs in the first cycle of a 3-cycle addition. Even though though the value of x isn't available after the jump occurs in the first cycle, it is available on exit from the partial schedule at the DEF, which is the point we're interested in. By definition, any multicycle operation bisected by a jump is guaranteed to finish execution in the split's partial schedule. So for the purposes of computing *splitGen*, we can pretend that every operation takes one cycle.

Similar reasoning applies to *splitKill*. Each node is added to the set $splitKill[c]$ where the cycle c is defined to be

$$\max(c_1, c_2)$$

where

$$c_1 = \max_{s \in R(node)} s.cycle$$

$$c_2 = \max_{s \in OL(node)} (s.cycle + 1)$$

$R(node)$ is the set of nodes reading $node$'s value;

$OL(node)$ is the set of conditional jumps for which $node$ is off-live, that is, the jumps that off-live read $node$.

The expression for c_1 again pretends that operations take only one cycle; any multicycle operations bisected by a split are guaranteed to finish execution in the partial schedule. The expression for c_2 is a little more subtle; it says that a value isn't dead until at least the cycle after a conditional jump for which the value is off-live. To see why, consider this schedule:

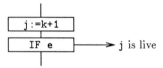

Suppose that j is read on the off-trace edge of the jump and that no succeeding operation in the schedule uses its value. Assuming the jump is scheduled in cycle i, the set $splitLive[i+1]$ is used to report the live values at the split; so the value of j must be kept alive up through cycle $i + 1$.

A similar analysis is used to derive the construction of *joinGen* and *joinKill*. Each node is added to *joinGen*[*LastCycle*(*node*) + 1]. That is, an operation's value isn't live until after the last cycle of the operation. For example:

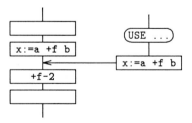

The join bisects the 2-cycle addition, and the value of x is not live on entry to the partial schedule (but it would be if the join were made one cycle later).

A value becomes dead no earlier than the last cycle of all its successors; that is, each node is added to $joinKill[c]$ where the cycle c is defined as:

$$\max_{s \in S(node)} LastCycle(s)$$

where $S(node)$ is the set of all successors, including jumps for which the node is off-live.

In the previous example, assuming the addition is the last use of **a**, **a** will be reported live on entry to the join's partial schedule. If the join were made one cycle later, **a** would be reported dead.

There is an obscure complication in computing $joinGen$ and $joinKill$. Consider this example:

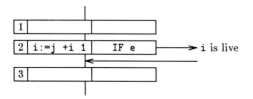

Suppose there are no operations reading the value of **i** on the schedule and that **i** is live on the off-trace edge of the IF. Then **i** is dead at the join. But unless special action is taken, **i** would be reported live at the join, because $joinGen[3]$ would contain the node for **i:=j +i 1**. So in general, a node is not added to $joinGen$ if its only successor is a conditional jump for which the node is off-live and the conditional jump is scheduled in the last cycle of node.

List Scheduling Versus Operation Scheduling

How does the list-scheduling code generator compare with Ruttenberg's operation scheduler? (In what follows, "list scheduling" refers to all of the code generator just described, including bottom-up-greedy.)

Operation scheduling does not form the schedule of instructions sequentially as in list scheduling. Instead it enumerates the nodes in some topological order, placing each node in the earliest possible cycle of the schedule, based on when and where its operands were scheduled. The general algorithm is similar to BUG, with temporal data structures keeping track of the cycles in which functional units, registers, and data paths are available. Each node has a list of triples:

<first cycle, last cycle, location>

specifying where and when the multiple copies of the node's value can be found. To schedule a node, the operation scheduler must consider all these possibilities: the multiple temporal locations of the operands, the different functional units capable of executing the node's operation and the cycles they are available, the multiple ways to move the operands to a candidate functional unit, and the destination register banks connected to a candidate functional unit. The operation scheduler uses branch-and-bound search to consider all combinations of these choices, finding the combination that will compute the node's value earliest. If it's necessary to copy the value of a node to be closer to a functional unit, the node's time/location triples are updated to reflect the additional locations occupied by the value.

You might think that deciding which code generator is better is simply a matter of running some benchmarks through both. Unfortunately, the operation scheduler's machine model is unrealistic, a small subset of the list scheduler's model. A machine consists of several clusters, and each cluster consists of several functional units connected by a complete crossbar and a single, highly ported register bank (for example, 3-in/6-out); the clusters don't all contain the same functional units. The memory banks are not distinguished by memory-bank disambiguation, that is, any vector reference can be done in any bank. In addition, only two programs were tested thoroughly on the operation scheduler, SOLVE (LU decomposition) and FFT (Fast Fourier Transform), with the inner loops unrolled only 4 times and with only small inputs (a 16 × 16 array for SOLVE, a 512 array for FFT). So the limited machine model and the lack of experiments makes comparisons of the implementations only marginally useful.

The code generated by the list scheduler ran slightly faster than the code generated by the operation scheduler:

	OS	LS	OS/LS
FFT	40163 instrs.	36345 instrs.	1.11
SOLVE	19649	17950	1.09

The results shown were the best for each code generator, choosing from all the various option settings. The operation scheduler's post-pass, which tries to fold data movements on top of other code, was used with the operation scheduler.

Examining the object code and the execution profiles (described in chapter 8) shows that both code generators produced about the same length schedules for the inner loops. But the operation scheduler doesn't handle induction variables very well—it doesn't ensure that induction variables end up in the same location at the end of an inner-loop trace as at the beginning. Consequently, the operation scheduler is forced to move the induction variables from their final to initial positions on the back edge of the loop; this extra copying accounts for the slightly poorer results of the operation scheduler.

The list scheduler ran about two times faster than the operation scheduler:

	OS	LS	OS/LS
FFT4	144 seconds	63 seconds	2.3
SOLVE4	231	138	1.7

These times don't include the operation scheduler's post-pass.

Finally, the list scheduler is somewhat smaller than the operation scheduler:

	OS	LS	OS/LS
Lines	3956	2957	1.34
Tokens	14489	10631	1.36

(Blank lines and comments weren't counted.)

Considering the unrealistic machine model used by the operation scheduler, the small number of benchmarks, and the fact that both code generators were implemented as research prototypes, these comparisons shouldn't be taken too seriously.

The current implementations aside, how do the two algorithms compare? Because operation scheduling and bottom-up-greedy use similar algorithms, operation scheduling will only perform significantly better than list scheduling if the simplifying assumption used in list scheduling is invalid. That is, list scheduling (including BUG) will do as well only if the choice of register banks, bank ports, and data paths are secondary to the choice of functional units. I've already argued that if registers and data paths were a primary factor, then the machine is probably ill-designed.

To get some feel for how good the assumption is, I compared the lengths of schedules as estimated by BUG against the lengths of the schedules actually produced by the list scheduler for three programs:

	LS cycles/BUG cycles		
Unrolling	8	16	32
FFT	1.14	1.17	
SOLVE1	1.04	1.04	1.05
TRID4	1.10	1.14	

The ratio "LS cycles/BUG cycles" is the sum of all the actual schedule lengths divided by the sum of the lengths estimated by BUG. For these benchmarks, BUG appears to be underestimating the schedule lengths by about 5–15%. This 5–15% is due solely to the fact that BUG doesn't account for limited data paths (buses and register ports). Thus, operation scheduling could hope to do at most 5–15% better than list scheduling on these benchmarks by avoiding contention for the data paths. Because at least some of that contention is unavoidable, operation scheduling most likely couldn't attain these upper bounds. So it appears that, based on these few benchmarks, the assumption made by BUG is pretty reasonable.

The current operation scheduling algorithm doesn't appear to do as well as BUG in taking account of the eventual destination of data. Consider this example:

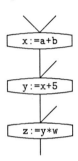

Suppose there were many adders but only a few multipliers in the machine. Because of the way BUG passes estimates up the DAG, the list scheduler would try to place both additions near the multiply. But the operation scheduler wouldn't take account of the multiply when placing the first addition; it would likely place the addition somewhere distant from a multiplier, requiring extra data movement. (However, it probably wouldn't be hard to add BUG-like propagation of estimates to operation scheduling.)

A more serious failing of the operation scheduler is that registers are not fully utilized. When a register is assigned to a node newly scheduled in cycle i, the register is reserved for cycles i through infinity—no other node can use the register after cycle i. After all the successors have been scheduled, however, the reservation on the register is cut back to the actual range of cycles $i:j$ in which the register is actually being used. For example, consider a DAG with 8 nodes N_1–N_8, in which N_2 and N_3 read N_1:

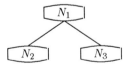

Suppose that the height of node 2 is much greater than the height of node 3. A likely scheduling order for the nodes might be 1, 2, 5, 6, 7, 3, 8, 4; a possible schedule might be:

1	N_4	N_8
2	N_1	
3	N_3	
4	N_2	
5	N_5	N_7
6	N_6	

When node 1 is scheduled in cycle 2 and assigned some register, the register is reserved for cycles $2:\infty$. When node 2 is scheduled, the reservation remains for $2:\infty$, since 3 is still unscheduled. Only after node 3 is scheduled in cycle 3 is the reservation cut back to cycles $2:4$. Because nodes 5, 6, and 7 occur in the scheduling order before 3, the reservation $2:\infty$ prevents them from using the register, even though they are eventually placed after cycle 4 and wouldn't interfere with the use of the register by nodes 1, 2, and 3.

In general, given some scheduling order $n_1, n_2, n_3, \ldots$, and two nodes n_i and n_j, where n_j is the last node in the order that is a successor of n_i, none of the nodes $n_{i+1}, \ldots, n_{j-1}$ will be able to use the register assigned to n_i, even if they are scheduled in cycles after all the successors of n_i. Without doing experiments on a realistic set of benchmarks, it's hard to say exactly how serious this restriction is (the few experiments with the operation scheduler used a machine model with a 200-register bank in each cluster.) Conceivably, an unacceptably larger number of registers might be required to prevent spilling in the inner loops. Note that list scheduling doesn't have this problem; because it forms instructions sequentially, registers remain allocated for exactly the cycles in which they are used.

How do the time complexities of the two algorithms compare? BUG takes $O(nf^2)$, where n is the number of nodes in the DAG and f is the maximum number of functional units implementing any one operation. List scheduling takes $O(rn \log n)$ worst-case (using separate data-ready queues for each functional unit), where r is the maximum number of register banks connected to the output of any unit. The observed behavior of list scheduling is strictly linear.

Ruttenberg mistakenly claims operation scheduling is $O(n)$, but in fact it is $O(n \log n)$ if any heuristic based on sorting is used (for example, height, depth, or execution frequency). But the linear constant factors are more important here (sorting a few hundred nodes in a DAG is very fast). The branch-and-bound search of operation scheduling takes time proportional to the product of:

f, the number of functional units that must be considered for any operation;

r, the number of register banks connected to the outputs of a functional unit;

the number of different data paths from an operand's location to a functional unit;

the number of different locations a value occupies over time (the number of <first cycle, last cycle, location> triples).

This product grows quickly as the size of the machine model increases, much faster than the f^2 factor in BUG and the r factor in list scheduling. Of course, it's not at all clear how the bounding of branch-and-bound will affect the operation scheduler's average behavior. Asymptotic upper bounds on time complexity just aren't very useful for comparing programs as complex as code generators— experimental observations are more meaningful. Nevertheless, based on the analysis above, the meager comparisons of the implementations, and the observed behavior of list scheduling, it's hard to see how operation scheduling could be any faster, and it's all too easy to believe that it will be slower.

The data and control structures used in operation scheduling are more complicated than in list scheduling. Operation scheduling requires many temporal data structures (structures indexed by cycle) to track the availability of resources and values. List scheduling only needs to remember availability for a small, fixed-length window starting at the current cycle. Operation scheduling's branch-and-bound control structure of operation scheduling is much hairier than the algorithms used in list scheduling.

Ruttenberg claims that operation scheduling provides a better framework for heuristics controlling evaluation order, the order in which nodes are placed on the schedule. This may be true, but does it matter? He ran only a few experiments measuring the effects of different heuristics, and the results were inconclusive; they don't contradict my assertion that heuristics fancier than simple node height aren't much better in realistic situations. Concentrating on other problems in the compiler are likely to result in more significant improvements, for example, induction variables or bookkeeper copying.

Chapter 8
Experiments

As I stated in the introduction, my thesis is: Ordinary scientific programs can be compiled for VLIWs, yielding order of magnitude speed-ups. Given the complexity of the Bulldog compiler, the only reasonable way to test this thesis is to run the compiler on a representative set of scientific programs.

To this end, I've assembled a library of benchmark routines intended to encompass a wide range of control and data structures encountered in scientific programming. I've compiled these programs and simulated their execution on a number of machine models. The results of these experiments strongly support my thesis.

The Ideal Machine Models

Assume we had an arbitrarily fast and parallel VLIW machine. What is the maximum amount of parallelism that trace scheduling and disambiguation can find? The ideal machine models help measure that amount, giving an upper bound on the parallelism we could expect to find on realistic hardware.

The **parallel ideal model** is a machine with an infinite number of functional units and registers. All operations take one cycle, and there is no communications delay between registers, functional units, and memory. The instruction word is infinitely wide; that is, the compiler may place as many operations as it can in an instruction. The set of operations implemented by the machine is exactly the set of intermediate-code operations.

The **sequential ideal model** is just like the parallel ideal model, except that it has only one functional unit (implementing all operations). As in the parallel model, operations take one cycle, there are an infinite number of registers, and there are no communication delays between elements. But only one operation may be executed per cycle.

The **ideal speed-up** for a program is the ratio of the execution time on the sequential model and the execution time on the parallel model. Intuitively, the ideal speed-up measures how much parallelism trace scheduling and disambiguation can find, independent of code generation for particular realistic hardware.

Code generation for the ideal machines is very simple. Because there is an infinite number of registers, register allocation is trivial. Each intermediate-code variable name is bound to a new register. Functional unit assignment is also trivial: Because there are no communication delays and the elements are completely connected, any functional unit implementing a given intermediate-code operation will suffice. To generate code for a trace, the nodes of the DAG are enumerated in a topological order. In the sequential model, each node is placed in a separate instruction. In the parallel model, all the nodes at a given depth are placed in the same instruction. (Remember that the parallel model has an infinite number of functional units.) Thus, the length of a schedule for the sequential model is exactly the number of nodes in the DAG, and the length of a schedule for the parallel model is the depth (or height) of the DAG. The same bookkeeping rules for code motions described in chapter 4 apply here as well.

The ELI Models

The **realistic ELI** (Enormously Long Instructions) models an 8-cluster VLIW. To date, no VLIWs have actually been built, so I can't say with 100% confidence how "realistic" the model is. However, its design is based closely on the ELI development work of Fisher, O'Donnell, and Sidell [Fisher 84].

The top of figure 8.1 shows the interconnection of the 8 clusters of the realistic ELI. Each cluster is independently connected to 4 others by long, slow buses. A move between clusters takes one full cycle, and each bus can transport one value every cycle. However, any one cluster can transmit at most 2 values and receive at most 2 values per cycle.

Each of the clusters is identical (almost). The bottom of figure 8.1 shows one cluster. A partial crossbar connects a front-door memory bank, two integer ALUs, a floating adder, a floating multiplier, a constant generator (not shown), and the bus interconnect to the neighboring clusters. One of the clusters also has the back-door memory port that talks to all the memory banks.

The top of figure 8.2 shows a floating adder unit. The adder reads and writes two register banks. Each bank has 16 registers; 1 value can be written and 2 values read every cycle (1-in/2-out). Each bank is also connected to the crossbar.

The floating multiplier and integer ALU units are similar to the floating adder. The integer ALU implements a full set of arithmetic and logical operations, including arithmetic comparisons and conditional jumps.

The bottom of 8.2 shows the front-door memory unit. It contains an integer ALU as well as the memory port, both sharing the two register banks (each 1-in/2-out). That ALU has a limited repertoire of arithmetic operations and is intended mainly for address arithmetic. The one back door of the realistic ELI is similar to a front door, except that it can address all memory banks.

Figure 8.3 shows the global-bus unit that connects the cluster with the neighboring clusters. A single 2-in/2-out register bank sits between the cluster crossbar and the interface to the global buses.

The constant generator (not shown) represents the immediate field of the instruction for the cluster; it can place one 12-bit integer (signed or unsigned, depending on context) on the cluster's crossbar every cycle.

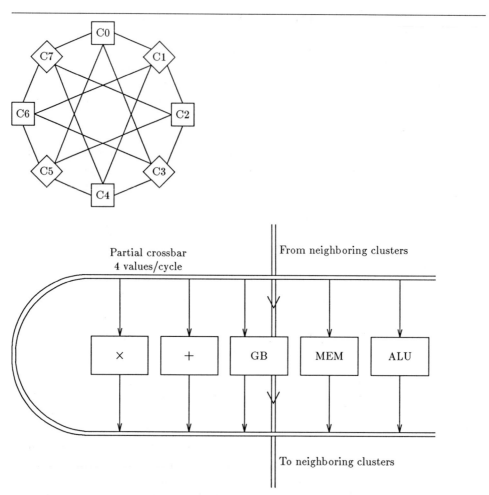

Figure 8.1. The 8-cluster realistic ELI.

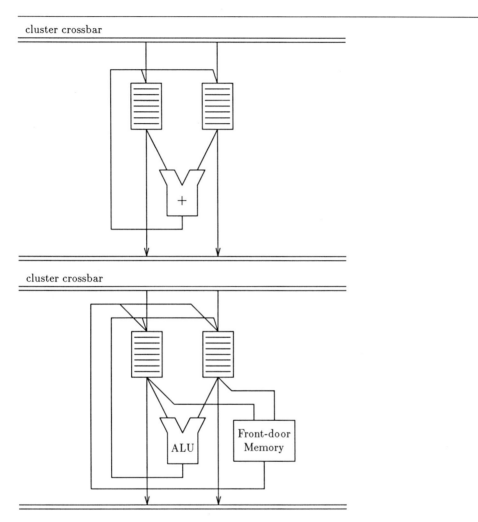

Figure 8.2. Floating adder and front-door memory units.

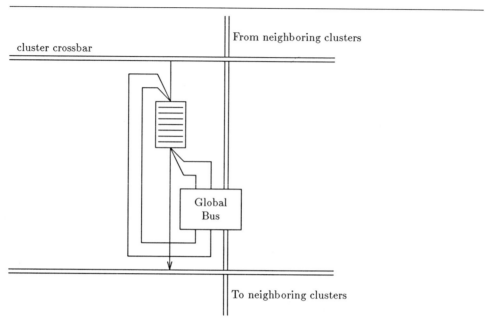

cluster crossbar

From neighboring clusters

Global
Bus

To neighboring clusters

Figure 8.3. Global-bus unit.

The pipeline delays of the various functional units are:

integer ALU	1 cycle
floating adder	3 cycles
floating multiplier	4 cycles
back-door memory	6 cycles
front-door memory	3 cycles

A new operation can be initiated every cycle on each pipeline.

The partial crossbar connects the register banks of all the units, but can transmit only 4 values per cycle. The functional units read and write values to the local banks only; the banks serve as buffers between the crossbar and the functional units.

Division isn't directly implemented by the machine. Instead, a 3-step Newton's method approximation is used [FPS 82]. The code for q:=y/x is expanded inline as:

```
r0:=RECIP(x)
r1:=r0 * (2 - x*r0)
r2:=r1 * (2 - x*r1)
r3:=r2 * (2 - x*r2)
q :=r3 * y
```

where `RECIP` is a one-cycle machine operator that provides an 8-bit approximation to `1/x` via table lookup.

The conditional-jump machine operations of the integer ALUs have one of the forms:

```
IF x relop y
IF-TRUE x
IF-FALSE x
```

where *relop* is one of the integer comparison operators $<, \leq, =, \neq, \geq, >$. Conditional jumps cannot test floating point values directly, on the assumption that a floating comparison would make a jump much longer than the one cycle allowed (see page 106). The front end of the compiler transforms conditionals with floating tests into a floating comparison followed by a boolean conditional jump. For example, `IF x>y` would be expanded into:

```
b:=x>y
IF-TRUE b
```

Appendix A contains the actual Lisp definition of the realistic ELI model.

The **sequential ELI** models a traditional pipelined machine like the MIPS [Hennessy 82], the CDC 6600, or the scalar part of the Cray-I. It is built with the same technology as the realistic ELI. Figure 8.4 shows the sequential ELI. There is one 1-in/2-out register bank servicing a floating adder, a floating multiplier, an integer ALU, a memory bank, and a constant generator. These pipelined functional units are identical to those of the realistic ELI. However, the machine can initiate at most one operation per cycle, subject to bandwidth limitations of the register bank.

Appendix A contains the Lisp definition of the sequential model.

The **realistic speed-up** for a program is the ratio of the execution time on the sequential ELI and the execution time on the realistic ELI. It is a rough measure of how much faster a VLIW is compared to a traditional machine built by the same people with the same chips, assuming a trace scheduling compiler is used for both machines. The realistic speed-up also indicates how effectively the VLIW is being utilized.

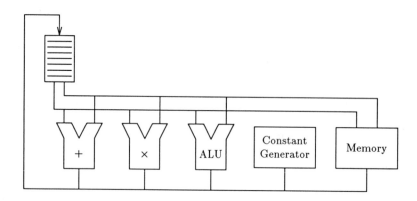

Figure 8.4. The sequential ELI.

The Benchmark Library

The library routines were converted directly from standard, portable Fortran into Tinylisp, mostly using the automatic conversion program written by John Ruttenberg and Joe Rodrigue. Any subroutines invoked by the main routines were defined to be inline and automatically expanded at each use at compile time. I added the needed assertions and manually performed various source optimizations described later and in chapter 6.

Appendix B contains the Tinylisp and the Fortran for some of the programs. The library consists of:

MATRIX MULTIPLY. A standard three-loop implementation. As described in chapter 6, loop merging was used to bank-disambiguate the column-vector accesses.

FFT. The complex Fast Fourier Transform, taken directly from Steiglitz [Steiglitz 74]. Chapter 6 describes the transformations made to bank-disambiguate the vector references and eliminate much of the loop overhead.

SOLVE. LU decomposition, used to solve linear systems of equations. SOLVE is similar to the routine in *Computer Methods for Mathematical Computations* [Forsythe 77].

SVD. Singular value decomposition, from *Computer Methods*. SVD is a powerful tool, used for such problems as general linear equations, linear least-squares, pseudo-inverses, approximating matrices, and evaluating determinants and finding singular matrices. Chapter 6 describes the transformations made to SVD. The computation of the matrix U of left-singular vectors was excluded from the benchmark version so that the routine could be squeezed through the Bulldog compiler. This omission isn't serious: The code computing U is very similar to other code in SVD, and in most applications of SVD, the left-singular vectors aren't needed.

TRID1, TRID2, TRID4. Three programs for solving tridiagonal linear systems. TRID1 uses the classical, two-loop method. Because its loops directly implement linear recurrences of the form:

```
a[i]:=f( a[i-1] )
```

there isn't much directly available parallelism. TRID2 uses a slightly more complicated algorithm whose loops have about twice the available parallelism as TRID1. TRID4 uses the method of cyclic reduction and has a lot of available parallelism [Rodrigue 82], but its many loops add quite a bit of overhead.

SIMPLE. SIMPLE is a Fortran program for doing fluid dynamics computation. SIMPLE was written and distributed by scientists at Lawrence Livermore National Laboratory as an example of production fluid dynamics code that parallel-computing researchers in academy could use as a realistic benchmark. I obtained my copy through Dennis Gannon at Purdue University.

I profiled the execution of SIMPLE on a DEC-2060 and found the most time-critical routines to be:

EOS	39%
NEWRZ	19%
CONDUC	18%

I selected EOS and NEWRZ for my benchmark library. I rejected CONDUC because it is essentially a tridiagonal solver, and tridiagonal solvers are already included in the library.

EOS. From SIMPLE. EOS performs equation-of-state calculations. The original routine in the benchmark is a scalar function that does a table lookup and then evaluates a polynomial. It is actually a family of four functions performing similar computations for different polynomials. For the library, I selected only the function for computing energy; the other three are very similar.

I vectorized the routine as described by Dubois [Rodrigue 82]. Also, following his personal advice, I increased the number of data boxes used by the table lookup from 4 to 25 in each direction, making the table lookup more realistic. The input data for these experiments were captured from a snapshot of the running SIMPLE program.

NEWRZ. Another routine from SIMPLE. The comment in the code for NEWRZ says:

> This routine calculates the new velocities, coordinates, and the density and change in specific volume for each zone.

It consists of three simple sets of doubly nested loops containing expressions of many floating additions and multiplies.

QK61. A core routine performing 61-point polynomial evaluations in QUAD-PAK, a state-of-the-art package for adaptive quadrature [Piessens 83]. The function being integrated is used in calculating generalized Bessel functions; such functions arise in analyzing the behavior of finite difference approximations to the Telegraph equation, and in certain types of visco-elastic equations. Profiles of running the top-level routine QAGE on a DEC-2060 showed that 90% of the execution time was spent in QK61 and the function being integrated.

QUANC8. Integration using adaptive quadrature, from *Computer Methods*. The function being integrated is the same as for QK61. QUANC8 is not considered state-of-the-art. I included QUANC8 because, unlike QK61, it contains all the high-level conditional control structure of the adaptive quadrature algorithm.

ZEROIN. Finding real zeros of a single function, from *Computer Methods*. The function being zeroed is used to analyze the behavior of 4th-order approximations to the wave equation.

The functions passed as parameters to the last three programs were expanded inline at each call. The trigonometric functions used by the parametric functions were also expanded inline.

There's one important source transformation that hasn't been discussed yet. Vector reductions, such as summing the elements, are common in scientific code, but they're typically written in a sequential style:

```
total:=0
FOR i:=0 TO n-1
    total:=total+v[i]
```

After unrolling, the additions to `total` must be done sequentially; even though the memory references can be done in parallel, the sequential additions are a bottleneck.

However, a simple transformation yields parallelism dependent only on the amount of unrolling (assume b, the number of memory banks, is 8):

```
total0:=0; total1:=0; ...; total7:=0
i:=0

LOOP
    IF i+0 >= n THEN EXITLOOP
    total0:=total0+v[i+0]
    IF i+1 >= n THEN EXITLOOP
    total1:=total1+v[i+1]
    ...
    IF i+7 >= n THEN EXITLOOP
    total7:=total7+v[i+7]
    i:=i+8

total:=((total0+total1) + (total2+total3)) +
       ((total4+total5) + (total6+total7))
```

Now, 8 independent sums are formed in parallel in the loop body, and at the end they are totalled. (Induction-variable simplification will replace each of the 8 different uses of i by separate variables that can be manipulated in parallel.)

Because reductions are so common, I added a Tinylisp language construct (a macro) for reductions. The above reduction would be expressed as:

```
total := VectorReduce( i:=0 to n-1, +, 0.0, v[i] )
```

which expands into the code shown.

Running the Experiments

The experiments reported here were all conducted within the same framework. The inner loops of a program were unrolled 1, 2, 4, 8, 16, and sometimes 32 times, and for each amount of unrolling, the program was compiled and simulated on the four machine models: the sequential and parallel ideal models and the realistic and sequential ELI models. From these runs I gathered various sets of statistics, presented below.

You'll notice in the tables there are often numbers missing for particular entries, and you'll probably think of other experiments you'd like to have seen run. I'm fully aware of the limitations of these experiments. The compilations and simulations were very expensive and time-consuming, and when I started I had little idea of exactly which source transformations to use. Consequently, I concentrated my efforts on running those experiments which seemed most crucial to proving or disproving my thesis. At the end of this chapter I'll discuss future possible experiments.

Trace Profiling

A simple but effective simulation tool for evaluating the performance of a program is the trace profiler. It records the number of machine instructions and operations actually executed for each trace, and at the end of simulation presents a concise table of the results. This helps identify the bottlenecks in programs, both in terms of absolute number of instructions executed in a trace and the local parallelism obtained for a trace. For example, a profile might show that 50% of execution time is spent in one particular trace of an inner loop and that the ratio of operations to instructions (the local parallelism) is only 1.5; the inner loop would then be a prime candidate for possible source or algorithmic transformations.

Execution Statistics

	Speed-up		Input size		Unrolling		% Partial		
Program	Ideal	Real.	Ideal	Real.	Ideal	Real.	Split	Join	Total
MATMUL	25.5	7.4	50^2	50^2	32	64	1	0	1
FFT	48.3	6.9	1024	1024	16	16	2	0	2
SOLVE	18.9	6.2	128^2	128^2	16	16/8	2	0	2
SVD	16.2	5.4	30^2	128^2	16/2	32/16	2	0	2
TRID1	2.7	.9	4096	4096	16	8	5	0	5
TRID2	3.8	1.2	4096	4096	16	8	10	0	10
TRID4	33.3	7.0	4096	4096	16/4	16/2	0	0	0
EOS	8.3	2.3	64^2	64^2	16	8	2	1	3
NEWRZ	19.8	7.6	60^2	49^2	8	16	2	0	2
QK61	10.2	4.5	–	–	2	4	0	0	0
QUANC8	8.1	–	–	–	4	–	–	–	–
ZEROIN	3.5	–	–	–	4	–	–	–	–

Ideal speed-up is the ratio of the execution times on the sequential and parallel ideal models.

Realistic speed-up is s/r, where r is the execution time of the realistic ELI and s is the best execution time on the sequential ELI over unrollings of 1, 2, 4, and 8.

Input size is the size of the input arrays.

Unrolling is the amount the inner loops were unrolled. Due to the limitations of the compiler, some programs had mixed unrolling; for example "16/8" indicates that the time-critical inner loops were unrolled 16 times, the other inner loops 8 times.

% Partial is the number of instructions executed in split and join partial schedules on the realistic ELI, as a percentage of the total number of instructions executed.

I didn't waste precious time running QUANC8 or ZEROIN on the realistic models. QK61 is a better test of adaptive quadrature, and the ideal speed-up for ZEROIN was so low that there was little point in confirming that its realistic speed-up would be small.

Only three programs had little ideal parallelism: TRID1, TRID2, and ZEROIN. This isn't surprising. TRID1 and TRID2 have inner loops that are simple recurrences of the form v[i] := f(v[i-1]). ZEROIN doesn't manipulate any arrays, and its control structure consists of a loop containing many data-dependent conditionals that evaluates the parametric function once each iteration.

The ideal speed-up of the other programs is limited only by the amount of unrolling and the size of the input. For example, the more the inner loop of MATMUL is unrolled, the more copies of the inner loop body can be done in parallel (provided the input arrays are big enough).

Of the programs with more than a little ideal parallelism, only EOS performed badly on the realistic machine (EOS is discussed in more detail below). The others achieved speed-ups from 4.5 (QK61) to 7.6 (NEWRZ).

Theoretically, realistic speed-ups greater than 8 are possible, since the realistic ELI can initiate much more than 8 times as many operations per cycle as the sequential ELI. But in practice, scientific programs tend to be limited either by memory bandwidth, floating adds, or floating multiplies, and for those the realistic ELI is only 8 times faster (because it has only 8 times as many memory banks or floating units).

Remember that the realistic speed-up is the ratio of the execution times on the sequential ELI and the realistic ELI, using trace scheduling with loop unrolling for both models. However, current sequential machines like the MIPS don't actually use trace-scheduling compilers, but rather compile one basic block at a time. A later section shows that trace scheduling results in significant improvements of execution time on the sequential ELI. So if we used a basic-block-only compiler for the sequential ELI instead of trace scheduling, the realistic speed-ups shown here would be somewhat larger.

The small percentage of time spent in partial schedules is quite encouraging. Even EOS, which spends a lot of its time doing table lookup and thus has a high proportion of conditionals, spends little time in partial schedules. The numbers support my claim that fancier methods for handling partial schedules aren't needed.

Compilation Statistics

Program	Unrolling	Size	RCS/SCS		% Copies Split	Join	Total	
MATMUL	64	435	8.7		102	1	103	
FFT	8	928	8.8		66	0	66	
	16	1693	16.1	(1.8)	126	0	126	(1.9)
SOLVE	8	1025	3.2		31	34	65	
	16/8	1853	5.7	(1.8)	65	79	144	(2.2)
SVD	8	7668	2.7		71	18	89	
	16	11378	4.0	(1.5)	104	14	118	(1.3)
TRID1	8	2888	14.9		134	0	134	
TRID2	8	3230	4.4		105	0	105	
TRID4	8/2	1285	1.4		24	1	25	
	16/2	1921	2.0	(1.4)	85	2	87	(3.5)
EOS	8	3189	1.2		90	28	118	
NEWRZ	16	1156	2.7		12	0	12	
QK61	4	2585	2.1		107	1	107	

Size is the number of instructions generated for the realistic ELI.

RCS/SCS (realistic code size/sequential code size) is the ratio of the number of instructions generated for the realistic ELI and the sequential ELI (with no unrolling). The numbers in parenthesis indicate the relative increase in realistic code size for those programs that were run with two different amounts of unrolling. For example, the code size of FFT unrolled 16 times is 1.8 times the code size of FFT unrolled 8 times.

% Copies is the number of intermediate-code copies produced during bookkeeping at splits and joins, expressed as a percentage of the total number of intermediate-code operations in the optimized flow graph. The numbers in parenthesis show the relative increase in that percentage for programs run with two different amounts of unrolling.

These numbers show that even with large amounts of unrolling, the size of the code generated is not unreasonable for a practical machine, even though there is a quite a bit of bookkeeper copying. Reassuringly, the copying (as a percentage of intermediate-code size) appears to increase only linearly with unrolling, not quadratically or exponentially as we feared. As discussed in chapter 6, most of the copying could probably be eliminated by taking advantage of the fact that the size of the input is a multiple of the number of banks b, eliminating most of the exit tests from the unrolled inner loops.

Here are the running times of the compiler:

Program	Unrolling	Traces	Total	% of Total			Relative increase			
				Opt	TS	CG	Total	Opt	TS	CG
MATMUL	64	27	39	76	5	19				
FFT	8	47	41	63	4	32				
	16	66	124	43	5	52	3.0	2.0	3.4	4.9
SOLVE	8	83	20	44	6	50				
	16/8	136	56	45	10	45	2.8	2.9	4.4	2.5
SVD	8	287	63	45	10	45				
	16	418	122	40	13	46	1.9	1.7	2.6	2.0
TRID1	8	21	9	53	10	37				
TRID2	8	21	30	63	9	27				
TRID4	8/2	80	39	58	7	35				
	16/2	52	68	71	5	24	1.7	2.2	1.2	1.2
EOS	8	207	62	23	10	67				
NEWRZ	16	42	138	83	3	14				
QK61	4	19	92	70	8	22				

Traces is the number of traces needed to compile the program.

Total is the number of CPU minutes consumed by the compiler running on a DEC-2060 with 1.5 megawords of memory.

% of Total shows the percentage of time spent in intermediate-code flow analysis and optimization (Opt), trace picking and bookkeeping (TS), and code generation (CG).

Relative increase shows the relative increase in the CPU times for those programs that were run with two different amounts of unrolling. For example, the compiler takes 3.0 times as long when the loops of FFT are unrolled 16 times instead of 8.

Obviously, the compiler is very slow. And these times are CPU times—the elapsed times (which I don't have) tend to be somewhat larger, since the large amounts of virtual memory paging by the compiler, mostly due to garbage collection, aren't fully included in the CPU time.

The Lisp system used to implement the compiler has only 2.2 megawords of virtual address space available for data (1.1 million cons cells). Because each program was unrolled as much as the limited address space allowed, there was often very little unallocated space left in the storage heap, and the Lisp system was forced to garbage collect quite frequently. (The amount of time spent in garbage collection is another statistic I should have collected.) Multiflow, Inc. has ported the compiler to a Symbolics 3600, whose CPU runs at about the same speed as the DEC-2060 but which has a much larger virtual address space; initial indications are that the compiler runs much faster (though certainly not as fast as a traditional compiler).

Roughly 1/3 to 2/3 of the time is spent in the intermediate-code analyses and optimizations; about one quarter to one half of the time is spent in code generation; and less than a tenth of the time is spent picking traces and book-keeping. Clearly, the first task in making the compiler faster is speeding up the intermediate-code optimizations.

The two- to three-fold increase in CPU time as unrolling is increased from 8 to 16 is encouraging. If that linear trend holds for larger amounts of unrolling, programs could be unrolled 32 or maybe even 64 times without much compiler-tuning needed, thus making a 16- or 32-cluster VLIW practical.

Sequential Speed-up

The following table shows the effect of unrolling for the sequential ELI:

Program	Sequential Speed-up	Unrolling	Input size
MATMUL	1.36	4	50^2
FFT	1.00	1	1024
SOLVE	1.87	2	88^2
SVD	1.36	4	64^2
TRID1	1.57	8	4096
TRID2	1.12	4	4096
TRID4	1.40	4	4096
EOS	1.01	2	64^2
NEWRZ	–	–	–
QK61	1.03	2	–

> **Sequential speed-up** is the ratio of the execution time on the sequential ELI with no unrolling and the execution time for the given unrolling. The speed-ups shown are the largest over unrollings of 1, 2, 4, and 8.

As you can see, modest amounts of unrolling yield quite significant speed-ups for a pipelined sequential machine. These increases are in addition to the speed-ups due to pipelined execution of basic blocks. Considering that pipelined execution will typically yield speed-ups from 1.5 to 2.5 [Kuck 78], and that the speed-ups for the MIPS due to block reorganization were no more than 10%, these speed-ups due to unrolling are quite important. At least for scientific code, simple unrolling can yield significant improvements, yet it has received almost no attention in academic compiler research, and as far as I know, no commercial compiler implements it automatically.

Speed-ups in Detail

This section shows how the speed-ups vary for every program according to unrolling and the input size n, and discusses some of the programs in detail. A general observation: Small input sizes (vectors of length less than, say, 30) don't yield nearly as much ideal or realistic parallelism as larger input sizes.

MATMUL.

Ideal Speed-up				
Unrolling	$n = 5^2$	10^2	25^2	50^2
1	2.3	2.4	2.3	2.3
2	3.5	4.1	4.3	4.5
4	4.1	5.9	7.3	8.3
8	5.0	6.9	10.7	13.7
16	4.5	8.4	15.1	19.8
32	3.7	6.9	16.5	25.5

Sequential Speed-up				
Unrolling	$n = 5^2$	10^2	25^2	50^2
1	1.00	1.00	1.00	1.00
2	1.01	1.11	1.26	1.30
4	0.74	1.00	1.20	1.36
8	0.56	0.70	0.99	1.22
16	0.29	0.48	0.77	0.96

Realistic Speed-up				
Unrolling	$n = 5^2$	10^2	25^2	50^2
8	1.86	2.92	5.31	7.36

FFT.

Ideal Speed-up						
Unrolling	$n = 32$	64	128	256	512	1024
1	2.9	3.1	3.3	3.4	3.5	3.6
2	4.4	4.9	5.3	5.6	5.9	6.1
4	5.7	6.5	7.2	7.8	8.4	8.9
4*	12.4	13.4	14.2	14.8	15.2	15.5
8	6.5	7.6	8.6	9.5	10.4	11.2
8*	20.8	23.3	25.2	26.7	27.9	28.8
16	6.8	8.1	9.3	10.5	11.6	12.6
16*	30.1	35.3	39.7	43.2	46.0	48.3

Sequential Speed-up						
Unrolling	$n = 32$	64	128	256	512	1024
1	1.00	1.00	1.00	1.00	1.00	1.00
2	0.79	0.81	0.82	0.83	0.84	0.85
4	0.57	0.59	0.62	0.64	0.65	0.67
8	0.34	0.36	0.39	0.41	0.43	0.45
16	0.18	0.20	0.22	0.23	0.25	0.26

Realistic Speed-up						
Unrolling	$n = 32$	64	128	256	512	1024
8	4.35	4.66	4.95	5.17	5.34	5.47
16	4.12	4.94	5.63	6.18	6.61	6.92

The starred rows for the ideal speed-ups indicate the special unrolling described in chapter 6. The special unrolling yields a four-fold increase in parallelism for the largest input. (The realistic experiments were all done with the special unrolling.)

Note that unrolling doesn't improve the running time of FFT on the sequential machine. This might be due to the fact that the body of the inner loop is quite large compared to most: It contains 10 vector references, a complex multiply and two complex additions. This is enough to keep the pipelines full without any unrolling, while unrolling merely increases the overhead due to extra induction variables created by loop-induction-variable simplification.

SOLVE.

Unrolling	Ideal Speed-up			
	$n = 16^2$	32^2	64^2	88^2
1	1.9	1.9	2.0	2.0
2	2.9	3.3	3.6	3.8
4	3.8	5.1	6.2	7.0
8	4.6	7.0	9.7	12.1
16	5.3	8.6	13.4	18.9

Unrolling	Sequential Speed-up			
	$n = 16^2$	32^2	64^2	88^2
1	1.00	1.00	1.00	1.00
2	1.45	1.70	1.83	1.87
4	1.34	1.65	1.82	1.87
8	0.84	1.05	1.21	1.27

Unrolling	Realistic Speed-up				
	$n = 16^2$	32^2	64^2	88^2	128^2
8	1.69	2.51	3.25	3.52	–
16/8	1.68	2.91	4.63	5.42	6.18

For inputs of size less than 64, SOLVE achieves less than 50% utilization of the realistic ELI. This is probably due to the overhead of the inner loops, which have the form:

```
FOR i:=1 TO n
    FOR j:=i TO n
        ...v[j]...
```

Trace profiling showed that SOLVE spends a large fraction of its time in the traces of outer loops, mostly in the initialization code of the inner loops. It might be possible to reduce this overhead either by improving the loop-induction-variable simplification in the front end, or by merging the outer loops with the inner loops, similar to the merging used for memory-bank disambiguation.

SVD.

Ideal Speed-up				
Unrolling	$n = 5^2$	10^2	20^2	30^2
1	1.8	2.0	2.1	3.1
2	2.2	3.0	3.6	5.5
4	2.6	4.0	5.9	9.5
8/2	2.6	4.3	7.2	12.8
16/2	2.5	4.5	8.4	16.2

Sequential Speed-up			
Unrolling	$n = 16^2$	32^2	64^2
1	1.00	1.00	1.00
2	1.24	1.30	1.33
4	1.17	1.29	1.36
8	1.01	1.17	1.29

Realistic Speed-up				
Unrolling	$n = 16^2$	32^2	64^2	128^2
8	2.00	2.55	2.89	–
16	2.24	3.18	4.16	–
32/16	2.29	3.32	4.43	5.38

SVD achieves even lower utilization of the realistic ELI than SOLVE, and only for very large inputs is the speed-up greater than 5. SVD has many more loops with greater nesting than SOLVE, and as with SOLVE, trace profiling showed SVD spending a large fraction of its time in the outer loops.

TRID1.

Unrolling	Ideal Speed-up $n = 256$	512	1024	2048	4096
1	1.4	1.4	1.4	1.4	1.4
2	1.9	1.9	1.9	1.9	1.9
4	2.3	2.3	2.3	2.3	2.3
8	2.5	2.5	2.5	2.6	2.6
16	2.7	2.7	2.7	2.7	2.7

Unrolling	Sequential Speed-up $n = 256$	512	1024	2048	4096
1	1.00	1.00	1.00	1.00	1.00
2	1.33	1.33	1.33	1.33	1.33
4	1.51	1.51	1.52	1.52	1.52
8	1.56	1.56	1.57	1.57	1.57

Unrolling	Realistic Speed-up $n = 256$	512	1024	2048	4096
8	.95	.95	.94	.94	.94

It's not surprising that TRID1 has so little parallelism. Its inner loops are recurrences of the form `v[i] := f(v[i-1])`, and each iteration is data-dependent on the previous iteration. Thus, the execution of successive iterations can't be overlapped much.

Notice that the realistic speed-up is less than 1.0; that is, the program executes faster on the sequential ELI than on the parallel realistic ELI. There are three possible reasons for this. First, there is some overhead due to the extra induction variables created when loops are unrolled 8 times. In loops with data-independent iterations, that overhead is far outweighed by the parallelism resulting from separate induction variables for each unrolling; but in the data-dependent loops of TRID1, there is no such resulting parallelism. Second, the code generator isn't perfect at allocating functional units, and it might have been a little too greedy in distributing the computation across the machine, resulting in communication delays. Third, even if the code generator allocates functional units perfectly (for example, by restricting computation to one cluster), a single cluster of the realistic ELI has more built-in communication delays than the sequential ELI. Which of these three reasons is the actual cause of the slowdown isn't important, though, since TRID1 is clearly an unsuitable algorithm for a parallel machine.

TRID2.

Ideal Speed-up					
Unrolling	$n = 256$	512	1024	2048	4096
1	3.2	3.2	3.2	3.2	3.2
2	3.5	3.5	3.5	3.5	3.5
4	3.7	3.7	3.7	3.7	3.7
8	3.8	3.8	3.8	3.8	3.8
16	3.8	3.8	3.8	3.8	3.8

Sequential Speed-up					
Unrolling	$n = 256$	512	1024	2048	4096
1	1.00	1.00	1.00	1.00	1.00
2	1.08	1.07	1.07	1.08	1.08
4	1.12	1.10	1.11	1.11	1.12
8	1.10	1.08	1.09	1.10	1.10

Realistic Speed-up					
Unrolling	$n = 256$	512	1024	2048	4096
8	1.20	1.20	1.19	1.19	1.19

Like TRID1, the inner loops of TRID2 are data-dependent recurrences that are inherently non-parallel.

TRID4.

Unrolling	Ideal Speed-up				
	$n = 256$	512	1024	2048	4096
1	3.2	3.3	3.3	3.3	3.4
2	5.2	5.6	5.8	5.9	6.0
4	8.9	10.1	11.0	11.4	11.7
8	13.7	17.2	19.8	21.6	22.7
16/4	16.5	22.1	27.1	30.9	33.3

Unrolling	Sequential Speed-up				
	$n = 256$	512	1024	2048	4096
1	1.00	1.00	1.00	1.00	1.00
2	1.27	1.29	1.31	1.31	1.32
4	1.31	1.34	1.37	1.39	1.40
8	1.25	1.31	1.35	1.37	1.39

Unrolling	Realistic Speed-up				
	$n = 256$	512	1024	2048	4096
8/2	3.05	3.56	3.96	4.24	4.41
16/2	3.83	4.86	5.79	6.51	7.01

The algorithm of TRID4, cyclic reduction, was designed explicitly for parallel machines, and the numbers demonstrate its superior parallelism compared to the previous two versions of TRID.

Comparing versions of TRID

The speed-ups obtained for the three versions of TRID say nothing about their relative performance. Even though one version might have a greater amount of parallelism, another might be faster in terms of absolute execution time.

The tables below compare the execution times of the three versions running on the parallel ideal machine, the sequential ELI, and the realistic ELI. The numbers shown are the ratio of the best time for the given program with the best time for TRID1.

	Ideal Speed-up Ratio				
	$n = 256$	512	1024	2048	4096
TRID1	1.0	1.0	1.0	1.0	1.0
TRID2	1.8	1.8	1.8	1.8	1.8
TRID4	3.1	4.2	5.1	5.8	6.3
	Sequential Speed-up Ratio				
	$n = 256$	512	1024	2048	4096
TRID1	1.0	1.0	1.0	1.0	1.0
TRID2	1.5	1.5	1.5	1.5	1.6
TRID4	0.8	0.8	0.9	0.9	0.9
	Realistic Speed-up Ratio				
	$n = 256$	512	1024	2048	4096
TRID1	1.0	1.0	1.0	1.0	1.0
TRID2	1.9	1.9	2.0	2.0	2.0
TRID4	3.3	4.3	5.3	6.1	6.6
Cray-I	4.0	5.0	5.8	6.2	6.5

Clearly, TRID4 is the fastest version for the realistic ELI; TRID2 is the fastest on the sequential ELI.

The row labeled "Cray-I" shows the ratio of the Cray-I execution times of a version using hand-coded, vectorized cyclic reduction and the standard scalar version (TRID1) compiled with the Cray Fortran compiler [Rodrigue 82]. Notice the similarity between those ratios and the ratios for TRID4. This supports my contention that the realistic and sequential ELI models correspond to reality.

For the smaller input sizes, the realistic TRID4 ratios are somewhat smaller than the Cray ratios. This means either that the realistic ELI doesn't handle small vectors as well as the Cray or else the realistic ELI executes scalar, data-dependent loops relatively faster than the Cray. Given that the parallelism available for scalar programs on the ELI far outweighs that available on the Cray, the latter explanation sounds more likely.

EOS.

Ideal Speed-up					
Unrolling	$n = 4^2$	8^2	16^2	32^2	64^2
1	2.1	2.2	2.3	2.5	2.6
2	2.6	2.7	3.1	3.6	4.1
4	2.7	3.1	3.7	4.6	5.8
8	2.7	3.3	4.1	5.3	7.3
16	3.0	3.5	4.3	5.8	8.3

Sequential Speed-up					
Unrolling	$n = 4^2$	8^2	16^2	32^2	64^2
1	1.00	1.00	1.00	1.00	1.00
2	0.96	0.97	0.96	1.00	1.01
4	0.88	0.91	0.91	0.99	1.01
8	0.77	0.86	0.86	0.92	0.95

Realistic Speed-up					
Unrolling	$n = 4^2$	8^2	16^2	32^2	64^2
8	1.32	1.50	1.58	1.86	2.29

The original version of EOS (from SIMPLE) was a scalar function that computed a simple polynomial after doing table lookups to compute some coefficients. The version used here has been vectorized as described in *Parallel Computations* [Rodrigue 82]. The routine accepts a vector of input values; it then does table lookups for each value in the vector, saving the coefficients in a temporary vector; then it computes the polynomials using a simple, vectorizable loop.

The table lookups are the bottleneck in achieving higher parallelism. Trace profiles showed that the computation of the polynomials was about 8 times faster on the realistic ELI than on the sequential ELI, but the realistic ELI wasn't any faster doing the table lookups. The table lookups are implemented using the cache-loop strategy described by Dubois in *Parallel Computations* (I'm doubtful whether any other technique would be faster on the ELI).

Supposedly, the input sizes used in practice are much larger than the 64^2 used here, maybe by a factor of 4 or more. If so, then the table lookups might become insignificant, since the hit ratio of the cache loop would increase. Unfortunately, running simulations with larger inputs was too expensive, and Yale wasn't willing to continue footing the bills.

QUANC8.

Unrolling	Ideal Speed-up
1	3.4
2	5.3
4	8.1

QUANC8 has only modest amounts of parallelism, primarily because the inner loop uses only 8-point polynomial evaluation. The state-of-the-art QK61 evaluates larger polynomials and has more ideal parallelism.

ZEROIN.

Unrolling	Ideal Speed-up
1	3.1
2	3.4
4	3.5

Unrolling doesn't effect the ideal speed-up of ZEROIN much. ZEROIN uses a bisection method to narrow the interval containing a zero, and for arbitrary functions, the compiler can't predict whether the right or left bisection will be chosen, and thus can't evaluate the next iteration of the loop in parallel with the current one. Perhaps n-ary sectioning might yield significant improvements, since then $n - 1$ evaluations of the parametric function could be done in parallel.

Experiments for the Future

Given the time, the next experiments I would have liked to run would measure the individual contribution of the standard optimizations, trace scheduling, and disambiguation. I would disable each in turn and in pairs and observe the degradation in performance for the realistic ELI. To disable trace scheduling, I would turn on the switch (that currently exists in the compiler) restricting traces to single basic blocks. To disable disambiguation, I would add a switch that causes all questions of the form, "Do v[i] and v[j] possibly refer to the same location?" to be answered with "maybe."

Next, I would like to try running other sorts of programs with different types of data structures other than simple arrays. Examples: How effectively can tables be searched using n-ary search? Intuitively, it seems that an n-ary search should do quite well on a VLIW with n clusters. What if the tables need to be updated? What about sorting? What about manipulating large objects like B-trees? How well would various sparse matrix techniques work?

All the variations on the particular heuristics of trace picking and code generation need to be thoroughly explored. How do they affect bookkeeper copying?

Execution time? Code size? Similarly, the loop transformations for memory-bank disambiguation and reducing loop overhead should be investigated more thoroughly.

The other obvious set of experiments I'd like to run would measure the effect of changing the machine models. For example, how well can the Bulldog compiler utilize hardware as the number of clusters ranges from 2 to 32? What happens if the bandwidth of crossbars and buses is changed? What happens if the machine is made more asymmetric, such as if not all clusters have the same set of functional units or if the cluster interconnections are skewed? Some measurements I made of various programs showed that rarely were more than 8 or 9 operations initiated per instruction, even though the 8-cluster ELI instruction is capable of initiating many times that. So what would be the effect of replacing each cluster with a pipelined sequential processor like the MIPS? Similarly, how many conditional jumps are needed per instruction for optimal performance? Examining some of the object code suggests that perhaps only 1 or 2 jumps per instruction would be sufficient, especially if multicycle jumps are allowed to overlap.

These sorts of hardware questions aren't crucial to my thesis, but rather explore the interaction between hardware, compiler, and program. Fully answering the questions would constitute another dissertation.

Chapter 9
Final Thoughts

I've presented strong evidence in support of my thesis: Ordinary scientific programs can be compiled for VLIWs, yielding order of magnitude speed-ups over traditional architectures. But this only begins to address the issues of making VLIWs and trace scheduling compilers practical. There is a world of difference between a prototype compiler constructed in academy for a simulated machine and an economically successful product.

Other Domains

I've concentrated on scientific programs only. Are there other classes of programs for which VLIWs and trace scheduling will work well?

The programs in the library that exhibited the least amount of parallelism were also the programs that had the smallest and least regular data structures. Considering the limited scope of my experiments, it would be foolish to make sweeping generalizations. But it does seem unlikely that VLIWs and trace scheduling would do well on programs that don't have large, regular control and data structures.

The data structures wouldn't necessarily have to be arrays. It's certainly possible that programs manipulating other regular data structures such as trees and lists might do well on VLIWs with trace scheduling, provided there was a high degree of regularity. However, even though systems and AI programs often use these data structures, often they don't spend a large fraction of their time in the code manipulating them—much, if not most of the time of such programs is spent in highly irregular control structures that have frequent conditionals manipulating small data structures. Thus, I doubt whether most AI or systems applications could take full advantage of VLIWs.

Scaling Up

My experiments only dealt with an 8-cluster VLIW offering roughly 8-fold parallelism. What about larger VLIWs?

With a little work, the current compiler could probably handle a 16-cluster VLIW. The main impediment (for a compiler) to larger machines is loop unrolling and the quadratic running time of the flow analyses and optimizations. In general, loops must be unrolled a multiple of n times for an n-cluster machine; for n larger than 16, the time of the flow analyses and optimizations becomes unacceptable. I discussed in chapter 2 improved algorithms requiring substantially less time. But even if they do prove to be better for large unrolled programs, I still doubt it would be practicable in the next few years to compile for VLIWs much larger than 64 or 128 clusters at the very most.

Automating the Transformations

The current compiler requires the programmer to manually apply many non-trivial source transformations. He must specify the amount of loop unrolling, conditional jump probabilities, and assertions for memory-reference and memory-bank disambiguation, and he must often significantly rewrite loops.

This extra work doesn't make VLIWs and the current compiler impractical, however. Today many people find it necessary (and economical) to resort to assembly language to get even adequate performance from LIWs and vector machines, since their compilers don't provide a good mapping from the source language to the capabilities of the machine. But the Bulldog compiler lets the programmer directly control VLIWs without descending to machine language; while tuning a program might be time-consuming, it involves much less work than programming a Cray-I or FPS-164 in assembly language.

Many of the simpler transformations could be automated without much difficulty. Adding obvious assertions, estimating jump probabilities, setting the amount of unrolling, and some of the simpler bank-disambiguation transformations are not that hard to implement. However, the more sophisticated control transformations needed for bank disambiguation are just now being researched; whether they can be implemented as part of a production compiler, I don't know. Since there will always be some programs like FFT that are beyond the capabilities of any near-future automatic methods, care must be taken to ensure that the automatic transformations added in don't preclude manually specified transformations.

A Better Approach?

Though it may well be economical for the next few years, I don't think that adding more and more sophisticated transformations to a Fortran compiler is the right long-term approach. I'm suspicious of any programming system that requires the programmer to translate his high-level intentions into a low-level language, only to have the compiler try to discover the original high-level intent of the programmer. Why not design a language more suited both for expressing the programmer's intentions and helping the compiler generate efficient code?

The time-critical kernels of most scientific programs consist mainly of array manipulations. But Fortran requires the programmer to specify the operations in terms of low-level scalar operations; he must specify many details irrelevant to the correct execution of his original array-oriented algorithm. An APL-like notation, where the programmer specifies the array operations directly, might be a better programming language for these programs than Fortran. Even Fortran 8x [ANSI 81] might be better, though I'm always doubtful about committee efforts.

The advantages of such an approach are obvious: The compiler needn't discover the original high-level intention of the programmer before picking a good implementation for the program. For example, current Fortran compilers for parallel machines go to great lengths analyzing the different classes of loops that occur in Fortran programs. But a compiler for an APL-like language wouldn't need to do that analysis; the language's operators explicitly indicate the type of array operation and thus determine the classes of loops that could be used to implement the operation.

Compilation for APL proper is quite difficult. But a subset of APL specifically chosen for scientific programming could be compiled much more easily, especially if various sorts of static declarations are added to the language. A VLIW compiler for this language could analyze an array expression and generate an efficient intermediate-code implementation that by construction would be automatically optimized, unrolled, disambiguated, and bank disambiguated. (Many, if not most, of the optimization techniques of a standard Fortran compiler, such as loop induction variable simplification, loop invariant motion, and common-subexpression elimination, serve mainly to optimize the low-level details peculiar to a Fortran program.)

Budd has implemented an APL compiler for traditional vector machines [Budd 84]. It's quite likely that it could be adapted for use on VLIWs without much difficulty. The APL compiler currently generates a machine-independent intermediate vector code. From that code it wouldn't be hard to generate good scalar intermediate code of the sort expected by the Bulldog compiler. That scalar code could then be fed directly into the trace scheduler.

Perhaps trace scheduling isn't even necessary in this approach. By construction, the intermediate-code loops generated would fall into a few simple classes, and the techniques used by the FPS-164 compiler might extend naturally to larger VLIW machines. In either case, eliminating the expensive standard flow analyses and optimizations would make larger VLIWs more practical.

Of course, there is a huge disadvantage in using a language that has no resemblance to Fortran. There are hundreds of millions of lines of Fortran code out in the real world, a very real incentive to stick with Fortran-like languages. Any alternative to Fortran must provide significant, clearly recognizable advantages to induce industry to leave Fortran behind.

VLIWs Versus Vector Machines

If VLIWs and trace scheduling work well only with programs that have a high degree of regularity in data and control, are VLIWs any better than vector machines?

So far, programs that run well on vector machines also run well on VLIWs. However, there is at least one task a VLIW can perform much better than a vector machine: The FFT shuffle is easy for a VLIW, but expensive on a vector machine [Rodrigue 82]. Whether there are other such tasks, I don't know. An advantage of the VLIW/trace-scheduling combination is that there is a direct mapping from the Fortran language level to the operations performed on the machine; whereas a frequent problem with vector machines is that even the "enhanced" Fortran supplied by the manufacturer doesn't always provide sufficient access to the machine's capabilities [Rodrigue 82].

Another problem with vector machines is that they aren't as efficient when manipulating short vectors. But my experiments indicate that maybe VLIWs don't do well with short vectors either.

Clearly, VLIWs can efficiently emulate the capabilities of vector machines. And VLIWs have the potential to degrade more gracefully in the face of programs only partially vectorizable, whereas vector machines are all-or-nothing. Unlike vector machines, VLIWs don't need two sets of hardware, one for normal scalar computation and one for vectors; for example, VLIWs don't have the large vector registers, the complex vector control units, or the high-bandwidth central memory controller needed for the Cray. Whether all this makes VLIWs economically advantageous is an open question. At least one start-up company is trying to make a commercial VLIW, so we should know more in a year or two.

Trace Scheduling for RISCs and LIWs

Trace scheduling would probably do better than traditional compilation for pipelined reduced-instruction-set processors like the MIPS and the FPS-164 (the 164 is an LIW machine, but LIWs have the same essential characteristics as RISCs).

My experiments show that even for a sequential pipelined machine, there is a significant payoff from trace scheduling. By unrolling the inner loops 2 to 4 times and picking traces that included several basic blocks, trace scheduling obtained a 30 to 80% improvement for many of the library programs running on the sequential ELI model. This improvement is in addition to the speed-up obtained simply by pipelining the operations on a per-block basis; Hennessy and Gross report that by generating code only one block at a time, they were able to obtain 2 to 10% speed-ups for the MIPS, compared to not doing any pipelining at all [Hennessy 83]. Of course, these speed-ups aren't strictly comparable because the MIPS and the sequential ELI are different machines and the benchmarks run were quite different. But the point is that trace scheduling can yield quite significant improvements in comparison to other methods, at least for scientific code.

Also, the Bulldog compiler's method for handling multicycle jumps (delayed jumps) appears to be somewhat better than the heuristics used for the MIPS [Gross 82]. Though benchmarks used for the MIPS were generally systems programs, not scientific programs, the fact that basic blocks in all programs tend to be short suggest that trace scheduling would obtain larger improvements for pipelined execution of jumps.

Trace scheduling should also work well for LIWs such as the FPS-164 and the MARS-432. The current FPS-164 Fortran compiler can only compile the simplest loops to take full advantage of the machine [Touzeau 84], whereas trace scheduling would provide about the same speed-up for almost all the loops likely to be run on the FPS-164.

Appendix A
The ELI Machine Models

This appendix contains the definitions of the realistic- and sequential-ELI machine models used in the experiments reported in chapter 8. See chapter 3 for the general machine model implemented by the compiler.

The "definition language" consists of a few procedures and special forms (macros) supplied by the compiler, plus Lisp itself. If you are familiar with Lisp, you shouldn't have any problem comprehending the gist of these definitions.

A resource class is defined using the special form:

```
(resource-class (name class-name) (size class-size) )
```

This returns a Lisp object representing a resource class with the given size and symbolic name. If the `size` clause is missing, a size of 1 is assumed.

A machine element (register bank, functional unit, or constant generator) is defined using the special form

```
(me -parts-)
```

where *-parts-* is a list of name/value pairs specifying the various parts of the machine element. For example:

```
(me (name           'r1)
    (type           'register-bank)
    (size           32)
    (read-ports     1)
    (write-ports    2)
    (read-resources (resource-class (name 'r1-read)
                                    (size 2) ) )
    (write-resources (resource-class (name 'r1-write) ) )
```

defines a 1-in/2-out register bank with 32 registers. As another example:

```
(me (name      'f+)
    (type      'functional-unit)
    (delay     2)
    (resources (resource-class (name 'f+) ) )
    (operators '(float fix fsub fadd fneg fabs fmin fmax fdiv flt
                 fgt feq fne fle fge frecip frsqrt fsc fsign-bit) ) ) )
```

defines a floating-adder functional unit with 3-cycle operations (a `delay` of 0 means the unit's operations take 1 cycle). The `operators` clause lists the intermediate-code operators implemented by the functional unit.

Machine elements are connected by using the `->` primitive:

> (-> *me1 me2 resource-class*)

This connects the output of *me1* with the input of *me2*. The *resource-class* is optional; if supplied, it is associated with the connection (see chapter 3). If *me1* or *me2* or both are lists of machine elements, connections are made between all pairs of elements taken from the respective lists. As a convenience:

> (<-> *me1 me2 resource-class*)

makes a two-way connection, and is equivalent to:

> (-> *me1 me2 resource-class*)
> (-> *me2 me1 resource-class*)

The definitions of the realistic and sequential models share a module of common definitions, the so-called "base" ELI model. The base definitions are given last.

The Realistic ELI

```lisp
;================================================================================
;
; REALISTIC ELI
;
; This code defines the realistic ELI model.
;
;================================================================================
(eval-when (eval load)
    (build '(list-scheduler:base-eli-model) ) )
(eval-when (compile load)
    (include list-scheduler:declarations) )
(defun rem.register-bank:new ( i &optional (read-ports 2) (write-ports 1) )
    (me (name            (!! 'c i 'r) )
        (type            'register-bank)
        (size            32)
        (read-ports      read-ports)
        (write-ports     write-ports)
        (read-resources  (resource-class (name (!! 'c i 'r-read) )
                                         (size read-ports) ) )
        (write-resources (resource-class (name (!! 'c i 'r-write) )
                                         (size write-ports) ) ) ) ) )
(defun rem.adder-subcluster:new ( i )
    (let ( (bank-a (rem.register-bank:new (!! i 'f+a) ) )
           (bank-b (rem.register-bank:new (!! i 'f+b) ) )
           (adder  (bem.adder:new       i) ) )
        (<-> adder bank-a)
        (<-> adder bank-b)
        '(,bank-a ,bank-b) ) )
(defun rem.multiplier-subcluster:new ( i )
    (let ( (bank-a     (rem.register-bank:new (!! i 'f*a) ) )
           (bank-b     (rem.register-bank:new (!! i 'f*b) ) )
           (multiplier (bem.multiplier:new   i) ) )
        (<-> multiplier bank-a)
        (<-> multiplier bank-b)
        '(,bank-a ,bank-b) ) )
(defun rem.frontdoor-subcluster:new ( i )
    (let ( (bank-a     (rem.register-bank:new (!! i 'ma) ) )
           (bank-b     (rem.register-bank:new (!! i 'mb) ) )
           (frontdoor  (bem.frontdoor:new    i) )
           (memory-alu (bem.memory-alu:new   i) ) )
        (<-> frontdoor  bank-a)
        (<-> frontdoor  bank-b)
        (<-> memory-alu bank-a)
```

```
        (<-> memory-alu bank-b)
        '(,bank-a ,bank-b) ) )
(defun rem.backdoor-subcluster:new ( i )
    (let ( (bank-a    (rem.register-bank:new (!! i 'ba) ) )
           (bank-b    (rem.register-bank:new (!! i 'bb) ) )
           (backdoor  (bem.backdoor:new      i) )
           (memory-alu (bem.memory-alu:new   (!! i 'b) ) ) )
        (<-> backdoor   bank-a)
        (<-> backdoor   bank-b)
        (<-> memory-alu bank-a)
        (<-> memory-alu bank-b)
        '(,bank-a ,bank-b) ) )

(defun rem.test-alu-subcluster:new ( i )
    (let ( (bank-a   (rem.register-bank:new (!! i 'ta) ) )
           (bank-b   (rem.register-bank:new (!! i 'tb) ) )
           (test-alu (bem.test-alu:new      i) ) )
        (<-> test-alu bank-a)
        (<-> test-alu bank-b)
        '(,bank-a ,bank-b) ) )

(defun rem.bus-subcluster:new ( i )
    '(,(rem.register-bank:new (!! i 'b) 2 2) ) )

(defun rem.cluster:new ( i unique-subcluster )
    (let*( (constant-generator (bem.constant-generator:new i) )
           (bus                (rem.bus-subcluster:new     i) )
           (subclusters
               '(,,bus
                 ,,unique-subcluster
                 ,,(rem.adder-subcluster:new      i)
                 ,,(rem.frontdoor-subcluster:new  i)
                 ,,(rem.test-alu-subcluster:new   i)
                 ,,(rem.multiplier-subcluster:new i) ) )
           (crossbar
               (resource-class (name (!! 'c i 'x) ) (size 4) ) ) )
        (-> subclusters       subclusters crossbar)
        (-> constant-generator subclusters crossbar)
        bus) )
```

```
;***============================================================================
;***
;*** Here is where the realistic model is actually constructed
;***
;***============================================================================

(machine-model.initialize)
(let ( (clusters (list:vector
            '(,(rem.cluster:new 0 (rem.backdoor-subcluster:new 0) )
              ,(rem.cluster:new 1 () )
              ,(rem.cluster:new 2 () )
```

```
                ,(rem.cluster:new 3 () )
                ,(rem.cluster:new 4 () )
                ,(rem.cluster:new 5 () )
                ,(rem.cluster:new 6 () )
                ,(rem.cluster:new 7 () ) ) ) ) )
    (loop (incr i from 0 to 7)
          (bind i+1 (mod (+ i 1) 8)
                i+3 (mod (+ i 3) 8) )
    (do
        (<-> ([] clusters i)
             ([] clusters i+1)
             1)
        (<-> ([] clusters i)
             ([] clusters i+3)
             1) ) ) )
(machine-model.finalize)
```

The Sequential ELI

```
;================================================================================
;
; A pipelined sequential model used for comparing with the realistic
; ELI model.  One operation can be initiated every cycle, and the register
; port can  read and write a value every cycle.
;
;================================================================================
(eval-when (eval load)
    (build '(list-scheduler:base-eli-model) ) )
(eval-when (compile load)
    (include list-scheduler:declarations) )
(machine-model.initialize)
(let*( (cycle
            (resource-class (name 'cycle) (size 1) ) )
        (register-bank
            (me (name          'r)
                (type          'register-bank)
                (size          #.(* 8 64) )
                (read-ports    3)
                (write-ports   1)
                (read-resources  (resource-class (name 'r-read)  (size 3) ) )
                (write-resources (resource-class (name 'r-write) (size 1)))))
        (constant-generator
            (me (name    'c)
                (type    'constant-generator)
                (resources (resource-class (name 'constant) ) )
                (constraint-function
                        'bem.me:constant:immediate?) ) )
        (fu1
            (me (name    'fu1)
                (type    'functional-unit)
                (delay   0)
                (resources cycle)
                (operators '(inot idiv isub ieq imax imin iadd ineg ior
                            ige ilt iand iabs bitrev iland ilor iash
                            ile ine ie0mod iexp igt isel fsel if-true
                            if-false if-ilt if-igt if-ieq if-ine if-ile
                            if-ige if-ie0mod fsign-bit isign-bit) ) ) )
        (fu3
            (me (name    'fu3)
                (type    'functional-unit)
                (delay   2)
                (resources cycle)
                (operators '(float fix fsub fadd fneg fabs fmin fmax fdiv
                            flt fgt feq fne fle fge frecip frsqrt fsc
```

```
                        vbase ivload fvload ipload fpload ivstore
                        fvstore ipstore fpstore) ) ) )
    (fu4
        (me (name      'fu4)
            (type      'functional-unit)
            (delay     3)
            (resources cycle)
            (operators '(fmul imul) ) ) ) )
    (<-> register-bank
        '(,register-bank ,fu1 ,fu3 ,fu4) )
    (-> constant-generator
        '(,register-bank ,fu1 ,fu3 ,fu4) )
    () )
(machine-model.finalize)
```

The Base ELI Definitions

```
;===============================================================================
;
; This module defines the basic units in common between the ideal and
; realistic ELI models.
;
;===============================================================================
(eval-when (compile load)
    (include list-scheduler:declarations) )
(defun bem.memory-alu:new ( i )
    (me (name      (!! 'c i 'm+) )
        (type      'functional-unit)
        (delay     0)
        (resources (resource-class (name (!! 'c i 'm+) ) ) )
        (operators '(inot isub iadd ineg ior iand iabs bitrev iland
                     ilor iland ilor iash) ) ) )
(defun bem.test-alu:new ( i )
    (me (name      (!! 'c i 't+) )
        (type      'functional-unit)
        (delay     0)
        (resources (resource-class (name (!! 'c i 't+) ) ) )
        (operators '(inot idiv isub ieq imax imin iadd ineg ior ige ilt
                     ile ine ie0mod iexp igt iand iabs iland ilor isel
                     fsel iland ilor if-true if-false if-ilt if-igt if-ieq
                     if-ine if-ile if-ige if-ieq if-ine if-ile if-ige
                     if-ie0mod fsign-bit isign-bit)))) 
(defun bem.adder:new ( i )
    (me (name      (!! 'c i 'f+) )
        (type      'functional-unit)
        (delay     2)
        (resources (resource-class (name (!! 'c i 'f+) ) ) )
        (operators '(float fix fsub fadd fneg fabs fmin fmax fdiv flt
                     fgt feq fne fle fge frecip frsqrt fsc fsign-bit) ) ) )
(defun bem.multiplier:new ( i )
    (me (name      (!! 'c i 'f*) )
        (type      'functional-unit)
        (delay     3)
        (resources (resource-class (name (!! 'c i 'f*) ) ) )
        (operators '(fmul imul) ) ) )
(defun bem.frontdoor:new ( i )
    (me (name      (!! 'c i 'm) )
        (type      'functional-unit)
        (delay     2)
```

```
            (resources (resource-class (name (!! 'c i 'm) ) ) )
            (operators '(vbase ivload fvload ipload fpload ivstore
                        fvstore ipstore fpstore) )
            (bank       i)
            (constraint-function
                        'bem.me:vn:ok-for-frontdoor?) ) )
(defun bem.backdoor:new ( i )
    (me (name       (!! 'c i 'bd) )
        (type       'functional-unit)
        (delay      5)
        (resources (resource-class (name (!! 'c i 'bd) ) ) )
        (operators '(vbase ivload fvload ipload fpload ivstore
                    fvstore ipstore fpstore) ) ) )
(defun bem.constant-generator:new ( i )
    (me (name       (!! 'c i 'c) )
        (type       'constant-generator)
        (resources (resource-class (name (!! 'c i 'c) ) ) )
        (constraint-function
                    'bem.me:constant:immediate?) ) )
(defun bem.me:constant:immediate? ( me constant )
    (?( (inump constant)
        (&& (< constant 2047)
            (> constant -2048) ) )
      ( (= 0 constant)
        t)
      ( (consp constant)
        (== 'address (car constant) ) )
      ( t
        () ) ) ) )
(defun load-constant? ( constant )
    (if (bem.me:constant:immediate? () constant) (then
        (!== 'load *ls.immediate-constant-action*) )
    (else
        t) ) )
(defun bem.me:vn:ok-for-frontdoor? ( me vn )
    (|| (! *fa.disambiguate-banks?*)
        (== (me:bank me) (oper:part (vn:oper vn) 'bank) ) ) )
```

Appendix B
Some of the Benchmark Programs

This appendix contains the Tinylisp and Fortran code for some of the benchmark programs. For programs that required major source transformations for memory-reference and memory-bank disambiguation, I've included both the original Tinylisp version and the transformed version used in the experiments. Unfortunately, space prevents me from including all the programs.

MATMUL

The original Tinylisp:

```
;================================================================================
;
; Matrix Multiply
;
;================================================================================

(def-block ( a  b  n ) ( c )
    (declare (a b c) float ( (1 56) (1 56) ) )
    (declare (n i j k) integer)

    (loop (incr i from 1 to n) (do
        (loop (incr j from 1 to n) (do
            (:= (c i j)
                (vector-reduce (incr k from 1 to n)
                            (unroll *unroll*)
                    + 0.0 (* (a i k) (b k j) ) ) ) ) ) ) ) )
    )
```

The transformed Tinylisp for MATMUL:

```
;==================================================================================
;
; Matrix Multiply
;
; Modified to minimize bank conflict.
;
;==================================================================================

(def-block ( a b n ) ( c )
    (declare (n i j k) integer)
    (declare (a b c) float ( (1 56) (1 56) ) )
    (declare (s0 s1 s2 s3 s4 s5 s6 s7) float)

    (loop (incr i from 1 to n) (do
        (loop (incr j from 1 to n by 8) (do
            (assert (=0-mod (- j 1) 8) )

            (:= s0 (:= s1 (:= s2 (:= s3 (:= s4 (:= s5 (:= s6 (:= s7 0.0)))))))))

            (loop l
                    (incr k from 1 to n)
                    (unroll *unroll*)
            (do
                (assert (=0-mod (- k (unroll-index l) ) *unroll*) )
                (:= s0 (+ s0 (* (a i k) (b k (+ j 0) ) ) ) )
                (:= s1 (+ s1 (* (a i k) (b k (+ j 1) ) ) ) )
                (:= s2 (+ s2 (* (a i k) (b k (+ j 2) ) ) ) )
                (:= s3 (+ s3 (* (a i k) (b k (+ j 3) ) ) ) )
                (:= s4 (+ s4 (* (a i k) (b k (+ j 4) ) ) ) )
                (:= s5 (+ s5 (* (a i k) (b k (+ j 5) ) ) ) )
                (:= s6 (+ s6 (* (a i k) (b k (+ j 6) ) ) ) )
                (:= s7 (+ s7 (* (a i k) (b k (+ j 7) ) ) ) ) ) )
```

```
(:= (c i j) s0)
(if (<= (+ j 1) n) .1 (then
    (:= (c i (+ j 1) ) s1) ) )
(if (<= (+ j 2) n) .1 (then
    (:= (c i (+ j 2) ) s2) ) )
(if (<= (+ j 3) n) .1 (then
    (:= (c i (+ j 3) ) s3) ) )
(if (<= (+ j 4) n) .1 (then
    (:= (c i (+ j 4) ) s4) ) )
(if (<= (+ j 5) n) .1 (then
    (:= (c i (+ j 5) ) s5) ) )
(if (<= (+ j 6) n) .1 (then
    (:= (c i (+ j 6) ) s6) ) )
(if (<= (+ j 7) n) .1 (then
    (:= (c i (+ j 7) ) s7) ) ) ) ) ) )
)
```

FFT

The original Fortran:

```
C
C FFT from "Introduction to Discrete Systems" by Kenneth Steiglitz
C
C
C Generates test signal S and obtains DFT F using FFT algorithm
C
C
      DIMENSION S( 1024 )
      COMPLEX   F( 1024 )
      N = 32
      DO 1 J = 1, N
          S( J ) = SIN( FLOAT( J - 1 ) * 3.141593/8. )
    1     CONTINUE
      CALL FTRANS( S, F, N )
      DO 2 J = 1, N
          FABS = CABS( F( J ) )
          JM = J - 1
          WRITE( 6, 3 ) JM, S( J ), F( J), FABS
    3     FORMAT( ' ', I6, ' SIGNAL=', F14.7, ' F=', 2F14.7,
    *             ' FABS=', F14.7 )
    2     CONTINUE
      STOP
      END


C
C Places Fourier transform of N-point signal S in F.
C
      SUBROUTINE FTRANS( S, F, N )
      DIMENSION S( 1024 )
      COMPLEX   F( 1024 )
      CALL SHUFF( S, F, N )
      LENGTH = 2
    1 CONTINUE
          DO 2 J = 1, N, LENGTH
              CALL COMBIN( F, J, LENGTH )
    2         CONTINUE

          LENGTH = LENGTH + LENGTH
          IF (LENGTH .LE. N)  GOTO 1
      RETURN
      END


C
C "Bit-reverses" the S array.  N (number of points) any power of 2.
```

```
C Result is put in F to prepare transform iteration.
C
      SUBROUTINE SHUFF( S, F, N )
      DIMENSION S( 1024 )
      COMPLEX   F( 1024 ), CMPLX
      DO 5 IFORT = 1, N
          I = IFORT - 1
          J = 0
          M2 = 1
  1       CONTINUE
              M1 = M2
              M2 = M2 + M2
              IF (MOD( I, M2 ) .LT. M1)  GOTO 3
                  J = J + N / M2
  3               CONTINUE
              IF (M2 .LT. N)  GOTO 1
          JFORT = J + 1
          F( IFORT ) = CMPLX( S( JFORT ), 0. )
  5       CONTINUE
      RETURN
      END


C
C Combines trasforms in F( J ) - F( N/2+J-1 ) and F( N/2+J ) - F( N+J-1 )
C into transform in F( J ) - F( N + J - 1 )
C
      SUBROUTINE COMBIN( F, J, N )
      COMPLEX F( 1024 ), EMJT, Z, CEXP
      EMJT = CEXP( ( 0., -1. ) * ( 6.283185/FLOAT( N ) ) )
      N2 = N / 2
      DO 1 L = 1, N2
          LOC1 = L + J - 1
          LOC2 = LOC1 + N2
          Z = EMJT ** (L - 1) * F( LOC2 )
          F( LOC2 ) = F( LOC1 ) - Z
          F( LOC1 ) = F( LOC1 ) + Z
  1       CONTINUE
      RETURN
      END
```

The original Tinylisp for FFT:

```
;================================================================================
;
; FFT adapted from "Introduction to Discrete Systems" by Kenneth Steiglitz
;
; This version uses precomputed complex exponentials.
;
;================================================================================
(def-block ( s n emjt ) ( f )
    (declare s     float ( (1 1024) ) )
    (declare n     integer)
    (declare emjt complex float ( (1 1024) ) )

    (declare f                      complex float ( (1 1024) ) )
    (declare (z f1)                 complex float)
    (declare (i j l loc1 loc2 length) integer)

    (loop (incr i from 1 to n)
          (unroll *unroll*)
    (do
        (:= j (bit-reverse (- i 1) n) )
        (:= (f i) (complex (s (+ j 1) ) 0.0) ) ) )


    (loop (step length from 1 using (+ length length)
                  while (<= (* 2 length) n) )
    (do
        (loop (incr j from 1 to n by (* 2 length) ) (do
            (loop (incr l from 1 to length)
                  (unroll *unroll*)
            (do
                (assert (>= l 1) )
                (assert (<= l length) )

                (:= loc1 (+ l (- j 1) ) )
                (:= loc2 (+ loc1 length) )

                (:= z (* (emjt (+ length (- l 1) ) ) (f loc2) ) )
                (:= f1 (f loc1) )
                (:= (f loc2) (- f1 z) )
                (:= (f loc1) (+ f1 z) ) ) ) ) ) ) ) )
    )
```

The transformed Tinylisp for FFT (the specially transformed shuffle follows):

```
;====================================================================
;
; FFT1 adapted from "Introduction to Discrete Systems" by Kenneth Steiglitz
;
; This version uses precomputed complex exponentials and unrolls the main
; loop specially.
;
;====================================================================
(def-block ( s n emjt ) ( f )
    (declare s    float ( (1 1024) ) )
    (declare n    integer)
    (declare emjt complex float ( (1 1024) ) )

    (declare f                       complex float ( (1 1024) ) )
    (declare (z f1)                  complex float)
    (declare (i j l loc1 loc2 length) integer)

    (loop la
         (incr i from 1 to n)
         (unroll *unroll*)
    (do
        (assert (=0-mod (- i (unroll-index la) ) *unroll*) )

        (:= j (bit-reverse (- i 1) n) )
        (:= (f i) (complex (s (+ j 1) ) 0.0) ) ) )

    (:= length 1)
    (loop l1
         (incr j from 1 to n by (* 2 length) )
         (unroll *unroll*)
    (do
        (assert (=0-mod (+ -1 (- j (* 2 length (- (unroll-index l1) 1) ) ) )
                        *unroll*) )

        (:= l 1)
        (assert (>= l 1) )
        (assert (<= l length) )
        (:= loc1 (+ l (- j 1) ) )
        (:= loc2 (+ loc1 length) )
        (:= z (* (emjt (+ length (- l 1) ) ) (f loc2) ) )
        (:= f1 (f loc1) )
        (:= (f loc2) (- f1 z) )
        (:= (f loc1) (+ f1 z) ) ) )


    (:= length 2)
```

```
(loop 12
      (incr j from 1 to n by (* 2 length) )
      (unroll *unroll//2*)
(do
      (assert (=0-mod (+ -1 (- j (* 2 length (- (unroll-index 12) 1) ) ) ) )
                      *unroll*) )

      (:= l 1)
      (assert (>= l 1) )
      (assert (<= l length) )
      (:= loc1 (+ l (- j 1) ) )
      (:= loc2 (+ loc1 length) )
      (:= z (* (emjt (+ length (- l 1) ) ) (f loc2) ) )
      (:= f1 (f loc1) )
      (:= (f loc2) (- f1 z) )
      (:= (f loc1) (+ f1 z) )

      (:= l 2)
      (assert (>= l 1) )
      (assert (<= l length) )
      (:= loc1 (+ l (- j 1) ) )
      (:= loc2 (+ loc1 length) )
      (:= z (* (emjt (+ length (- l 1) ) ) (f loc2) ) )
      (:= f1 (f loc1) )
      (:= (f loc2) (- f1 z) )
      (:= (f loc1) (+ f1 z) ) ) )

(:= length 4)
(loop 14
      (incr j from 1 to n by (* 2 length) )
      (unroll *unroll//4*)
(do
      (assert (=0-mod (+ -1 (- j (* 2 length (- (unroll-index 14) 1) ) ) ) )
                      *unroll*) )

      (:= l 1)
      (assert (>= l 1) )
      (assert (<= l length) )
      (:= loc1 (+ l (- j 1) ) )
      (:= loc2 (+ loc1 length) )
      (:= z (* (emjt (+ length (- l 1) ) ) (f loc2) ) )
      (:= f1 (f loc1) )
      (:= (f loc2) (- f1 z) )
      (:= (f loc1) (+ f1 z) )

      (:= l 2)
      (assert (>= l 1) )
      (assert (<= l length) )
      (:= loc1 (+ l (- j 1) ) )
```

```
(:= loc2 (+ loc1 length) )
(:= z (* (emjt (+ length (- 1 1) ) ) ) (f loc2) ) )
(:= f1 (f loc1) )
(:= (f loc2) (- f1 z) )
(:= (f loc1) (+ f1 z) )

(:= 1 3)
(assert (>= 1 1) )
(assert (<= 1 length) )
(:= loc1 (+ 1 (- j 1) ) )
(:= loc2 (+ loc1 length) )
(:= z (* (emjt (+ length (- 1 1) ) ) ) (f loc2) ) )
(:= f1 (f loc1) )
(:= (f loc2) (- f1 z) )
(:= (f loc1) (+ f1 z) )

(:= 1 4)
(assert (>= 1 1) )
(assert (<= 1 length) )
(:= loc1 (+ 1 (- j 1) ) )
(:= loc2 (+ loc1 length) )
(:= z (* (emjt (+ length (- 1 1) ) ) ) (f loc2) ) )
(:= f1 (f loc1) )
(:= (f loc2) (- f1 z) )
(:= (f loc1) (+ f1 z) ) ) )
```

```
(loop (step length from 8 using (+ length length)
                 while (<= (* 2 length) n) )
(do
    (assert (=0-mod length 8) )

    (loop lb (incr j from 1 to n by (* 2 length) ) (do
        (assert (=0-mod (- j (unroll-index lb) ) *unroll*) )

        (loop lc
            (incr l from 1 to length)
            (unroll *unroll*)
        (do
            (assert (=0-mod (- l (unroll-index lc) ) *unroll*) )
            (assert (>= l 1) )
            (assert (<= l length) )

            (:= loc1 (+ l (- j 1) ) )
            (:= loc2 (+ loc1 length) )

            (:= z (* (emjt (+ length (- l 1) ) ) (f loc2) ) )
            (:= f1 (f loc1) )
            (:= (f loc2) (- f1 z) )
            (:= (f loc1) (+ f1 z) ) ) ) ) ) ) )
)
```

The transformed shuffle of FFT; I've elided the middle sections:

```
;==================================================================================
;
; FFT SHUFFLE
;
; This is a special 64-unrolling of the shuffle part of FFT.  The bank
; of every memory access is known at compile time.
;
;==================================================================================

(def-block ( s n emjt ) ( f )
    (declare s     float ( (0 1023) ) )
    (declare n     integer)
    (declare emjt complex float ( (0 1023) ) )

    (declare f                     complex float ( (0 1023) ) )
    (declare (z f1)                complex float)
    (declare (i j l loc1 loc2 length d) integer)
    (declare (i0 i1 i2 i3 i4 i5 i6 i7) integer)

    (assert (=0-mod n 64) )

    (:= d (// n 8) )
    (assert (>= d 8) )
    (assert (=0-mod d 8) )

    (loop (incr i0 from 0 to (- d 1) by 8) (do
        (:= i1 (+ i0 d) )
        (:= i2 (+ i1 d) )
        (:= i3 (+ i2 d) )
        (:= i4 (+ i3 d) )
        (:= i5 (+ i4 d) )
        (:= i6 (+ i5 d) )
        (:= i7 (+ i6 d) )

        (assert (=0-mod i0 8) )

        (:= i (+ i0 0) )            (:= j (bit-reverse i n) )
        (assert (=0-mod (- j 0) 8) ) (:= (f i) (complex (s j) 0.0) )
        (:= i (+ i0 1) )            (:= j (bit-reverse i n) )
        (assert (=0-mod (- j 0) 8) ) (:= (f i) (complex (s j) 0.0) )
        (:= i (+ i0 2) )            (:= j (bit-reverse i n) )
        (assert (=0-mod (- j 0) 8) ) (:= (f i) (complex (s j) 0.0) )
        (:= i (+ i0 3) )            (:= j (bit-reverse i n) )
        (assert (=0-mod (- j 0) 8) ) (:= (f i) (complex (s j) 0.0) )
        (:= i (+ i0 4) )            (:= j (bit-reverse i n) )
        (assert (=0-mod (- j 0) 8) ) (:= (f i) (complex (s j) 0.0) )
        (:= i (+ i0 5) )            (:= j (bit-reverse i n) )
```

```
(assert (=0-mod (- j 0) 8) )  (:= (f i) (complex (s j) 0.0) )
(:= i (+ i0 6) )               (:= j (bit-reverse i n) )
(assert (=0-mod (- j 0) 8) )  (:= (f i) (complex (s j) 0.0) )
(:= i (+ i0 7) )               (:= j (bit-reverse i n) )
(assert (=0-mod (- j 0) 8) )  (:= (f i) (complex (s j) 0.0) )


(:= i (+ i1 0) )               (:= j (bit-reverse i n) )
(assert (=0-mod (- j 4) 8) )  (:= (f i) (complex (s j) 0.0) )
(:= i (+ i1 1) )               (:= j (bit-reverse i n) )
(assert (=0-mod (- j 4) 8) )  (:= (f i) (complex (s j) 0.0) )
(:= i (+ i1 2) )               (:= j (bit-reverse i n) )
(assert (=0-mod (- j 4) 8) )  (:= (f i) (complex (s j) 0.0) )
(:= i (+ i1 3) )               (:= j (bit-reverse i n) )
(assert (=0-mod (- j 4) 8) )  (:= (f i) (complex (s j) 0.0) )
(:= i (+ i1 4) )               (:= j (bit-reverse i n) )
(assert (=0-mod (- j 4) 8) )  (:= (f i) (complex (s j) 0.0) )
(:= i (+ i1 5) )               (:= j (bit-reverse i n) )
(assert (=0-mod (- j 4) 8) )  (:= (f i) (complex (s j) 0.0) )
(:= i (+ i1 6) )               (:= j (bit-reverse i n) )
(assert (=0-mod (- j 4) 8) )  (:= (f i) (complex (s j) 0.0) )
(:= i (+ i1 7) )               (:= j (bit-reverse i n) )
(assert (=0-mod (- j 4) 8) )  (:= (f i) (complex (s j) 0.0) )


... and so on for i2, i3, i4, i5, and i6...

(:= i (+ i7 0) )               (:= j (bit-reverse i n) )
(assert (=0-mod (- j 7) 8) )  (:= (f i) (complex (s j) 0.0) )
(:= i (+ i7 1) )               (:= j (bit-reverse i n) )
(assert (=0-mod (- j 7) 8) )  (:= (f i) (complex (s j) 0.0) )
(:= i (+ i7 2) )               (:= j (bit-reverse i n) )
(assert (=0-mod (- j 7) 8) )  (:= (f i) (complex (s j) 0.0) )
(:= i (+ i7 3) )               (:= j (bit-reverse i n) )
(assert (=0-mod (- j 7) 8) )  (:= (f i) (complex (s j) 0.0) )
(:= i (+ i7 4) )               (:= j (bit-reverse i n) )
(assert (=0-mod (- j 7) 8) )  (:= (f i) (complex (s j) 0.0) )
(:= i (+ i7 5) )               (:= j (bit-reverse i n) )
(assert (=0-mod (- j 7) 8) )  (:= (f i) (complex (s j) 0.0) )
(:= i (+ i7 6) )               (:= j (bit-reverse i n) )
(assert (=0-mod (- j 7) 8) )  (:= (f i) (complex (s j) 0.0) )
(:= i (+ i7 7) )               (:= j (bit-reverse i n) )
(assert (=0-mod (- j 7) 8) )  (:= (f i) (complex (s j) 0.0) )

) ) ) )
```

TRID4

The original Fortran:

```
      PARAMETER  N1=800
      PARAMETER  N2=400
      PARAMETER  LMAX=20, LMIN=21, LMAXP=21

      DIMENSION A(N1), B(N1), C(N1), D(N1), X(N1)
      DIMENSION SCA(N2),SCB(N2),SCC(N2),SCD(N2)
      DIMENSION RB(N1)
      DIMENSION NL(LMAXP), ML(LMAXP), IO(LMAXP), JO(LMAXP)
      REAL CYC1,CYC2,CYCLES,CYCPP
      INTEGER ORDER
      OPEN(UNIT=6,DEVICE='TTY:')
c
c------Print version information -------
c
      WRITE(6,63)
 63   FORMAT('  ORDER. CYCLES (TOTAL). CYCLES PER POINT.',
     1       '  REL. ERROR IN 2- AND MAX-NORMS.'/1X,79('=')/)
c
c-----------------------------------------------------------------------------
c
      DO 25 ICOUNT = 1,1
      RORDER = 200. * ICOUNT
      ORDER  = 200  * ICOUNT
C
      DIAG = 11.
      SUB  = -3.
      SUPER= -5.
C
      B(1) = DIAG
      DO 1 I = 2,ORDER
      B(I) = DIAG
      A(I) = SUB
 1    C(I-1) = SUPER
      A(1) = 0.
      C(ORDER) = 0.
      D(1) = B(1) + C(1)
      DO 15 I = 2,ORDER
 15      D(I) = A(I) + B(I) + C(I)
      D(ORDER) = A(ORDER) + B(ORDER)
c
c---------- call tridiagonal solver ----------
c
      CYC1 = 0
      CYC2 = 0
c     call timer(cyc1)
```

```
c     call tridag(order,a,b,c,d,x)
c
c*****CUT ONE*****

      NC=ORDER
      N = NC
      LEVEL = 0
      I0(LEVEL + 1) = N
      J0(LEVEL + 1) = 0

      DO 500 L = 1, LMAX
      I1 = I0(L)
      J1 = J0(L)
      NL(L) = N
      IF (N .LE. LMIN) GO TO 600
      M = (N+1) / 2
      MM = M - 1
      ML(L) = M
       I = I1
       J = J1 - 1
      DO 200 II = 1, M
       I = I + 1
       J = J + 2
       B(I) = B(J)
       D(I) = D(J)
  200  RB(I)    = 1.0/B(J+1)

       I = I1
       J = J1
      DO 210 II = 1, MM
       I = I + 1
       J = J + 2
       SCA(II) = A(J+1) * RB(I)
       SCC(II) = C(J-1) * RB(I)

       A(I+1) = A(J) * SCA(II)
       C(I)   = C(J) * SCC(II)

       A(I+1) = -A(I+1)
       C(I)   = -C(I)

       SCB(II)  = C(J) * SCA(II)
       SCD(II)  = D(J) * SCA(II)

       B(I+1) = B(I+1) - SCB(II)
       D(I+1) = D(I+1) - SCD(II)

       SCB(II)  = A(J) * SCC(II)
       SCD(II)  = D(J) * SCC(II)
```

```
        B(I) = B(I) - SCB(II)
        D(I) = D(I) - SCD(II)

210   CONTINUE

C      CALL BOTCHD(...)

       IF (2*M .NE. N) GO TO 220

       TA  = A(J1+1)    / B(J1+N)
       TC  = C(J1+N-1) / B(J1+N)

       A(I1+1)  =  - TA * A(J1+N)
       B(I1+1)  =  B(I1+1) - TA * C(J1+N)
       D(I1+1)  =  D(I1+1) - TA * D(J1+N)
       B(I1+M)  =  B(I1+M) - TC * A(J1+N)
       C(I1+M)  =  - TC * C(J1+N)
       D(I1+M)  =  D(I1+M) - TC * D(J1+N)
       GOTO 230

220   A(I1+1)  =  A(J1+1)
       C(I1+M)  =  C(J1+N)

230   CONTINUE

       IO(L+1) = IO(L) + M
       JO(L+1) = JO(L) + N
       N        = M
500   LEVEL    = LEVEL + 1
c
c
c
600   CONTINUE
c
c*****CUT TWO*****
c
       NB = N
       NM = NB - 1
c
       DO 6010 I = 1, NB
       IF ( B(J1+I) .EQ. 0.D+0) B(J1+I) = 1.0D-38
6010    CONTINUE
c
       SCA(J1+1) = 1.D0 / B(J1+1)
       DO 6015 I = 2, NM
6015  SCA(J1+I)=1.D+0 / (B(J1+I) - A(J1+I) * C(J1+I-1) * SCA(J1+I-1))
c
c  Invert tridiagonal part on Q
```

```
c
      SCB(J1+1) = A(J1+1) * SCA(J1+1)
      DO 6020 I = 2, NM
6020  SCB(J1+I) = - A(J1+I) * SCB(J1+I-1) * SCA(J1+I)
      SCB(J1+NM) = SCB(J1+NM) + C(J1+NM) * SCA(J1+NM)
C
      DO 6030 J = 2, NM
      I = NB - J
6030  SCB(J1+I) = SCB(J1+I) - C(J1+I) * SCA(J1+I) * SCB(J1+I+1)
      RCAQ =  1.D+0 /
     1    (B(J1+NB) - C(J1+NB) * SCB(J1+1) - A(J1+NB) * SCB(J1+NM))
c
c  End precomputation. The following are all the calcs invovling D
c
      X(J1+1) = D(J1+1) * SCA(J1+1)
      DO 6040 I = 2, NM
6040  X(J1+I) = (D(J1+I) - A(J1+I) * X(J1+I-1)) * SCA(J1+I)
c
      DO 6050 J = 2, NM
      I = NB - J
6050  X(J1+I) = X(J1+I) - C(J1+I) * SCA(J1+I) * X(J1+I+1)
C
      X(J1+NB) = (D(J1+NB)-C(J1+NB)*X(J1+1)-A(J1+NB)*X(J1+NM))*RCAQ
      DO 6060 I = 1, NM
6060  X(J1+I) = X(J1+I) - X(J1+NB) * SCB(J1+I)
c
c*****CUT TWO*****
c
      IF (LEVEL .EQ. 0) RETURN
c
c
c
      DO 900 LL = 1, LEVEL
      L = LEVEL + 1 - LL
      M = ML(L)
      N = NL(L)
      I1 = I0(L)
      J1 = J0(L)

      I = I1
      J = J1 - 1
      DO 800 II = 1, M
      I = I + 1
      J = J + 2
 800  X(J) = X(I)

      MM = M - 1

      I = I1
```

```
      J = J1
      DO 810 II = 1, MM
      I = I + 1
      J = J + 2

      SCA(II)  = A(J) * X(J-1)
      SCC(II)  = C(J) * X(J+1)
      SCB(II)  = D(J) - SCA(II)
      SCD(II)  = SCB(II) - SCC(II)
 810  X(J)     = SCD(II) * RB(I)

      IF (2*M .EQ. N)
     1    X(J1+N) = ( D(J1+N) - A(J1+N)*X(J1+N-1) -C(J1+N)*X(J1+1) )
     2                / B(J1+N)

 900  CONTINUE
c---------------------------------------------------------------------------

c*****CUT ONE*****
c
c     call timer(cyc2)
c
c----------compute cycles ----------
c
      CYCLES = CYC2 - CYC1
      CYCPP = CYCLES / ORDER
c
c---------errors in 2 and max norms ----------
c
      ERRMAX = 0.
      ERR2 = 0.
      DO 3 I = 1, ORDER
      ABSERR = ABS(1.-X(I))
      ERR2 = ERR2 + ABSERR*ABSERR
 3    ERRMAX = AMAX1(ERRMAX,ABSERR)
      RELERR = SQRT(ERR2) / SQRT(RORDER)
c
c--------- print results ----------------------
c
      WRITE(6,62)ORDER, CYCLES,CYCPP,RELERR,ERRMAX
 62   FORMAT(1X,I6,2E16.5,5X,2E16.5)

 25   CONTINUE

      STOP
      END
```

The transformed Tinylisp for TRID4:

```
;===============================================================================
;
; Tridiagonal Solver using cyclic reduction.
;
;===============================================================================

(def-block ( a b c d order ) ( x )
    (declare (a b c d) float ( (1 20000) ) )
    (declare order      integer)
    (declare x          float ( (1 20000) ) )
    (declare (x0 x1 x2 x3 x4 x5 x6 x7 x8 x9) float)

    (declare (sca scb scc scd) float   ( (1 10000) ) )
    (declare rb             float   ( (1 20000) ) )
    (declare (nl ml i0 j0)  integer ( (1 21) ) )
    (declare (i i1 ii j j1 l level ll lmax lmin m mm n nb nc nm) integer)
    (declare (rcaq ta tc sca-ii scb-ii scc-ii scd-ii prev-sca prev-scb
                   prev-x)
             float)

    (:= lmin 21)
    (:= lmax 20)

    (:= j1   0)      ;*** J1 is live here, but live analysis doesn't know
                     ;*** that the loops execute > 0 times.  To avoid a minor
                     ;*** compiler bug, we assign J1 to force it to be live.

        ;***
        ;*** cut one
        ;***
    (:= nc    order)
    (:= n     nc)
    (:= level 0)
    (:= (i0 1) n)
    (:= (j0 1) 0)

    (loop ll (incr l from 1 to lmax) (do
        (:= i1    (i0 l) )
        (:= j1    (j0 l) )
        (:= (nl l) n)

        (if (<= n lmin) (then
            (leave ll 0) ) )

        (:= m     (// (+ n 1) 2) )
        (:= mm    (- m 1) )
        (:= (ml l) m)
```

```
(loop 12
     (incr ii from 1 to m)
     (incr i  from (+ i1 1) )
     (incr j  from (+ j1 1) by 2)
     (unroll *unroll2*)
(do
    (assert (>= (- i j) 10) )
    (assert (=0-mod (- i (unroll-index 12) )           *unroll2*) )
    (assert (=0-mod (- j -1 (* 2 (unroll-index 12) ) ) *unroll2*) )

    (:= (b i)     (b j))
    (:= (d i)     (d j))
    (:= (rb i)    (//n 1.0 (b (+ j 1) ) ) ) ) ) ) )

(loop 13
     (incr ii from 1 to mm)
     (incr i  from (+ i1 1) )
     (incr j  from (+ j1 2) by 2)
     (unroll *unroll2*)
(do
    (assert (>= (- i j) 10) )
    (assert (=0-mod (- ii (unroll-index 13) )          *unroll2*) )
    (assert (=0-mod (- i (unroll-index 13) )           *unroll2*) )
    (assert (=0-mod (- j (* 2 (unroll-index 13) ) )    *unroll2*) )

    (:= sca-ii       (* (a (+ j 1) ) (rb i) ) )
    (:= scc-ii       (* (c (- j 1) ) (rb i) ) )

    (:= (a (+ i 1) ) (- (* (a j) sca-ii) ) )
    (:= (c i)        (- (* (c j) scc-ii) ) )

    (:= scb-ii       (* (c j) sca-ii) )
    (:= scd-ii       (* (d j) sca-ii) )
    (:= (b (+ i 1) ) (- (b (+ i 1) ) scb-ii) )
    (:= (d (+ i 1) ) (- (d (+ i 1) ) scd-ii) )

    (:= scb-ii       (* (a j) scc-ii) )
    (:= scd-ii       (* (d j) scc-ii) )

    (:= (b i)        (- (b i) scb-ii) )
    (:= (d i)        (- (d i) scd-ii) )

    (:= (sca ii) sca-ii)
    (:= (scb ii) scb-ii)
    (:= (scc ii) scc-ii)
    (:= (scd ii) scd-ii) ) )
```

```
(if (= n (* 2 m) ) (then
    (:= ta               (//n (a (+ j1 1) )        (b (+ j1 n) ) ) )
    (:= tc               (//n (c (- (+ j1 n) 1) ) (b (+ j1 n) ) ) )

    (:= (a (+ i1 1) ) (- 0.0          (* ta (a (+ j1 n) ) ) ) )
    (:= (b (+ i1 1) ) (- (b (+ i1 1) ) (* ta (c (+ j1 n) ) ) ) )
    (:= (d (+ i1 1) ) (- (d (+ i1 1) ) (* ta (d (+ j1 n) ) ) ) )
    (:= (b (+ i1 m) ) (- (b (+ i1 m) ) (* tc (a (+ j1 n) ) ) ) )
    (:= (c (+ i1 m) ) (- 0.0          (* tc (c (+ j1 n) ) ) ) )
    (:= (d (+ i1 m) ) (- (d (+ i1 m) ) (* tc (d (+ j1 n) ) ) ) ) )

    (else
        (:= (a (+ i1 1) ) (a (+ j1 1) ) )
        (:= (c (+ i1 m) ) (c (+ j1 n) ) ) ) ) )

    (:= (i0 (+ 1 1) ) (+ (i0 1) m) )
    (:= (j0 (+ 1 1) ) (+ (j0 1) n) )
    (:= n             m)
    (:= level         (+ level 1) )
    ) )

    ;***
    ;*** cut two
    ;***
(assert (=0-mod j1 8) )
(:= nb  n)
(:= nm  (- nb 1) )

(loop 14
    (incr i from 1 to nb)
    (unroll *unroll1*)
(do
    (assert (=0-mod (- i (unroll-index 14) ) *unroll1*) )
    (:= (b (+ j1 i) ) (select (= 0.0 (b (+ j1 i) ) )
                            1.0e-38
                            (b (+ j1 i) ) ) ) ) ) )

(:= prev-sca (:= (sca (+ j1 1) ) (//n 1.0 (b (+ j1 1) ) ) ) ) )
(loop 15
    (incr i from 2 to nm)
    (unroll *unroll1*)
(do
    (assert (=0-mod (- i 1 (unroll-index 15) ) *unroll1*) )
    (:= prev-sca (:= (sca (+ j1 i) )
        (//n 1.0 (- (b (+ j1 i) )
                    (* (a (+ j1 i) ) (c (- (+ j1 i) 1) )
                    prev-sca) ) ) ) ) ) )

    ;***
```

```
;*** Invert tridiagonal part on Q ---
;***
(:= prev-scb (:= (scb (+ j1 1) ) (* (a (+ j1 1) ) (sca (+ j1 1) ) ) ) )
(loop 16
     (incr i from 2 to nm)
     (unroll *unroll1*)
(do
    (assert (=0-mod (- i 1 (unroll-index 16) ) *unroll1*) )
    (:= prev-scb (:= (scb (+ j1 i) )
        (- (* (a (+ j1 i) ) prev-scb (sca (+ j1 i) ) ) ) ) ) ) )
(:= (scb (+ j1 nm) ) (+ (scb (+ j1 nm) )
                        (* (c (+ j1 nm) ) (sca (+ j1 nm) ) ) ) )


(:= prev-scb (scb (+ j1 nb -1) ) )
(loop 17
     (incr j from 2 to nm)
     (decr i from (- nb 2) )
     (unroll *unroll1*)
(do
    (assert (=0-mod (- j 1 (unroll-index 17) ) *unroll1*) )
    (assert (=0-mod (+ i 1 (unroll-index 17) ) *unroll1*) )
    (:= prev-scb (:= (scb (+ j1 i) )
        (- (scb (+ j1 i) )
           (* (c (+ j1 i) ) (sca (+ j1 i) ) prev-scb) ) ) ) )

(:= rcaq
    (//n 1.0 (- (- (b (+ j1 nb) )
                   (* (c (+ j1 nb) ) (scb (+ j1 1) ) ) )
                (* (a (+ j1 nb) ) (scb (+ j1 nm) ) ) ) ) )


    ;***
    ;*** End precomputation.  The following are all the calcs invovling
    ;*** D.
    ;***
(:= prev-x (:= (x (+ j1 1) ) (* (d (+ j1 1) ) (sca (+ j1 1) ) ) ) )
(loop 18
     (incr i from 2 to nm)
     (unroll *unroll1*)
(do
    (assert (=0-mod (- i 1 (unroll-index 18) ) *unroll1*) )
    (:= prev-x (:= (x (+ j1 i) )
        (* (- (d (+ j1 i) ) (* (a (+ j1 i) ) prev-x) )
           (sca (+ j1 i) ) ) ) ) )

(:= prev-x (x (+ j1 nb -1) ) )
(loop 19
     (incr j from 2 to nm)
     (decr i from (- nb 2) )
     (unroll *unroll1*)
```

```
(do
    (assert (=0-mod (- j 1 (unroll-index 19) ) *unroll1*) )
    (assert (=0-mod (+ i 1 (unroll-index 19) ) *unroll1*) )
    (:= prev-x (:= (x (+ j1 i) )
        (- (x (+ j1 i) ) (* (c (+ j1 i) ) (sca (+ j1 i) )
                          prev-x) ) ) ) ) )

(:= (x (+ j1 nb) )
    (* (- (- (d (+ j1 nb) )
          (* (c (+ j1 nb) ) (x (+ j1 1) ) ) )
        (* (a (+ j1 nb) ) (x (+ j1 nm) ) ) )
      rcaq) )

(loop 110
    (incr i from 1 to nm)
    (unroll *unroll1*)
(do
    (assert (=0-mod (- i (unroll-index 110) ) *unroll1*) )
    (:= (x (+ j1 i) )
        (- (x (+ j1 i) ) (* (x (+ j1 nb) ) (scb (+ j1 i)))))))

;***
;*** cut two
;***
(if (!= level 0) (then

    (loop 111 (incr ll from 1 to level) (do
        (:= l    (- (+ level 1) ll) )
        (:= m    (ml l) )
        (:= n    (nl l) )
        (:= i1   (i0 l) )
        (:= j1   (j0 l) )

        (loop 112
            (incr ii from 1 to m)
            (incr i  from (+ i1 1) )
            (incr j  from (+ j1 1) by 2)
            (unroll *unroll2*)
        (do
            (assert (>= (- i j) 10) )
            (assert (=0-mod (- i (unroll-index 112) )              *unroll2*))
            (assert (=0-mod (- j -1 (* 2 (unroll-index 112) ) ) *unroll2*))

            (:= (x j) (x i) ) ) )

        (:= mm (- m 1) )
        (loop 113
            (incr ii from 1 to mm)
            (incr i  from (+ i1 1) )
```

```
        (incr j  from (+ j1 2) by 2)
        (unroll *unroll2*)
(do
    (assert (>= (- i j) 10) )
    (assert (=0-mod (- ii (unroll-index 113) )        *unroll2*) )
    (assert (=0-mod (- i (unroll-index 113) )         *unroll2*) )
    (assert (=0-mod (- j (* 2 (unroll-index 113) ) ) *unroll2*) )

    (:= (sca ii) (* (a j) (x (- j 1) ) ) )
    (:= (scc ii) (* (c j) (x (+ j 1) ) ) )
    (:= (scb ii) (- (d j) (sca ii) ) )
    (:= (scd ii) (- (scb ii) (scc ii) ) )
    (:= (x j)    (* (scd ii) (rb i) ) ) ) ) )

(if (= n (* 2 m) ) (then
    (:= (x (+ j1 n) )
        (//n (- (- (d (+ j1 n) )
                    (* (a (+ j1 n) ) (x (- (+ j1 n) 1) ) ) )
                (* (c (+ j1 n) ) (x (+ j1 1) ) ) )
            (b (+ j1 n) ) ) ) ) )

) ) ) )
```

NEWRZ

The original Fortran:

```fortran
      SUBROUTINE NEWRZ( DTN, DTNPH, R, Z, U, V, AJ, ENERGY, P, Q, TEMP,
     X     RHO, DTAU, MASS, NBC, KMN, LMN, KMX, LMX )

c         this routine calculates the new velocities, coordinates,
c         and the density and change in specific volume for each zone.

      REAL R(33,33)
      REAL Z(33,33)
      REAL U(33,33)
      REAL V(33,33)
      REAL AJ(33,33)
      REAL ENERGY(33,33)
      REAL P(33,33)
      REAL Q(33,33)
      REAL TEMP(33,33)
      REAL RHO(33,33)
      REAL DTAU(33,33)
      REAL MASS(33,33)
      REAL NBC(33,33)

C     COMMON /MAIN/ C
C     X R(33,33),Z(33,33),U(33,33),V(33,33),AJ(33,33)
C     X,ENERGY(33,33),P(33,33),Q(33,33),TEMP(33,33)
C     X,RHO(33,33),DTAU(33,33),MASS(33,33),NBC(33,33)

C
C     COMMON /KLSPACE/ KMN,LMN,KMX,LMX
C     DATA P1D6 /0.166666666666667/ C
C     DATA VCUT /1.0E-5/          C

      P1D6 = 0.166667
      VCUT = 1.0E-5

c     compute acceleration and new velocities

      DO 100 L=LMN,LMX
        DO 110 K=KMN,KMX
          AU = (P(K,L)+Q(K,L)) * (Z(K,L-1)-Z(K-1,L)) +
     X         (P(K+1,L)+Q(K+1,L))*(Z(K+1,L)-Z(K,L-1)) +
     X         (P(K,L+1)+Q(K,L+1))*(Z(K-1,L)-Z(K,L+1)) +
     X         (P(K+1,L+1)+Q(K+1,L+1))*(Z(K,L+1)-Z(K+1,L))
          AW = (P(K,L)+Q(K,L)) * (R(K,L-1)-R(K-1,L)) +
     X         (P(K+1,L)+Q(K+1,L)) * (R(K+1,L)-R(K,L-1)) +
     X         (P(K,L+1)+Q(K,L+1)) * (R(K-1,L)-R(K,L+1)) +
```

```fortran
     X          (P(K+1,L+1)+Q(K+1,L+1)) * (R(K,L+1)-R(K+1,L))
                AUW = RHO(K,L)*AJ(K,L)+RHO(K+1,L)*AJ(K+1,L)
     X             +RHO(K,L+1)*AJ(K,L+1)+RHO(K+1,L+1)*AJ(K+1,L+1)
                AUW = 2./AUW
                AU  = -AU*AUW
                AW  =  AW*AUW
                U(K,L) = U(K,L)+DTN*AU
                V(K,L) = V(K,L)+DTN*AW
                IF(ABS(U(K,L)) .LE. VCUT) U(K,L) = 0.0
                IF(ABS(V(K,L)) .LE. VCUT) V(K,L) = 0.0
  110      CONTINUE
  100 CONTINUE

c      advance coordinates to time (n+1)

      DO 200 L=LMN,LMX
        DO 210 K=KMN,KMX
           R(K,L) = R(K,L)+DTNPH*U(K,L)
           Z(K,L) = Z(K,L)+DTNPH*V(K,L)
  210      CONTINUE
  200 CONTINUE

c      jacobian area in (r,z) plane
c      volume = volume/2pi (cm**3/radian)
c        mass =   mass/2pi (gm/radian)

      KMNP = KMN + 1
      LMNP = LMN + 1
      DO 300 L=LMNP,LMX
        DO 310 K=KMNP,KMX
           AJ1 = R(K,L)* (Z(K-1,L)-Z(K,L-1))
     X         + R(K-1,L)* (Z(K,L-1)-Z(K,L))
     X         + R(K,L-1)*(Z(K,L)-Z(K-1,L))
           AJ3 = R(K-1,L)*(Z(K-1,L-1)-Z(K,L-1))
     X         + R(K-1,L-1)*(Z(K,L-1)-Z(K-1,L))
     X         + R(K,L-1)*(Z(K-1,L)-Z(K-1,L-1))
           AJ(K,L) = 0.5*(AJ1+AJ3)
           VOL = P1D6*((R(K,L)+R(K-1,L)+R(K,L-1))*AJ1 +
     X                 (R(K-1,L)+R(K-1,L-1)+R(K,L-1))*AJ3 )
           VN = 1.0/RHO(K,L)
           RHO(K,L) = MASS(K,L)/VOL
           VNP = 1.0/RHO(K,L)
           DTAU(K,L) = VNP-VN
  310      CONTINUE
  300 CONTINUE

      RETURN
      END
```

The transformed Tinylisp for NEWRZ:

```
;===============================================================================
;
; NEWRZ, from SIMPLE
;
; This routine calculates the new velocities, coordinates, and the density
; and change in specific volume for each zone.
;
; The argument KMN is assumed = 2 to make the bank disambiguation work
; correctly.   This is a realistic assumption, as far as I can tell from the
; SIMPLE code.
;
;===============================================================================

(defmacro def-column-major ( name )
    '(def-tinylisp-macro ,name ( x y )
        (list ',(atomconcat name '-array) y x) ) )

(def-column-major r)
(def-column-major z)
(def-column-major u)
(def-column-major v)
(def-column-major aj)
(def-column-major p)
(def-column-major q)
(def-column-major rho)
(def-column-major dtau)
(def-column-major mass)

(def-block (dtn dtnph r-array z-array u-array v-array aj-array p-array
            q-array rho-array mass-array kmn lmn kmx lmx)
           (u11 v11 r11 z11 aj11 rho11 dtau11)

    (declare (dtn dtnph) float)
    (declare (kmn kmx lmn lmx) integer)
    (declare (u11 v11 r11 z11 aj11 rho11 dtau11) float)

    (declare r-array    float ((1 #.*newrz.max-s*) (1 #.*newrz.max-s*)))
    (declare z-array    float ((1 #.*newrz.max-s*) (1 #.*newrz.max-s*)))
    (declare u-array    float ((1 #.*newrz.max-s*) (1 #.*newrz.max-s*)))
    (declare v-array    float ((1 #.*newrz.max-s*) (1 #.*newrz.max-s*)))
    (declare aj-array   float ((1 #.*newrz.max-s*) (1 #.*newrz.max-s*)))
    (declare p-array    float ((1 #.*newrz.max-s*) (1 #.*newrz.max-s*)))
    (declare q-array    float ((1 #.*newrz.max-s*) (1 #.*newrz.max-s*)))
    (declare rho-array  float ((1 #.*newrz.max-s*) (1 #.*newrz.max-s*)))
    (declare dtau-array float ((1 #.*newrz.max-s*) (1 #.*newrz.max-s*)))
```

```
(declare (aj1 aj3 au auw aw p1d6 ukl vcut vkl vol vn vnp) float)
(declare (l l-1 l+1 k k-1 k+1 kmnp lmnp) integer)
(declare (pkl pkl+1 pk+1l pk+1l+1)         float)
(declare (qkl qkl+1 qk+1l qk+1l+1)         float)
(declare (rhokl rhokl+1 rhok+1l rhok+1l+1) float)
(declare (ajkl ajkl+1 ajk+1l ajk+1l+1)     float)
(declare (zk-1l-1 zkl-1 zk-1l zkl zk+1l)   float)
(declare (rk-1l-1 rkl-1 rk-1l rkl rk+1l)   float)

(:= p1d6 0.166667)
(:= vcut 1.e-5)

    ;*** compute acceleration and new velocities
    ;***
(loop (incr l from lmn to lmx) (do
    (:= l-1 (- l 1))
    (:= l+1 (+ l 1))

    (:= pk+1l   (p kmn l))
    (:= pk+1l+1 (p kmn l+1))

    (:= qk+1l   (q kmn l))
    (:= qk+1l+1 (q kmn l+1))

    (:= rhok+1l   (rho kmn l))
    (:= rhok+1l+1 (rho kmn l+1))

    (:= ajk+1l   (aj kmn l))
    (:= ajk+1l+1 (aj kmn l+1))

    (:= zkl    (z (- kmn 1) l))
    (:= zk+1l  (z kmn      l))

    (:= rkl    (r (- kmn 1) l))
    (:= rk+1l  (r kmn      l))

    (loop l1
          (incr k from kmn to kmx)
          (unroll *unroll*)
    (do
        (assert (=0-mod (- k (unroll-index l1) 1) *unroll*))

        (:= k-1 (- k 1))
        (:= k+1 (+ k 1))

        (:= pkl      pk+1l)
        (:= pkl+1    pk+1l+1)
        (:= pk+1l   (p k+1 l))
        (:= pk+1l+1 (p k+1 l+1))
```

```
(:= qkl      qk+1l)
(:= qkl+1    qk+1l+1)
(:= qk+1l    (q k+1 l))
(:= qk+1l+1  (q k+1 l+1))

(:= rhokl      rhok+1l)
(:= rhokl+1    rhok+1l+1)
(:= rhok+1l    (rho k+1 l))
(:= rhok+1l+1  (rho k+1 l+1))

(:= ajkl      ajk+1l)
(:= ajkl+1    ajk+1l+1)
(:= ajk+1l    (aj k+1 l))
(:= ajk+1l+1  (aj k+1 l+1))

(:= zk-1l   zkl)
(:= zkl     zk+1l)
(:= zk+1l   (z k+1 l))

(:= rk-1l   rkl)
(:= rkl     rk+1l)
(:= rk+1l   (r k+1 l))

(:= au
    (+ (+ (+ (* (+ pkl qkl)      (- (z k l-1) zk-1l))
             (* (+ pk+1l qk+1l) (- zk+1l (z k l-1))))
          (* (+ pkl+1 qkl+1)     (- zk-1l (z k l+1))))
       (* (+ pk+1l+1 qk+1l+1) (- (z k l+1) zk+1l))))
(:= aw
    (+ (+ (+ (* (+ pkl qkl)      (- (r k l-1) rk-1l))
             (* (+ pk+1l qk+1l) (- rk+1l (r k l-1))))
          (* (+ pkl+1 qkl+1)     (- rk-1l (r k l+1))))
       (* (+ pk+1l+1 qk+1l+1) (- (r k l+1) rk+1l))))
(:= auw
    (+ (+ (+ (* rhokl ajkl)      (* rhok+1l ajk+1l))
          (* rhokl+1 ajkl+1)) (* rhok+1l+1 ajk+1l+1)))
(:= auw (//n 2.0 auw))
(:= au (* (- au) auw))
(:= aw (* aw auw))

(:= ukl (+ (u k l) (* dtn au)))
(:= vkl (+ (v k l) (* dtn aw)))
(:= (u k l) (select (<= (abs ukl) vcut) 0.0 ukl))
(:= (v k l) (select (<= (abs vkl) vcut) 0.0 vkl)))))))

;*** advance coordinates to time (n+1)
;***
(loop (incr l from lmn to lmx) (do
```

```
    (loop 12
         (incr k from kmn to kmx)
         (unroll *unroll*))
    (do
        (assert (=0-mod (- k (unroll-index 12) 1) *unroll*))

        (:= (r k l) (+ (r k l) (* dtnph (u k l))))
        (:= (z k l) (+ (z k l) (* dtnph (v k l)))))))))

    ;*** jacobian area in (r,z) plane
    ;*** volume = volume2pi (cm**3radian)
    ;*** mass =   mass2pi (gmradian)
    ;***
(:= kmnp (+ kmn 1))
(:= lmnp (+ lmn 1))

(loop (incr l from lmnp to lmx) (do
    (:= l-1 (- l 1))
    (:= l+1 (+ l 1))

    (:= rkl-1 (r (- kmnp 1) l-1))
    (:= rkl   (r (- kmnp 1) l))

    (:= zkl-1 (z (- kmnp 1) l-1))
    (:= zkl   (z (- kmnp 1) l))

    (loop 13
         (incr k from kmnp to kmx)
         (unroll *unroll*))
    (do
        (assert (=0-mod (- k (unroll-index 13) 2) *unroll*))

        (:= k-1 (- k 1))
        (:= k+1 (+ k 1))

        (:= rk-1l-1 rkl-1)
        (:= rkl-1   (r k l-1))
        (:= rk-1l   rkl)
        (:= rkl     (r k l))

        (:= zk-1l-1 zkl-1)
        (:= zkl-1   (z k l-1))
        (:= zk-1l   zkl)
        (:= zkl     (z k l))

        (:= aj1
           (+ (+ (* rkl (- zk-1l zkl-1)) (* rk-1l (- zkl-1 zkl)))
              (* rkl-1 (- zkl zk-1l))))
        (:= aj3
```

```
            (+ (+ (* rk-11    (- zk-11-1 zkl-1))
                  (* rk-11-1 (- zkl-1 zk-11)))
               (* rkl-1 (- zk-11 zk-11-1)))))
      (:= (aj k l) (* 0.5 (+ aj1 aj3)))
      (:= vol
          (* p1d6
             (+ (* (+ (+ rkl rk-11) rkl-1) aj1)
                (* (+ (+ rk-11 rk-11-1) rkl-1) aj3))))
      (:= vn (//n 1.0 (rho k l)))
      (:= (rho k l) (//n (mass k l) vol))
      (:= vnp (//n 1.0 (rho k l)))
      (:= (dtau k l) (- vnp vn))))))))


(:= u11     (u    1 1) )
(:= v11     (v    1 1) )
(:= r11     (r    1 1) )
(:= z11     (z    1 1) )
(:= aj11    (aj   1 1) )
(:= rho11   (rho  1 1) )
(:= dtau11  (dtau 3 3) ) )
```

References

[Aho 77]   A. V. Aho and J. D. Ullman.
              Principles of Compiler Design.
              Addison-Wesley, 1977.

[Allen 84]   John R. Allen and Ken Kennedy.
              Automatic loop interchange.
              In *Proceedings of the SIGPLAN '84 Symposium on Compiler
                  Construction*, pages 233–246. Association for Computing Ma-
                  chinery, June 1984.

[ANSI 81]   Proposals approved for Fortran 8x.
              American National Standards Institute, Inc., 1981.
              Cited in Allen [Allen 84].

[Banerjee 79] Uptal Banerjee.
              Speedup of ordinary programs.
              Technical Report UIUCDS-R-79-989, University of Illinois De-
                  partment of Computer Science, October 1979.
              Cited in Nicolau [Nicolau 84].

[Barrett 79] William A. Barrett and John D. Couch.
              Compiler Construction: Theory and Practice.
              Science Research Associates, Chicago, 1979, pages 581–587.

[Budd 84]   Timothy A. Budd.
              An APL compiler.
              ACM Transactions on Programming Languages and Systems
                  6(3):297–313, July 1984.

[Chow 84]   Frederick Chow and John Hennessy.
              Register allocation by priority-based coloring.
              In *Proceedings of the SIGPLAN '84 Symposium on Compiler
                  Construction*, pages 222–232. Association for Computing Ma-
                  chinery, June 1984.

[Fisher 79]　　J. A. Fisher.
The optimization of horizontal microcode within and beyond basic blocks: An application of processor scheduling with resources.
U.S. Department of Energy Report COO-3077-161, Courant Mathematics and Computing Laboratory, New York University, October 1979.

[Fisher 80]　　Joseph A. Fisher.
2^n-way jump microinstruction hardware and an effective instruction binding method.
In *The 13th Annual Microprogramming Workshop*, pages 64–75. Association for Computing Machinery and IEEE Computer Society, November 1980.

[Fisher 81]　　Joseph A. Fisher.
Trace scheduling: A technique for global microcode compaction.
IEEE Transactions on Computers C-30(7):478–490, July 1981.

[Fisher 82]　　Joseph A. Fisher.
Computer systems architecture at Yale.
Research Report 241, Yale University, Department of Computer Science, July 1982.

[Fisher 83]　　Joseph A. Fisher.
Very long instruction word architectures and the ELI-512.
In *The 10th Annual International Symposium on Computer Architecture*, pages 140–150. IEEE Computer Society and Association for Computing Machinery, June 1983.

[Fisher 84]　　Joseph A. Fisher and John J. O'Donnell.
VLIW machines: Multiprocessors we can actually program.
In *Compcon 84*, pages 299–305. IEEE Computer Society, February 1984.

[Fisher 84b]　　Joseph A. Fisher, John R. Ellis, John C. Ruttenberg, and Alexandru Nicolau.
Parallel processing: A smart compiler and a dumb machine.
In *Proceedings of the SIGPLAN '84 Symposium on Compiler Construction*, pages 37–47. Association for Computing Machinery, June 1984.

[Forsythe 77]   George E. Forsythe, Michael A. Malcolm, and Cleve B. Moler.
Computer Methods for Mathematical Computations.
Prentice-Hall, 1977.

[Foster 72]   C. C. Foster and E. M. Riseman.
Percolation of code to enhance parallel dispatching and execution.
IEEE Transactions on Computers 21(12):1411–1415, December 1972.
Cited in Nicolau [Nicolau 84].

[FPS 82]   *APAL64 Programmer's Guide.*
Floating Point Systems, Portland, Oregon, 1982.

[Gross 82]   Thomas R. Gross and John L. Hennessy.
Optimizing delayed branches.
In *15th Annual Workshop on Microprogramming*, pages 114–120.
IEEE Computer Society and Association for Computing Machinery, December 1982.

[Harrison 77]   William H. Harrison.
Compiler analysis of the value ranges for variables.
IEEE Transactions on Software Engineering SE-3(3):243–250, May 1977.

[Hennessy 82]   J. L. Hennessy, N. Jouppi, J. Gill, F. Baskett, A. Strong, T. R. Gross, C. Rowen, and J. Leonard.
The MIPS machine.
In *Compcon 82*, pages 2–7. IEEE Computer Society, February 1982.
Cited in Hennessy [Hennessy 83].

[Hennessy 82b]
John Hennessy.
Symbolic debugging of optimized code.
ACM Transactions on Programming Languages and Systems 4(3):323–344, July 1982.

[Hennessy 83]   John Hennessy and Thomas Gross.
Postpass code optimization of pipeline constraints.
ACM Transactions on Programming Languages and Systems 5(3):422–448, July 1983.

[Jones 80]   Anita K. Jones and Edward F. Gehringer, editors.
                The Cm* multiprocessor project: A research review.
                Technical Report CMU-CS-80-131, Computer Science Depart-
                    ment, Carnegie-Mellon University, July 1980.

[Kuck 72]   D. J. Kuck, Y. Muraoka, and S.-C. Chen.
                On the number of operations simultaneously executable in For-
                    tran-like programs and their resulting speedup.
                IEEE Transactions on Computers C-21(12):1293–1310, Decem-
                    ber 1972.
                Cited in Nicolau [Nicolau 84].

[Kuck 78]   David J. Kuck.
                The Structure of Computers and Computations.
                John Wiley and Sons, New York, 1978, pages 312.

[Lah 83]   Jehkwan Lah and Daniel E. Atkins.
                Tree compaction of microprograms.
                In *The 16th Annual Microprogramming Workshop*, pages 23–33.
                    Association for Computing Machinery and IEEE Computer
                    Society, October 1983.

[Landskov 80]
                David Landskov, Scott Davidson, Bruce Shriver, and Patrich W.
                    Mallet.
                Local microcode compaction techniques.
                ACM Computing Surveys 12(3):261–294, September 1980.

[Linn 83]   Joseph L. Linn.
                SRDAG compaction: A generalization of trace scheduling to in-
                    crease the use of global context information.
                In *The 16th Annual Microprogramming Workshop*, pages 11–22.
                    Association for Computing Machinery and IEEE Computer
                    Society, October 1983.

[Lisp-84 84]   Association for Computing Machinery.
                *Conference Record of the 1984 Symposium on LISP and Func-
                    tional Programming*, August 1984.

[Martin 83]   Joanne L. Martin, Ingrid Y. Bucher, and Tony T. Warnock.
Workload characterization for vector computers: Tools and techniques.
Technical Report LA-UR-82-3213, Los Alamos National Laboratory, 1983.
Cited in Fisher [Fisher 84b].

[Micro-12 79]   Association for Computing Machinery.
12th Annual Microprogramming Workshop, November 1979.

[Micro-16 83]   Association for Computing Machinery and IEEE Computer Society.
The 16th Annual Microprogramming Workshop, October 1983.

[Nicolau 81]   Alexandru Nicolau and Joseph A. Fisher.
Using an oracle to measure parallelism in single instruction stream programs.
In *The 14th Annual Microprogramming Workshop*, pages 171–182. Association for Computing Machinery and IEEE Computer Society, October 1981.

[Nicolau 84]   Alexandru Nicolau.
Parallelism, Memory Anti-aliasing and Correctness Issues for a Trace-Scheduling Compiler.
PhD thesis, Yale University, December 1984.

[Numerix 83]   *MARS-432 Programmer's Reference Manual*.
Preliminary edition, Numerix Corporation, Newton, Massachussetts, 1983.

[Padua 80]   D. A. Padua, D. J. Kuck, and D. H. Lawrie.
High speed multiprocessors and compilation techniques.
IEEE Transactions on Computers 29(9):763–776, September 1980.
Cited in Nicolau [Nicolau 84].

[Piessens 83]   R. Piessens.
QUADPACK: A Subroutine Package for Automatic Integration.
Springer-Verlag, New York, 1983.

[Rau 81]   B. R. Rau, C. D. Glaeser.
                Some scheduling techniques and an easily schedulable horizontal
                architecture for high performance scientific computing.
                In *The 14th Annual Microprogramming Workshop*, pages 183–
                198. Association for Computing Machinery and IEEE Com-
                puter Society, October 1981.

[Rau 82]   B. Ramarkrishna Rau, Christopher D. Glaeser, and Raymond L.
                Picard.
                Efficient code generation for horizontal architectures: Compiler
                techniques and architectural support.
                In *The 9th Symposium on Computer Architecture*, pages 131–
                139. IEEE Computer Society and Association for Computing
                Machinery, April 1982.

[Riseman 72]   E. M. Riseman and C. C. Foster.
                The inhibition of potential parallelism by conditional jumps.
                IEEE Transactions on Computers 21(12):1405–1411, December
                1972.
                Cited in Nicolau [Nicolau 84].

[Rodrigue 82]   Garry Rodrigue (editor).
                Parallel Computations.
                Academic Press, 1982.

[Ruttenberg 83]
                J. C. Ruttenberg and J. A. Fisher.
                Lifting the restriction of aggregate data motion in parallel pro-
                cessing.
                In *Tenth Annual International Symposium on Computer Archi-
                tecture*, pages 211–215. Association for Computing Machinery,
                March 1983.

[Ruttenberg 85]
                John C. Ruttenberg.
                Delayed-Binding Code Generation for a VLIW Supercomputer.
                PhD thesis, Yale University, June 1985.
                Expected.

[Sandewall 78]
    Erik Sandewall.
    Programming in the interactive environment: The Lisp experience.
    ACM Computing Surveys 10(1):35-72, March 1978.

[Sites 78]
    Richard L. Sites.
    Instruction ordering for the Cray-I computer.
    Technical Report CS-023, Department of Electrical Engineering and Computer Science, University of California at San Diego, July 1978.
    I remember reading this six years ago. I've talked to Sites, who remembers his work on this problem quite well, but doesn't remember writing the tech report. I've also talked to the secretary responsible for distributing UCSD Computer Science reports, and she claims this report really does exist. But I haven't yet received a copy.

[Steele 84]
    Guy L. Steele, Jr..
    Common Lisp: The Language.
    Digital Press, Maynard, Massachussetts, 1984.

[Steiglitz 74]
    Kenneth Steiglitz.
    An Introduction to Discrete Systems.
    John Wiley and Sons, New York, 1974.

[Touzeau 84]
    Roy F. Touzeau.
    A Fortran compiler for the FPS-164 scientific computer.
    In *Proceedings of the SIGPLAN '84 Symposium on Compiler Construction*, pages 48-57. Association for Computing Machinery, June 1984.

[Tjaden 70]
    G. S. Tjaden and M. J. Flynn.
    Detection and parallel execution of independent instructions.
    IEEE Transactions on Computers 19(10):889-895, October 1970.
    Cited in Nicolau [Nicolau 84].

Index